Local Authority Financial Management and Accounting

by

Paul Cook

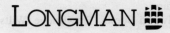

Published by Longman Information and Reference,
Longman Group UK Ltd, 6th Floor,
Westgate House, The High, Harlow, Essex CM20 1YR
Telephone: Harlow (0279) 442601; Fax: Harlow (0279) 444501;
Telex: 81491 Padlog.

© Longman Group UK Ltd 1993

A catalogue record for this book is available from the British Library

ISBN 0-582-21088-7

Typeset by The Midlands Book Typesetting Company,
Loughborough, Leicestershire
Printed and Bound by Redwood Books, Trowbridge, Wiltshire

To Juliana

Francisca Okeneme
School of Postgraduate studies
Faculty of Management
Middlesex - University
England - United Kingdom

Preface

Local government finance seems to be enjoying increasing topicality, if only because of the rapid succession of rates, poll tax and council tax. Certainly the current system is somewhat complicated. This is no help to the non-specialist managers in councils who are being asked to take on ever wider finance responsibilities. These range from devolved budgets to negotiating a service level agreement for financial services with the experts themselves.

The purpose of this book is to provide an insight into some of the main financial processes in councils, and some thoughts on how to get the best out of the system. It is not intended to be an exhaustive guide, rather to give a flavour of the topics covered.

As well as the aspects every council manager will be involved in — budgets, audit, and so forth — it deals with more specialised areas such as borrowing and investments. This should enable managers to make an assessment of how well finance departments perform, something of a change of roles.

Finally, the odd reminiscence has been included, if only to demonstrate that even such a dreary subject as council finance has its lighter moments.

The statutory position is generally that which appertained in December 1992.

Paul Cook

Contents

1 An introduction to local government finance

A tale — doubtless apocryphal — may serve to encapsulate the simplicity of councils' financial management. During the early 1980s, a London weighting increase was declared for certain groups of council workers. Officials then met to discuss how this cost burden should be reflected in councils' spending targets, thus providing more government assistance to the London authorities. After some mathematics, the paradoxical answer was discovered. The way to direct additional resources to London was to increase the targets of the councils outside London.

Certainly many of the rules and regulations governing councils' financial activities are far from straightforward. Yet the policies and trends underlying these restrictions are clear enough. So, in this first chapter, we run briefly through the main developments affecting councils' finances. To provide more insight into how the system works, we also look at how the treasurer or finance director of a council exercises his or her individual role. We conclude by looking at the influence of the local authority associations, and the professional accounting body CIPFA to which virtually all treasurers belong.

Current finance issues

The range of council services is wide, and all have their associated financial problems. There are, however, five main trends which show a common pattern affecting all council functions.

The method of raising local taxes remains in question

In 1990, the long-standing rates system was abolished as a means of taxing local residents. It was replaced by the ill-fated poll tax, which proved extremely unpopular. In order to reduce its effects, the central government grant to councils was increased to a historically high level. The new council tax (a modified form of the old rates system) is as yet untried, and came into operation on 1 April 1993.

Compulsory competitive tendering (CCT) affects a wide range of council services

In 1980, action was taken by the government to promote greater efficiency in council building departments. From this year onwards, councils have been required to win an increasing proportion of their own building work in competition with outside contractors. They must also achieve a minimum level of profitability

1

on their building activities. In 1988, compulsory competition (or CCT) was extended to other manual labour activities such as refuse collection and grounds maintenance. Latest government plans would further develop CCT by applying it to white collar or professional services, including the finance function.

The reorganisation of councils into unitary authorities

A programme of reorganisation is currently under way, with a general objective of replacing the two-tier county–district structure by unitary authorities where appropriate.

Limitation of council expenditure generally, and expenditure limitation for individual authorities

For some decades, limitation of public expenditure has been a pre-occupation of central government. This has led to pressure on local government to restrain its expenditure, particularly its taxation demands. Although in the 1970s there was a measure of council expenditure limitation in response to government exhortation, the 1980s and 1990s have seen the enactment of explicit expenditure limitation powers applied by government to individual councils' budgets.

Devolution, outsourcing and the enabling authority

All major council services have seen policy changes to move the emphasis of service delivery away from local authority control. In education, this has been achieved by devolving managerial responsibility for schools down to governors. In social services, community care legislation changes the emphasis of councils' role away from direct provision of care to that of assessor of client needs, and purchaser of care from a variety of sources. Similarly, in the housing service, a progressive reduction in the capital allocation given to councils has forced them into more of an enabling role, with much of new development being undertaken by housing associations.

We look briefly at the effects of these trends on council finance.

Local taxation

No issue has been more effective in creating public interest in local government finance than the short-lived poll tax. Few taxes are popular, and with hindsight the old rates system which applied up to 1990 was by no means unsatisfactory. Long stated deficiencies of the system though were that it made no concession for persons living alone in high value properties, and that the level of rates charged varied widely from council to council without any corresponding increase in the value of services provided. In fact, by the mid-1980s some of the worst impositions of high spending councils had been eliminated by the introduction of *rate-capping*. Councils were also prevented from raising supplementary rates during the year, even if cash requirements exceeded their original budget plans. The system of central grant to councils had also been refined. Under *block grant*, government distribution of money to councils was constructed to produce a standard rate nationwide for a standard level of service. (This never worked properly, of course.)

However, the government remained committed to the reform of local taxation, and to the introduction of the poll tax or community charge. The economic and political implications of this measure have been rehearsed ad nauseam, but the poll tax had a particular impact on councils' own financial organisation.

The rating system, so long established, had become familiar and easy to operate. Thus this aspect of financial management had become something of a backwater. The confirmation of the poll tax, with only a short time allowed for authorities to achieve its introduction, suddenly thrust revenue collection into an unexpected prominence.

Most councils managed, however, to contradict their own gloomy predictions by having staffing and computer systems ready and operating for the poll tax. Certainly the effort of doing so produced new self-confidence in treasurers' ability to cope with such developments, but a more long-lasting and ominous result was the proof that financial management in councils could be comprehensively altered without internal administrative disaster ensuing. Another portentous by-product of the poll tax introduction was the trend of increasing reliance by councils on outside consultancies for project management, and IT work.

The political imperative of replacing the poll tax was thus capable of swift execution, given councils' earlier success in poll tax implementation. The property-based council tax has already enabled councils to reduce revenue collection staff numbers, and the necessary computer developments have generally been accomplished with quiet efficiency. Yet to be established are the success in operation of the new tax, and indeed the future of local taxation at all.

As we see in a later chapter, councils' revenue raising powers are at their nadir.

- *The proportion of council funding supplied by central grant is at an all-time high. This calls into question the need for local taxation at all.*
- *The system of government grant, when taken in combination with capping powers, means very little local discretion as to the amount of revenue raised locally.*
- *Not paying local taxes has become ingrained as a habit with a significant proportion of the population.*

The effective and efficient operation of the council tax is thus seen by some commentators as a final chance for councils' continued autonomy. Were the tax to be abandoned, then local funding might be dispensed with entirely. The current central grant to councils is *unhypothecated*. This means that, although its value is determined by the spending need for various council functions (education, social services, etc), councils are largely free to apply their total grant in accordance with their own priorities. (In practice this freedom is limited as councils would argue the grant totals allow little extra money once basic statutory duties have been fulfilled.) If there were no power of local taxation, it would be extremely tempting to central government to exert much tighter control over how councils spent the grant paid to them.

Before we leave the area of local taxation, we examine the principle of *gearing*, which is a key consideration in many finance issues. Put simply, the principle is this. Local funding represents only a small proportion of total finance. The effect of a small reduction in external support is to produce an exaggerated increase in the local tax requirement. This is shown in Table 1.1.

Table 1.1: Illustration of gearing effect

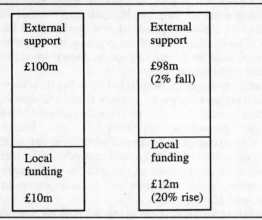

Given a £110m budget funded by 9 per cent local funding (£10m), and 91 per cent central funding, the table shows the effect of a 2 per cent reduction in external support. In order to rebalance the budget, a 20 per cent increase in the local tax level is necessary to compensate for the change.

The gearing effect means that apparently tiny moves in central support to councils can produce a destabilising effect on local taxes. Were councils financed to a much greater degree by their own local taxes, they would have a much stronger basis on which to absorb variations in government grant.

Compulsory competitive tendering (CCT)

CCT has had much effect on the way councils operate their finances. Back in the mid-1970s, there was general concern within local government itself as to the inefficiency of council building departments. Any inefficiency was encouraged by the method of accounting for the costs of direct labour work. This was simply to recharge internal customers with the actual cost of carrying out works — however high. This used to mean for example that, if the year end accounts showed the direct labour organisation (or DLO) to have incurred a loss, then the charges for building work in other committees' accounts would be revised appropriately. A further source of disquiet was the generous work study based bonus schemes then in wide use.

Tales abound of the inadequacies of such schemes. In one authority, council refuse collectors continued to be paid a bonus for collecting rubbish from long demolished estates. The plumbing work values in another were based on highly skilled soldering work to lead piping, and workmen walking to jobs with tools and materials in a wheelbarrow. In reality, most work simply entailed screwing together pieces of plastic pipe, and workmen speeding around housing estates by car.

The concept was thus developed that DLOs should be required to quote a fixed price in advance of work being undertaken, and that only that charge should be allowed in their accounts. This passed into law in the 1980 Local Government Planning and Land Act, and the relevant provisions still remain in force. Councils were required to win work by competitive tender for jobs exceeding £10,000 in value. Lower priced maintenance work was also to be competed for, with councils allowed an annual threshold of competition-free work. This threshold was reduced year-on-year by government regulation.

At the same time, councils are required to earn a 5 per cent rate of return on the capital employed in DLO work. Failure to achieve the rate of return necessitates a special report to the Department of the Environment. Successive failures may lead to closure of the DLO, or statutory restrictions on the type of work it may undertake.

These new controls on direct labour work effected some clear improvements in DLO efficiency, even if the expected rate of increase in the use of outside contractors did not materialise. Some amusing results stemmed from the 5 per cent requirement. Accountants soon twigged that the way to achieve the desired ratio was not to maximise the profit numerator, but to minimise the capital employed divisor. By leasing operational assets (excluded from DLO capital calculations) and transferring assets to other departments' control, some 100 per cent plus rates of return were soon in evidence. By and large though, the trimming of DLO operations offered evidence of the beneficial effects of CCT.

In 1988, the scope of CCT was extended to other traditional council direct labour areas, notably refuse collection, cleaning, and grounds maintenance. Again, many councils were able to eliminate problematical bonus schemes and inefficient working practices in driving down the cost of direct labour operations to tender winning prices. Government permitted some councils to use their capital programmes to fund the redundancy costs of CCT preparation, or winding down DLOs after contracts had been lost.

Thus far, CCT has been concentrated on manual labour services, but there is a clear government policy to apply CCT to professional services too. The threat of staff needing to compete for the council's own finance or legal work within the next few years has been a powerful stimulus to the development of internal markets and service level agreements. A further proposed extension of CCT is its application to the housing management function, which is one of the political priorities in many authorities.

As we see at various stages of this book, the need to operate financial services in a competitive and cost-effective manner is becoming one of the overriding factors in council financial management.

Local government reorganisation

Given all the financial difficulties facing councils, the process of reorganisation in the shire county areas adds an additional element of complexity. Perhaps this reflects a British propensity to reform its public institutions and local government structures rather than perfect the efficiency of their operation. Table 1.2 summarises the present structure, and shows the reorganisation that affected the (former) metropolitan areas in 1986.

Table 1.2: Local government structures and reorganisation

Metropolitan areas: London, Greater Manchester, Merseyside, South Yorkshire, Tyne & Wear, West Midlands, West Yorkshire

(a) **Outside London**

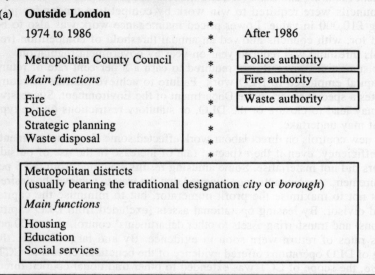

1974 to 1986

After 1986

Metropolitan County Council

Main functions

Fire
Police
Strategic planning
Waste disposal

Police authority

Fire authority

Waste authority

Metropolitan districts
(usually bearing the traditional designation *city* or *borough*)

Main functions

Housing
Education
Social services

The 1986 reorganisation thus transferred the strategic functions exercised by the metropolitan counties over to specialist authorities. The position was different in London.

(b) **London**

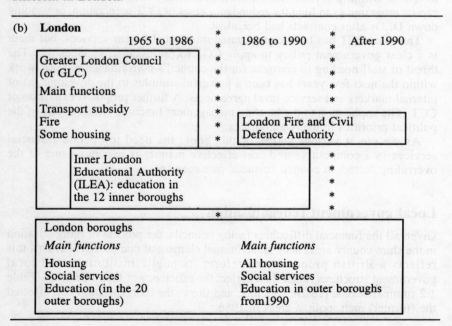

1965 to 1986

1986 to 1990

After 1990

Greater London Council
(or GLC)

Main functions

Transport subsidy
Fire
Some housing

London Fire and Civil
Defence Authority

Inner London
Educational Authority
(ILEA): education in
the 12 inner boroughs

London boroughs

Main functions

Housing
Social services
Education (in the 20
outer boroughs)

Main functions

All housing
Social services
Education in outer boroughs
from 1990

Table 1.2: (continued)

(c) **Current structure in the shire countries**

The shire areas include Kent, Essex, Lancashire and North Yorkshire.

County Council *Main functions* Education Social services Highways Fire Police	Reform is to be carried out in 5 stages over the period 1994 to 1998 As yet, there is no clear policy as to the structure to be introduced, and it will not necessarily be uniform across the country
District councils (Some still bear their historical title of city or borough.) *Main functions* Housing Poll Tax collection Benefits Leisure	

The pattern of reorganisation in London was thus to give all major functions to the boroughs, and to remove the inner/outer distinction by making the inner boroughs, too, responsible for education. The London Boroughs and metropolitan authorities are now close to the concept of *unitary authorities*, with a single council exercising all the main local government functions in its area.

The present reorganisation revisits the problem of whether local government operates more effectively as a two-tier county/district structure, or with single unitary authorities. In fact, the existing two-tier structure outside London has been a source of contention since its introduction in 1974. The dissatisfactions were largely removed in the metropolitan areas with their 1986 reorganisation.

Some of the key factors in the reorganisation debate are now summarised.

Sources of dissatisfaction in shire districts

In 1974, during the last reorganisation in the shire areas, some large county boroughs suffered the loss of key functions such as education and social services to their county council. These authorities included cities such as Derby, Portsmouth, Nottingham and Leicester. Ever since, these authorities and other, smaller districts have argued that with their traditional sense of local identity, they would make a much better job of delivering the major services than a remote county administration.

Shire districts are obliged to collect local taxes on behalf of their county, which precepts on them for its requirements. Districts often feel that they are unjustly held accountable for county tax increases, as local residents often fail to appreciate the difference between district and county.

Counties, having a much larger core of central administrators by virtue of the magnitude of their operations, are readily seen as excessively bureaucratic and costly. A view is often expressed that districts have the more difficult services to manage, including poll or council tax collection and the payment of benefits. It is difficult to generate much consumer satisfaction with these, unlike the more caring functions of education or social services.

Some factors in favour of retaining the counties

Counties would argue there are many reasons to retain the present two-tier structure, and in some areas to have a single unitary authority based on the old county area.

- *Any reorganisation is invariably a costly exercise, and it is extremely difficult to establish objective evidence that unitary districts would provide local government services more cheaply.*
- *Counties are able to achieve economies of scale in purchasing arrangements, and staffing structures. If, for example, a county were split into four unitary districts, it would need four chief education officers, not one.*
- *Many counties have established a record over the years of high professional expertise in areas such as finance and information technology. These long-run benefits would be difficult to retain in any reorganisation.*

It is probably fair to say that the shire counties, established in the historic Local Government Act of 1888, have been in politicians' sights for some years now. Yet some of the Local Government Commission's early pronouncements seem to envisage quite large unitary authorities.

Certainly, given all the changes being made within local government at the moment, reorganisation will not be entirely welcome to council staff. Just a few of the practical financial management difficulties that can arise with such an event will now be indicated. The sheer mechanics of ensuring that transferred staff are on the payroll, or of stopping outlying establishments paying into long-closed bank accounts ought not to be underestimated.

Closing the accounts of the abolished councils

All debtors, creditors and assets of the old authorities must be transferred into the accounts of the new authority. This is usually not as simple as it might seem, as the staff who prepared the old accounts have often retired or gone on to different jobs. More than likely, the authorities operated different computer systems, and prepared their accounts on different principles anyway.

Preparing accurate budgets for services

Council budgets are normally prepared on an incremental method, with political attention focused on the changes from last year's budget. This is impossible when whole functions, such as social services, have been split between a number of successor authorities. The new authority's budget for the function inevitably relies on a fair amount of guesswork. In combining budgets for the new services with their existing services, many injustices can arise. Some services will be given much more money than they need, others too little. It can take some years to correct these imbalances.

Transferring assets and contractual liabilities

Often council assets are not formally registered, having been in council use since living memory. However, on transfer to a successor authority, much work is necessary to establish the precise ownership of land and the terms of leases. If the successor council takes over a recently completed capital project, it will need to ensure it has full documentation and information. Any post-completion deficiencies will need to be pursued by officers who probably had no involvement at all in the original contract.

Depletion of reserves and balances

This phenomenon is not limited to reorganisations, as it is quite customary for expenditure to surge immediately prior to a change of administration at any council. This may range from signing-up contracts for pet projects at the eleventh hour, to last minute regradings for favoured officers. It was certainly noticeable in the 1974 reorganisation that many soon-to-be-defunct district councils had furnished their residents with new sports centres, to be run at the successor council's expense. More seriously, the ongoing commitments of predecessor councils' schemes, and a lack of balances, may create financial difficulties for the new authority.

A further difficulty with reorganisation is that it is always extremely difficult to make an ex-post assessment of whether any savings have accrued from the changes made. Simply to compare the cost of local government within a geographical area before and after the restructuring is unlikely to provide an answer. It will then be virtually impossible to determine how far changes are due to different political policies in the new authorities, rather than to any intrinsic merit in the new structure. For ease of reference, the timetable for reorganisation is summarised below.

- The review will be carried out in five stages, with the first new authorities in place by 1994. The final reviews will take place in 1996, with the last set of new authorities in operation by 1998.
- The first tranche of shire counties chosen for review are believed to represent areas where significant dissatisfaction exists with the present structure. It covers Avon, Gloucestershire, Somerset, Cleveland, Durham, Derbyshire, Humberside, Lincolnshire, North Yorkshire, and the Isle of Wight.
- The Local Government Commission has been asked to concentrate on the indirect costs in comparing one structure for an area with another. This may mean that reduced management structures in larger authorities have to be weighed against the extra costs of accommodating the reorganised council.

The limitation of council expenditure

A source of increasing frustration to both councillors and officers is the power of government to limit the expenditure plans of individual councils. This is, in fact, quite a recent feature of the local government financial scene, yet it has already become a basic fact of council life.

Table 1.3 sets out the steps towards the present arrangements, whereby every single local authority is eligible to be 'capped'. Before the financial year 1992/93, any council with a budget below £15m was exempt from capping. This dispensation protected many small district councils.

A Treasury mandarin once encapsulated the nature of the central/local government relationship by explaining that councils had always been part of the public expenditure system. The trouble was they didn't realise that they were. The process since 1979 of correcting that misconception has not been without its problems on either side.

Table 1.4 sets out the process from a different perspective, explaining the changes in government grant to councils over this period. These changes would have achieved capping virtually without the need for an explicit power.

Before 1979, councils had the best of both worlds. In the first place, government planned public expenditure in *real terms*. This meant that, as inflation took effect, the actual cash paid to councils was updated accordingly. Secondly, and equally advantageously, there was a strong element of *resource equalisation* in the grant calculation.

In calculating the grant paid to councils, an adjustment was made to bring each individual council's tax base up to the national average. A council with a low average ratable value per head of population was thus funded by the government as a notional ratepayer, meeting (with some limitations) whatever level of rate the council chose to set.

It must be admitted this formulation was not ideal from a government standpoint as, whilst it was exhorting councils to reduce their expenditure, it was simultaneously financing the overspending. Hence the introduction of the block grant system.

Block grant made, for the first time, an explicit government assessment of how much each council needed to spend to provide a reasonable level of services. With characteristic ingenuity, this was termed the *grant related expenditure assessment (GRE)*. Essentially, if a council spent at its GRE, then it would be paid enough block grant to enable its rate poundage to be set at the standard level decreed by the government.

Table 1.3: Progress to universal capping

1981/82	Block grant introduced, meeting nearly 60 per cent of relevant expenditure.
1982/83	Individual councils set targets, grant abatement for high spending.
1983/84	Penalties can apply even for councils spending below the government set GRE.
1985/86	Rate capping comes into effect.
1986/87	Legislation changes basis of grant calculation away from council accounts to government assumptions as to individual councils' spend.
1992/93	Capping applies to all councils.

Table 1.4: Systems of central grant to councils

Period and system	Increased for extra local spending?	Switches resources from tax rich-councils to tax-poor?	Settlement cash limited?
Before 1979			
Rate support grant (RSG) and the old rates system	Partly	Yes	No
1980 to 1990			
Block grant and the old rates system	Central funding could actually decrease if council was well in excess of government spending guide	Yes, but only for spending up to the standard level	Yes
1990 to 1992			
Poll tax, nationally set non-domestic rates, and revenue support grant (RSG)	Grant fixed, whatever council spends	No, non-domestic rates, are redistributed in proportion to council populations	Yes
1993 onwards			
Council tax, nationally set non-domestic rates, and revenue support grant (RSG)	Grant fixed, whatever council spends	Yes, as grant distribution reflects the local tax base. NNDR as above	Yes

The sting in the tail was the addition to this basic approach of a system of targets and penalties to induce councils to trim their budgets. Once a council pushed its expenditure much beyond the GRE, then its block grant entitlement went into reverse. The combination of increased local funding, and decreased central grant exerted a powerful gearing effect on rate bills. (Perversely the same mathematics did marvellous things to councils spending well below their GRE, who found that the less money they spent the more central grant they earned.)

This concentration on council expenditure levels fostered a considerable degree of *creative accounting*. As grant penalties usually got severer year on year, it made sense to move expenditure into earlier financial years by various means. In particular, contributions into reserves were classed as expenditure for grant calculation purposes. These could thus be charged in earlier years of low penalty rates, and used (penalty free) in later years of high penalty rates.

Other schemes avoided immediate charging of expenditure altogether, such as *deferred purchase arrangements*. Under these an independent company would carry out works on the council's behalf (relieving its revenue budget), in return for some future long-term repayment.

A further source of government disquiet was that, as the benefits system gave full relief for local taxes to the poorest sections of the community, those residents immune from local taxes might have a particular perspective on local tax levels. The revamping of the benefits system that accompanied poll tax in 1990 thus introduced a maximum 80 per cent relief, in the interests of more local accountability.

More importantly, there were major changes in the grant system. Grant was divorced from an individual council's expenditure level, and became more closely linked to government assessment of what councils should spend (now termed the *standard spending assessment (SSA)*). As grant was now fixed independently of expenditure, it could not be augmented by creative accounting.

Similarly, the principle of resource equalisation was largely abandoned. Business rates were excluded from the calculation by a change to central collection and redistribution on a per capita basis. The local tax base was now equalised only to reflect the number of inhabitants in a council area, without the relationship to general wealth inherent (albeit imperfectly) in the old rates system. The equalisation principle has now been reintroduced for the council tax element of local funding.

Thus government has moved from the status of a notional ratepayer, contributing its share to the locally determined tax level, to the provider of a fixed cash sum who also restricts any attempt to boost the level of local financing. The position has eased only slightly under council tax. Under this long-term trend, the focus of council decision making remains firmly on reduction of services and cuts in expenditure and staffing levels.

Devolution, outsourcing and the enabling authority

A few years ago, the then secretary of state for the environment communicated his vision of *the enabling authority*. Why should councils rely on their own workforce to provide local services? Why must they operate independently of other public sector agencies? Wouldn't the ideal local authority consist of a small executive board, placing and monitoring external contracts for all its services?

This thinking has grown apace, and has become allied to the concept of devolving financial control away from council power centres down to service units or even service users.

Perhaps the first manifestation of this principle on a national scale was the development of local management of schools (LMS). For some years a number of shire counties had transferred increasing power to their schools, and away from the central education office. These local experiments were taken up with enthusiasm in the 1988 Education Reform Act.

However councils were soon left wondering whether they were simply being excluded from an education service that was beginning to take the form of direct dealings between central government and individual schools. Certainly government emphasis is currently on the advantages available to schools that opt out of council control entirely.

In social services, councils had long been a direct provider of care to various groups. This was often at the expense of confused and overlapping responsibilities with local health authorities. Clearly in, say, care of the elderly, there are obvious overlaps between the functions of the two bodies.

Under community care, councils become responsible for assessing client need in the wider sense, and then purchasing that care from the range of available agencies. With an eye to enablement, the initial funding arrangements give councils an irresistible financial advantage to purchase much of that care from the private sector.

Direct council provision is also under threat in the other major council service, housing. Not only have council capital spending permissions been cut over the years, but the housing management function is soon to be subject to CCT.

Summary of finance trends

In some respects, what we have seen as the general picture of council finances seems ominous for the long-term future of local government.

- Its expenditure is under strict central control, and downward pressure limits the scope for local political initiative.
- There is a fair possibility it may lose its taxation powers, with consequent threats to its local spending autonomy.
- Its direct workforce is being successively whittled away by the need to compete for the council's own work with outside contractors. Once major functions are externalised, the likelihood of resurrecting an in-house operation is low.
- In much of the country, its attention will be diverted from operating services by a complex and costly reorganisation.
- The value of money under councils' direct political control is being further depleted by the loss of responsibilities (such as the recent incorporation of further education colleges, or opt-out schools), or the devolution of budgets to service users.

But it is perhaps not surprising that such a degree of change is taking place, given that council financial management operated in a fairly constant pattern for many years prior to 1979. Certainly the split of many council departments into independent purchaser and contractor sides has brought new perceptions as to the basis and cost of council services. In this book we therefore seek to explain the current financial management practices of councils. Whether central government policy will lead to a more effective and thoughtful provision of local government services remains to be seen.

Before we look in detail at the finance structures within individual councils, we examine some management trends that have become part of council internal operations, and how these affect finance.

Management trends

One of the strengths (or weaknesses?) of local government is the ability of new ideas to gain almost universal acceptance with great rapidity. This is perhaps because of the openness with which councils exchange ideas and information about management practices, given that there is little need for commercial confidentiality. Three particularly important ideas have relevance to the finance function:

- *the use of* **service level agreements**, *and the restructuring of councils into quasi-independent business units or trading accounts;*
- *priority given by councils to fulfilling customer needs and the quality of council services;*
- *devolution of central professional functions to service managers.*

Over the last decade, the effect of these ideas has been to reduce the past autonomy of the central finance department, and hopefully to make it more reactive to service needs. These processes are still continuing.

Service level agreement

Some years ago, the centre of influence in many councils was the legal (or town clerk's) department and the treasurer's department. These professional departments came first in the municipal pecking order. From the mid-1970s, councils began to appoint chief executives as head of their officer staff, but often this post has a less direct managerial control over the specialist chief officers than might be supposed. Many chief officers have statutory duties in their own right, and the authority of central professional departments was jealously guarded.

The pressure of CCT on service managers has caused greater scrutiny of the scale of the central overhead over the last few years. Service level agreements are a mechanism for translating this scrutiny into genuine control. Under service level agreements, central departments are expected to negotiate with their service customers as to the scale and cost of the professional services provided.

Since these agreements were first espoused by CIPFA in 1988, developments have moved on quickly. In a discussion paper published in 1992, the Institute considers the splitting of the traditional finance department into a central purchasing unit and various business units. The purchasing unit buys the financial services needed by the council from the business units, payroll, budget and so forth. This step has already been taken in a number of councils.

This would seem to be a logical mirroring of the enabling concept, as there is no overriding reason why the director of finance's responsibilities must be discharged by staff under the director's own management. However, the enforcement of an internal market in councils may not be without pitfalls.

Advantages of internal markets
- *Work is oriented towards agreed (fee earning) objectives.*
- *The necessity of providing services within agreed cost is a stimulus to efficiency.*
- *Voluntary competition is sound preparation for compulsory external competition.*

14

Disadvantages of internal markets
- *Effort is wasted in the bureaucracy of preparing and operating the agreements.*
- *Sections will limit their work to fee-earning activities, rather than operating in the council's wider interest.*
- *Duplication could occur with more than one internal unit competing for the same work.*

If finance departments become split on the client : contractor basis shown in Table 1.5, it may well have the advantage of defining much more clearly the precise objectives of the various specialist functions that comprise the finance role. Whether this will serve councils better than the traditional omniscient finance department remains to be seen over the next few years.

Table 1.5: Finance department structures

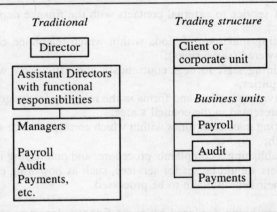

Certainly, it is curious to observe the enthusiasm with which many finance directors have advocated the use of external agencies for council finance work, in preference to the very staff they are responsible for managing.

Quality and customer care

Most councils now place considerable importance on the quality of service provision. In this, they are little different from industry, and much of the thinking relies on the teachings of management gurus such as Tom Peters. Information and systems used to control the quality of services usually relate very effectively to financial management.

As an example, it is quite difficult to set a budget for housing repairs if there are no clear standards as to what service will be provided, but if there is a clear statement on the quality of repairs service to which the council is committed, it becomes much easier to define the budget. Such a quality commitment might include exactly what repairs the council (as opposed to the tenant) is responsible for, how quickly the various types of repair will be dealt with, and what redress the tenant has if repairs are not carried out to an acceptable standard. As quality criteria are set for more and more council services, it should be possible to establish, much more directly, the effects of increasing or decreasing the budget for a particular service.

Finance departments are large service providers in their own right, both internally (such as providing financial advice or internal audit to service managers), and externally (in paying benefits, or collecting local taxes). (The categorisation of council tax collection as a local government *service* has a little irony, as it seems unlikely most residents would view this activity as such.) A finance department should have its own policies on quality, covering perhaps some of the following areas.

- Services to internal users ought to be specified in service level agreements.
- Service targets can be set for internal customers, such as how quickly correspondence is dealt with, or the acceptable level of down-time for a computer system.
- Quality of service to external contacts with the finance department might include:
    —setting maximum periods within which telephone calls should be answered (say 5 rings);
    —training staff to deal courteously and efficiently with telephone enquiries;
    —providing leaflets and forms in the minority languages significantly represented in the council's area;
    —setting maximum times within which correspondence should be dealt with;
    —establishing a complaints procedure, and publicising its availability.
- Clear targets should be set for services, such as how long claimants must wait for their benefit claim to be processed.

A possibility being explored by some finance departments is to secure accreditation by an independent body (such as British Standard 5750) for some or all of their financial services. This entails comprehensive documentation of all procedures, the establishment of quality control procedures, and reviews by external quality auditors.

Although quality is more perceptible in front line services, it is a principle that increasingly is affecting council finance operations. It will thus have continuing importance over the next few years.

Devolution of finance functions

We have already referred to the diminishing role of central finance departments, with the development of service level agreements and sometimes their reorganisation into a small central client unit, purchasing specialist services from independent business units. A further diminution in finance numbers over recent years reflects the extent to which services have taken over their own financial management.

Some of the ways the traditional finance role has changed are set out below.

Processing payments and collecting income

Councils have traditionally been slow payers of their suppliers. Many used extremely lengthy and cumbersome payment procedures, where invoices collected in service departments passed through various management controls before being sent in batches to the finance department for eventual payment.

Systems now in use log order details, and enable service users to check invoices and input payments directly. This is much speedier. The central finance role becomes limited to controlling the overall payment position with suppliers, and seeing that the system is operated within agreed procedures for security reasons.

Similarly, miscellaneous income used to be recovered by departments sending details of debts to a central income section. This section would issue an invoice, and control recovery of the debt. Systems now enable invoices to be originated by service providers, who are also able to take a more active role in credit management.

Budgets and financial advice

The strength of departmental financial management has always varied from council to council. Certain changes have moved the balance towards localised financial management within service departments. These include:

— greater availability of financial information through networked systems;
— the ability to carry out accounting or budgetary calculations locally using spreadsheets or database facilities;
— many councils send senior finance staff to work nominally under the control of a service chief officer, and in that department, so as to achieve better understanding and control of service finance.

We have seen earlier how local government itself is in a transitional phase, and all the financial problems that entails. To complicate the picture, we have also seen that financial management within councils is changing. Not only must financial activities be controlled by service level agreements and business criteria, but finance staff are soon likely to be competing for their own jobs against outside firms and consultants. A growing number of councils are jumping the gun by outsourcing or contracting out finance work voluntarily. Other councils have restructured their finance departments into arms' length client and contractor units. Allied to these changes is the increasing financial self-management practised by service departments.

Whereas in the 1970s, one finance department was broadly like another, there is currently a great deal of variation across the country in structure, use of outside agencies, and relationships with other departments. Some of these changes may be largely cosmetic. Will it make a tremendous difference to council employees whether they are paid their monthly salary by the finance department or by the payroll business unit? (Or by an outside payroll bureau?) Other changes are far-reaching, and it is impossible to say yet whether they lead to council finances being operated more effectively in the public interest.

It might well be that, within a decade, there will be a new vogue preaching the merits of a strong, centralised finance department. At least our brief review has shown that finance staff are as uncertain about their own future role as other service managers might be. With that confused agenda, we now examine some of the key elements of financial management within councils.

The basis of council financial management

How councils raise money, and how it is spent

The author was once involved in judging a series of council annual reports. These abounded in diagrams to the effect that rates were excellent value, and reminded residents of all the services they received for a daily expenditure less than that of buying a pint (milk or beer depending on the council's rate level).

In fact, as Table 1.6 shows, local taxes represent only a small contribution to council costs. Thus to pursue our analogy, that trivial daily expenditure is matched fivefold from other sources. The consequent pressures on local taxation because of this gearing have already been discussed earlier.

Table 1.6: Local authority income sources 1990/91

Government grants		
Revenue support grant	16%	
Specific grants	22%	
Non-domestic rates	17%	
Total government funding		55%
Council resources		
Interest earned on balances	2%	
Sale of land and property	5%	
Borrowing	2%	
Other income (including using reserves from earlier years)	9%	
Total council resources		18%
Charges for services		11%
Poll tax		16%
		100%

The total value of income received by councils was some £62 billion.

Source: Department of the Environment (DOE).

Table 1.7 shows how the £62 billion of income was spent, and gives some indication of the relative importance of council functions.

Table 1.7: Expenditure on services 1990/91

	%
Education	33
Housing	22
Social services	9
Police	8
Local transport	7
Other services	21
	100

Source: DOE.

The five main functions specified represent nearly 80 per cent of council expenditure. Equally, the range of activities encompassed in other services is very wide. A recent DOE summary of council functions prepared in relation to council reorganisation lists 206 Acts of Parliament relative to council services. Many of the lesser council functions which do not immediately spring to mind are of much importance to local residents, and include coast protection, electoral registration, and control of dangerous dogs.

The DOE list also includes some more unusual statutes, such as the Hypnotism Act 1952 or the Game Act 1831. The stifling weight of legislation under which councils are obliged to operate is a matter to which we return later.

One major source of local/central disputes is the extent to which government funding levels allow councils to fulfil even their minimum statutory responsibilities. Councils have so many duties that, once these obligations have been met, the scope for local discretion or political initiative can seem very limited. As we see later, government would argue that central funding allocations are calculated with the precise objective of equipping councils to provide a standard level of service.

The level of council borrowing and investments

As we saw in Table 1.6, borrowing is a small (2 per cent) element of the overall financing of council expenditure. This figure represents the net increase in councils' external capital borrowing during the year. The total debt under council management is much higher, consisting of all the accumulated borrowings incurred in earlier decades when capital programmes were much higher in real terms.

This council capital debt is estimated at some £60 billion, with about 80 per cent owed to the government-backed Public Works Loan Board (PWLB) . Other council borrowing consists of short-term loans from banks and other financial institutions, which is used to meet council costs pending receipt of budgeted income.

Most councils have some cash reserves, placed on deposit with banks or building societies through the money markets. Interest earned on these balances (which amount to over £10 billion), is used to finance council services.

Much larger investments are held by council pension or superannuation funds, totalling some £40 billion. These are mostly in the form of shares quoted on the London Stock Exchange.

Council financial procedures

The operation of council finances is governed by a series of procedures. These provide the framework within which individual services are operated.

The council's annual budget

All councils must have an annual revenue budget for the various services they provide. Setting this budget is linked into statutory deadlines for setting the council tax or precept. The budget is used during the financial year to monitor spending against approved levels. Special procedures usually apply to reallocate financial resources during the financial year.

The capital programme

Councils maintain a separate budget for their capital schemes. These are items of long-term value to the council such as buying property, or constructing roads. Because of the longer-term nature of these projects, and the difficulties in controlling expenditure on them, capital programmes usually cover a three-year period as a minimum. Once a scheme is approved into the council's capital programme, it will usually continue to its completion, provided construction ever starts in the first place.

Council tax and precept setting

The revenue budget and capital programme identify the planned expenditure of the council during the coming year. Before the financial year begins, the council must translate this into a tax demand on local residents. In Chapter 4 we see in greater detail how the level of council tax charged is calculated.

The shire counties derive their council tax income by precepting on the districts within their area. Those districts then issue council tax bills which cover both their own needs and the sums precepted by the county.

In calculating their council tax needs, both counties and districts must set items such as government grant (RSG) and their share of the nationally set non-domestic rate against their expenditure. Tax demands can also be limited by using reserves accumulated from earlier financial years.

The accounting system

Councils are required to publish their accounts annually. These published accounts are known as the statement of accounts. Often the publication combines the accounts with a report on the council's activities. The rules under which the accounts are prepared are laid down in local government law, and in accounting standards issued by the CIPFA accounting body.

Councils differ from the corporate sector in that, during the year, they use the same framework of accounts to monitor their expenditure to date against budget. This can cause problems because:

—accounting adjustments made at the year-end to accord with accounting standards may cause abrupt changes in the figures from earlier budget control reports;

—many of the accounting entries required for the published accounts do not become known until the year-end, such as the amount to be provided for doubtful debts, and these items are sometimes not covered at all in budget control reports.

Accounting systems are usually operated on a mainframe computer, and offer sophisticated facilites to extract data and use it for planning and control calculations.

Audit

Councils have two categories of auditor checking their activities. As with any organisation they are required to have external auditors. External auditors are appointed by the independent Audit Commission. About 70 per cent of audits are undertaken by the Commission's own District Audit Service, and the rest by major firms of chartered accountants.

Council audits are unusually wide ranging in that, as well as checking the accuracy of the published accounts (auditors call this giving an opinion on the accounts), auditors must examine the council's management arrangements and whether these ensure value for money is achieved in council services.

Auditors also have a quasi-judicial power to enquire into illegal or fraudulent expenditure. They may seek permission from a court to surcharge those responsible for the money involved. If those responsible are councillors they may be banned from office for 5 years.

The audit fee charged to a medium-sized council may be around £100,000.

The other category of auditor is internal audit, whose staff are normally under the supervision of the treasurer. Their work is less tightly defined, but as well as reviewing the adequacy of council financial systems, they investigate any allegations or suspicions of fraud that may arise. Internal audit is a powerful investigative unit in any council: often it comes to be known as the eyes and ears of the treasurer.

Financial regulations

To ensure officers and councillors carry out the financial aspects of their work with due propriety, councils adopt a set of financial regulations. These are issued from time to time by the treasurer, and the treasurer is usually empowered to make such regulations without needing the approval of a council committee.

Financial regulations may seem fairly mundane on a first reading, but they establish important ground rules as to how officers should deal with finance. They are often the test of whether an officer has acted correctly or not. All officers and members should have a copy of their council's financial regulations, and be well versed in those regulations affecting their particular area of activity. The types of subject that regulations cover include the following.

Income and banking

— procedures for raising accounts to collect in money for services provided by the council;

— any relevant VAT rules;

— who has authority to write off any debt due to the council (this usually consists of a scheme of increasing seniority needed as the amount increases, with debts above a certain sum, say £1000, needing committee approval);

— rules about how often money collected by officers must be paid into the council's bank account.

Purchasing and stores

— who has authority to order goods and services;

— whether any committee authority is needed for large items (many councils have a rule that there is automatic approval to purchase any item in the council's approved revenue budget or capital programme);

— how often stocks must be checked to stock records, and by whom;

— whether there are obligations to use specific suppliers for some goods and services (the council may have negotiated advantageous terms for bulk contracts on some items).

Financial regulations are usually an uneasy compromise between a guide to correct financial management and a list of potential disciplinary charges. Suffice it to say that any person who acts in accordance with them is likely to have a sound defence.

Standing orders

Council standing orders are the rules by which council business is conducted at the political level. They also control the awarding of contracts. Standing orders are usually prepared by the council's chief legal officer, but must be approved by the full Council (i.e. the regular meeting of all elected councillors of a particular local authority).

A favourite CIPFA examination question used to be explaining the difference between financial regulations and standing orders. In practice, there is little overlap as the list below shows:

Matters covered in standing orders

— What committees are formed.

It would not be practical for all councillors to deal as a body with managing all the council's functions. Hence service committees are formed. Some committees are required by law (e.g. an education committee), but with most services it is up to the Council whether it has a single committee for a function, or committees combining several functions. The representation of individual political parties on committees is controlled by statutory rules, and is broadly in line with the number of seats they hold on the council as a whole.

— The terms of reference of committees.

Despite being of the same political persuasion, chairs of different committees often hold opposing views on a particular issue. It is thus important to have clear terms of reference for the different committees. If a committee acted outside its terms of reference, that decision could potentially be subject to judicial review.

— What sub-committees are formed.

Bigger committees have smaller committees upon their backs to bite 'em. In a large council, the range and diversity of committees and sub-committees is sometimes quite remarkable. Unless they are well co-ordinated and managed, this can soon clog up the council machinery, and prejudice the management of services.

— Rules for the conduct of meetings.

Many councillors are experts on standing orders, and try to liven up the committee process with esoteric points of order. Rules of meeting may include:

—the statutory rules about giving the public adequate notice of any committee meeting (usually at least three days);
—rules on what can be discussed in confidential session (i.e. with no press or public present). Much of this is covered in statute;
—powers of the chair. These are much more wide ranging than the famous casting vote (which means that the chair has one vote in the normal voting process, and a further vote if the result is a tie). They may include deciding on whether a particular report should be taken at all by the meeting, dealing with unruly behaviour, and best of all, interpreting the standing orders. The chair's decision, as with any referee, is usually final.

Another important area covered by standing orders is the declaration of members' interests. Members must declare a *pecuniary interest*. Put simply, they should not vote on any matter where they stand to profit personally from the decision. An extreme example of pecuniary interest would be if a councillor were a director of a building firm bidding for a contract. In those circumstances, the member should declare such an interest at the start of the meeting, leave the room when that item is discussed, and not vote on it. Not to declare a pecuniary interest is a criminal offence. There are also non-pecuniary interests which councillors may find advisable to declare. If, for example, a councillor is a member of a golf club, it might not be appropriate to vote on a planning matter relating to the club.

— Contract standing orders.

Unfortunately, local government history has many instances of corruption in relation to contracts. Standing orders should provide rules on such matters as:

—who is allowed to tender for a contract (many councils use an approved list which should be chosen from in strict rotation);

23

—tender opening procedures. All tenders should be returned in a standard envelope, so that the sender could not be determined before opening (an unscrupulous officer could destroy some of the tenders). A tender panel should be formed, including persons not involved with preparing the tender documentation. All the tenders should be opened at the same time.

Council officers

The role of council officers, or more specifically chief officers, is determined by both their statutory duties and political accountability. Major chief officers, chief executive, finance, education, social services, legal, have direct duties imposed by statute. In extreme cases, these duties may require the chief officer to prevent councillors taking a particular course of action.

In most councils, it is a nice judgement to establish exactly how far the management of services is controlled by councillors and committees. Certainly, committees receive the advice of chief officers on all the matters they discuss, though such advice is not always accepted.

In practice, much of the management of services is delegated to chief officers (the precise extent may be covered in standing orders) yet, whilst massive transactions may go ahead without any committee approval (e.g. deciding to borrow £1 million at a particular interest rate), other apparently trivial matters (such as a £1000 grant to a voluntary group) may dominate the council's political scene for weeks on end.

Councillors

The most influential councillor is normally the leader of the majority party. The leader usually has a key role in the council's finances, and is looked to by officers to explain the policies and strategies required by the majority group, and which are thus likely to gain committee approval.

Other key members include the deputy leader and the chief whip of the majority party.

Chairs of committees have a powerful role as we have already seen. They often establish close working relationships with their departmental chief officer, gaining a wide understanding of that particular council function. Time-honoured local government practice is to cultivate one's chair, who may then be looked to to fight the department's corner in political debate.

Councillors come from a wide range of backgrounds and professions, ranging from business leaders to manual workers in other local authorities. It is important for officers to be able to gauge the response of particular members or groups of members.

Many councils are in the position where no one political grouping has sufficient seats to control it. A council being hung makes officer's lives all the more complex.

Certainly, councillors are to be admired for dealing with the great volumes of paperwork that are inflicted on them by officers. The author recalls a particularly thorough reader of council agendas whose day-time employment was a train driver. That he found the time for all this reading was a little alarming.

Councillors are responsible for pursuing complaints and queries by local residents, and these are usually addressed directly to the relevant chief officer, rather than through the formal committee system.

The office of mayor is essentially non-political, and is usually voted to a member of the majority party with a long record of council service. Quite often the mayoral year is succeeded by reduced political influence on return to normal member status.

Committees

The process of a committee meeting can seem rather perfunctory. In many councils there is a procedure whereby the meeting proper is preceded by a call-over, which allows councillors to ask officers detailed questions about the reports.

The political groups then meet, without officers in attendance, to decide how they will vote on the various items. Thus when the committee proper begins, councillors from the majority party may have very little they wish to say about the items.

The chair asks officers to present each report in turn. Officers soon become attuned to whether a presentation is actually required; if not, a brief 'as on paper chair' suffices. Political debate is usually focused on a few key items on the agenda. Members are entitled to question officers on any aspect of the reports, and often have a happy knack of lighting on the one area of uncertainty. Whilst this is good practice for officers at thinking on their feet, their key consideration in advising a committee is in tendering sound and adequate written advice.

A respite to the routine of committee meetings is the receiving of deputations from groups with a particular concern in items on the agenda. This is an excellent opportunity for councillors to deliver political speeches, thus the deputations part of the agenda can take far longer than the main business.

Minutes of committees are an essential source of reference as to the authority for decisions, and subsequent officer action.

Full council usually meets monthly, and receives the minutes of all the council's committees. Part of the proceedings may include a form of prime minister's question time, when opposition councillors can question the leader of the council on any matter relating to council services.

There are certain decisions which may only be taken in full council. These include setting the council tax.

Role of the treasurer

A council's chief financial officer has various statutory responsibilities, including preparing the published accounts, providing an internal audit service, and collecting the council tax. Under S114 of the Local Government Act 1988, for example, the treasurer may prevent the council entering into an unlawful action, or incurring expenditure beyond its resources. The issue of a S114 notice (in practice a very rare event) legally prevents the action for a 21 day period. As the external auditor must be informed, any attempts by the council to continue the action after 21 days would in practice need to be with the auditor's consent.

Much of the treasurer's role though is determined by how a particular individual chooses to exercise his or her office. Apart from a few specific duties, legislation is vague. The oft-cited section 151 of the Local Government Act 1972 states baldly '. . . every local authority shall make arrangements for the proper administration of their financial affairs and shall secure that one of their officers has responsibility for the administration of those affairs'. Treasurers' discretion as to their duties is exercised within an informal framework of common practice between councils on financial matters.

Nearly all treasurers are members of the CIPFA accounting body, and the guidance issued by the CIPFA on council financial management usually gains wide acceptance. Most of the guidance issued by CIPFA is in the form of codes of practice or advice, and is not mandatory on CIPFA members. The institute has disciplinary procedures, though these are rarely applied and certainly not in relation to non-compliance with accounting standards.

A further factor in establishing a common approach amongst treasurers is the frequent interchange of staff between councils. Although some treasurers have achieved their post after several promotions at the same council, most have worked for a number of different authorities. Council finance is a small world, and few councils have developed their financial procedures in isolation.

There are also various groups established at which treasurers exchange views on issues, ranging from national groupings such as the association of district council treasurers, down to county-based meetings of the county treasurer and all the district treasurers within that county's area.

Some of the main aspects of the treasurer's role are now explained.

Member of the council's management team

Most councils are controlled (subject to political oversight!) by a management team or board of the chief executive and chief officers. Finance is one of the key chief officers, and is thus likely to have an input to most issues of corporate importance.

Specialist in key finance areas

The treasurer is often required, or chooses, to make a direct personal input in specialist areas such as treasury management, or pension fund investment.

Value for money

Many treasurers consider they have a clear duty to oversee the value for money achieved in council services, and to report on deficiencies to the chief officer board or to the relevant committee of the council. Sometimes this responsibility is conceived as a wider duty to local tax payers. This can create some friction with other chief officers, who are not in a position to oversee the treasurer's activities in a reciprocal manner.

Departmental manager

Finance is usually quite a large department, and the treasurer has all the normal responsibilities of departmental management. There is a particular onus on finance to manage itself efficiently, as a failure to do so will damage its credibility to advise other departments on such issues. (Having said that, many interesting stories could be told of the organisational problems encountered within finance departments, though dealt with 'in camera'.)

Financial advice

The treasurer must advise both councillors and other chief officers on any financial aspect of their services. Given the wide range of council services, this is an exacting responsibility.

Audit

Councillors and chief officers have an expectation that the treasurer will provide an effective review and investigation service. Treasurers are often called on to carry out major disciplinary reviews and investigations.

Before leaving the role of the treasurer, it is important to stress the wide divergence of management styles practised by incumbents of this post. Whereas some concentrate their attention on the strategic financial issues facing the council, others take a greater interest in the details of their department's activities.

One treasurer, now retired, had a particular obsession with the need for staff to keep their desks tidy. He would wait until late on a Friday afternoon, and then roam the deserted department looking for examples of untidiness. These would incite a note 'Mr Smith, your desk is untidy'. Failure to take corrective action would result in a three-month transfer to the dreaded motor tax department.

Another treasurer used to make a point of reading through the whole of the council's abstract of accounts, hundreds of pages of figures, prior to its publication. He usually concluded this examination by throwing it on to the desk of the chief accountant with a terse 'there's a mistake in that'. As nobody dared to ask him exactly where the mistake was, many hours of checking usually ensued. There never was a mistake, it was just his way of keeping staff on their toes.

Important agencies in council finance

We conclude this introductory chapter with a brief look at some of the outside agencies that play a role in council finance.

The Department of the Environment and other Ministries, including the Treasury

The Department of the Environment (DoE) is the medium by which central government controls on councils are exercised. Its responsibilities range from the preparation of new legislation for consideration by parliament, down to the collection of expenditure statistics from individual councils. Many services require joint control, such as education where Department of Education policies need to be co-ordinated into the overall pattern of council services and expenditure as set by the DoE. Expenditure totals, accounting procedures and borrowing and investment policy are all under Treasury control.

The Audit Commission

The Audit Commission oversees the external audit of local authorities. Since 1990, its role has been extended to include audit of the health service. Its functions are dealt with in some depth in Chapter 3.

The local authority associations

The associations represent the views of member councils on a wide range of issues including finance. They include:
— the association of county councils (ACC);
— the association of metropolitan authorities (AMA), covering London boroughs and the metropolitan areas;
— the association of London authorities (ALA), and the London boroughs association (LBA) which are based on different political groupings.

CIPFA, the Association of Accounting Technicians (AAT), and other accounting bodies.

CIPFA provides the majority of council treasurers, and senior finance staff. The AAT is a lower level qualification relevant to junior managerial and technical finance posts. The UK has a fragmented accountancy profession, and the Institute of Chartered Accountants has also had a role in the development of council accounting practice in recent years.

The Department of the Environment

The department's remit requires it to develop new legislation and promote government initiatives in consultation with councils. Yet is must also adopt a monitoring role for their activities. Not surprisingly, many councils find it difficult to reconcile the two tasks, and a fair amount of criticism is directed at the department.

The situation can quite easily arise where a council is successfully lobbying one section of the DoE for more money, whilst a different section is imposing expenditure limitation on the council.

Council finance staff will naturally have a keen understanding of the practicalities of proposed legislation, and may feel their views are not sufficiently listened to during consultation exercises. Some policy changes are brought in by government in the teeth of council opposition, whereas on other occasions proposals are significantly altered in view of comments received.

There are formal DoE/local authority groups on various policy areas, though there is also a fair degree of informal discussion. Some of the main DoE roles are as set out below.

- Collects statistics from all councils on their revenue and capital expenditure.
- Issues borrowing permissions to councils for financing their capital programmes.
- Manages the payment of revenue support grant and housing subsidy to councils.
- Monitors council DLOs for anti-competitive practices, and takes remedial action where appropriate.
- Prepares the methodology for calculating council standard spending assessments.
- Issues capping directions to councils, and deals with appeals.
- Publishes consultation papers on new legislation.
- Prepares statutory instruments to give effect to ministerial powers, such as when particular legislation becomes operative, or the percentage of capital receipts councils are allowed to use for new spending.
- Publishes circulars explaining the operation of new legislation.

The question of government circulars is an interesting one, as some years ago these were usually accepted by councils as an authoritative interpretation of the law. In the present climate of relationships, circulars are now more often categorised as exhortation, and council lawyers pore over the relevant legislation looking for more favourable constructions.

The local authority associations

The associations provide a wider political platform for councils, and are used by DoE as the basis of consultation on most finance issues. The major task of the year is usually to develop the local authority side of the rate support grant negotiations.

Some of the associations' manoeuvres on RSG must come as welcome entertainment to the government side. On a recent occasion the chair of one association went public on his dissatisfaction with the negotiating line he had previously agreed with the others. Unfortunately, this was *before* the associations met the DoE to present their joint view.

Preparation of the local authority side of the RSG negotiations is an important task, as the ultimate settlement can have a very damaging effect on particular councils. Much of the work on the councils' side is to calculate the cost of operating services, given realistic assumptions on pay, prices, and new duties to be undertaken by councils. These calculations usually exceed the amount of money the government believes councils need to run their services.

The role of the associations in finance issues are summarised as follows.

- The associations have a structure which mirrors the political complexion of their member councils. This means for example that, if there is a change in which political party controls the majority of districts, the views of that particular association are likely to change too.

- The associations have committees dealing with the major functions that concern their members. They comment on government policy proposals, and publish their own reports with views on how council services should be operated or reorganised.
- The associations operate with a small secretariat of professional staff. Much of the advice provided to association committees is given by staff from member local authorities, so a particular council's treasurer may be appointed as the association's advisor on capital finance.
- Given the rapid rate at which political events develop, and the need for associations to react quickly to government announcements, the professional staff of the associations can have a very influential role. They have a privileged position in terms of access to information, and can be relied on to be well ahead of council staff on the state of play on most issues. There is often some tension arising between the associations' council-type committee management and the need for the secretariat to use initiative when the situation demands.
- Associations are used by member councils as a source of information and guidance on any aspect of local authority services. The associations are largely financed by the subscriptions of member councils, and are based in central London, within easy reach of the DoE and parliament.

The Chartered Institute of Public Finance and Accountancy

The CIPFA accounting institute has an influential role in council finance and it is worth examining it in a little detail. As Table 1.8 shows, it has some 9000 working members of whom just over half work in council finance departments. Virtually all council treasurers are CIPFA qualified.

The institute owes its influence to a long history of monopoly in council accounting matters though, as government has taken a more direct role in council finances, this dominance has been threatened. It was formed in 1885 as the Institute of Municipal Treasurers and Accountants. It had a two-tier membership until 1979, consisting of fellows and associates. Fellowship was conferred to treasurers, and only fellows were eligible to sit on the institute's ruling council.

In 1979, the institute changed to its present name, widening its charter to encompass the entire public sector. The two-tier membership was abandoned. More recently, the voting structure for the council was altered to allocate seats specifically for non-local government members.

The present council thus includes some members yet to reach the rank of finance director or treasurer, and local government representatives are in only a small majority.

In recent years, CIPFA has been concerned at its ability to survive on its low membership basis. Two attempts to merge with the much larger Institute of Chartered Accountants were rejected by the general membership of that institute. In a 1992 strategy document, CIPFA proposed extending its membership to public sector managers. Its own membership rejected the inclusion of non-accountant members.

In the mid-1980s the institute derived significant income from its consultancy activities, though most of these activities have now become established as independent companies in their own right.

The institute has had some success at developing membership outside its traditional local government base, though perhaps not to the extent hoped. The increasing number of members in other categories of employment has created a demand for changes in the services provided by the institute, yet clearly the level of influence in local authority accounting needs to be maintained.

Table 1.8: The Chartered Institute of Public Finance and Accountancy

(a) *Membership of the UK accounting bodies*

Body	Members	Students
Institute of Chartered Accountants in England and Wales (ICAEW)	97,720	15,325
Institute of Chartered Accountants in Scotland (ICAS)	13,022	1,500
Institute of Chartered Accountants in Ireland (ICAI)	7,584	2,600
The Chartered Association of Certified Accountants (ACCA)	38,000	83,000
The Chartered Institute of Management Accountants (CIMA)	31,991	54,718
CIPFA	11,092	3,442
Totals	199,409	160,585

One sometimes wonders how the economy can function at all with under 200,000 accountants to guide its fortunes.

(b) *Analysis of CIPFA membership by employment*

		%*
Health	975	11
Local government	4,892	54
National audit	744	8
Water	273	3
Other	2,190	24
Retired	2,018	—
Total	11,092	

* Excluding retired

Table 1.8: (continued)

(c) *How CIPFA derives its income*

Membership subscriptions	9%
Student and exam fees	5%
Publications and journals	33%
Courses and conferences	33%
Grants and sponsorship	6%
Other income	14%

Source: CIPFA annual report 1992.

- *The CIPFA council has 35 members, and includes committees as follows:*
  —professional;
  —technical (overseeing accounting and audit guidance);
  —management (running the institute);
  —health;
  —local government (including specialised local authority accounting);
  —disciplinary.
- *CIPFA publishes a financial information service (FIS — pronounced fizz), which is an encyclopaedic guide, in 30 loose-leaf volumes, to public finance in general and council finance in particular.*
- *CIPFA also publishes numerous guidance booklets on accounting and financial management.*

Summary

In this introductory chapter we have summarised some of the main current developments in local government finance. In later chapters we shall examine many of these subjects in greater detail.

2 Budgets, accounting and service finance

There are probably few areas of the financial domain where there is a greater divergence between theory and practice than budgeting. According to the textbooks a budget is a plan, expressed in financial terms, which encapsulates an organisation's strategy and is used to control its activities. Unfortunately in real local government life, the strategy options are tightly restrained. Moreover, councils are political organisations. Often budget decisions owe more to behind the scenes political bartering than to academic budget techniques. A further impediment to a guide on budget procedures is that each council has developed its own particular method of reaching its annual budget, so rather than restate budget theory, this chapter concentrates on some of the practical aspects of budgeting.

We then look briefly at the accounts which record the actual financial results of the council. Whilst these are more widely standardised than budgets, we still hope to demonstrate a few tricks of the trade.

Finally we summarise finance issues on some of the major council services.

Budget setting

In the 1970s there was a fairly consistent pattern between different councils as to the approach used in budget setting. Now, in the 1990s, there is a whole spectrum. This ranges from a continuing adherence to the centralised and intricate 1970s methods, to a business-oriented system for a council split into mini-trading units. Table 2.1 summarises some of these options.

Table 2.1: Review of budget methods

Method	Principles
Traditional, with inflation adjustment	The starting point for the budget is the previous year's budget. (This is sometimes described as an *incremental* approach.) The previous budget is updated for inflation, detailed head by detailed head. A central contingency for further inflation and adjustments is maintained. This is allocated out to departments as the year progresses.
	The principle behind this approach is to maintain services in 'real' terms. For example, if social workers are granted a higher pay award than the

33

Table 2.1: (continued)

local government average, more money would be directed into the social services budget.

This approach was prevalent in a period when:

— there was no statutorily enforceable limit on council expenditure (remember only as recently as financial year 1985/86 was rate-capping introduced);

— government grant to councils was adjusted during the financial year to reflect inflation increases.

Basically, the traditional approach was a good method of maintaining all services at an adequate base level. It concentrated attention on growth bids for any extra resources that the council chose to provide for itself by rate increases.

Cash-based budgets

A trend of restriction on council spending levels by the government, and the decision to pay government grant at a once and for all cash figure each year, outmoded the traditional system. To replace it, budgets came to be allocated to committees on a cash basis. This dispensed with the need to mete out the central inflation contingency during the year. Other trends developed, including

— financial management was increasingly undertaken by departments themselves, rather than relying on central accounting expertise in the finance department. In some authorities this has been accompanied by a transfer of accountants out to service departments.

— more flexibility to vary the pattern of spend within the cash allocation. Under a traditional system, the budget was subdivided into innumerable *heads* or *votes*. Strict rules used to be in force as to transferring money from one vote to another (known as *virement*). Under a cash system, the justification for close scrutiny of virement disappears, as the overriding objective becomes not breaching the cash total.

The cash limit system is essentially a means of ensuring that council expenditure does not exceed fixed cash resources. No longer is the objective to maintain a constant service base.

Competitive and distributed budgeting

Many council functions are now subject to compulsory competitive tendering (CCT). The only budgetary objective of these departments or committees (if the council chooses to operate them at all) is to meet government financial criteria and survive in business.

Table 2.1: (continued)

Other major functions are subject to special accounting arrangements. Housing, one of the main council functions, is *ring-fenced*. There is no opportunity to divert resources to housing at the expense of other functions.

The other major council service, education, also has special budgetary considerations. Not only have schools increasing control of their own finances, but they can choose to opt out of council control altogether. If they do so, the council's government grant will be redirected accordingly.

Finally, a vigorous internal market system is now found in more and more authorities. This means that departments such as architects, or even internal audit, are reliant on demand for services from service departments to maintain their existence.

The upshot of these developments is that, rather than representing a coherent council policy, budgets reflect a variety of external demands and requirements.

Having rehearsed this budget theory, you will probably be able to identify your own council's procedures somewhere within the spectrum. What really matters is being conversant and gaining facility in your own council's rules and procedures. One of the undying traits of the council bureaucrat is to increase his or her own budget at the expense of everybody else's. You have been warned.

Before we move into the detailed process of budget calculation though, let's briefly consider some general issues which are relevant.

Financial strategy

A long-term financial strategy may sound like something of a luxury, given the present local authority expenditure controls. However, there are many strategic choices available to councils in running their finances. Table 2.2 demonstrates some of these. It is obviously a bit of a fine distinction whether these are financial strategies or service strategies. The reason we highlight them is:

—if adopted, they will have a continuing effect on the financial position of the council as a whole, and most of its services;
—they are normally set as ground rules which apply to the whole budget process.

Financial strategy is not always clearly articulated. Sometimes the relevant guidance is hidden away in committee resolutions on specific matters, which then set a future precedent. However, in your approach to the budget, it is essential to have an understanding of the way the council is moving generally. If, for example, it is part of its strategy to increase fees and charges faster than inflation, you will need very detailed justification for a budget which assumes charge reductions.

Table 2.2: Examples of financial strategy options

Area of budget	Strategy options
The level of council debt	If a council pays off or reduces its external borrowing, then long-term financial advantages will accrue to its revenue account. Interest will be saved, and there would be no need to set aside money each year for debt redemption.
	Debt could be reduced by increasing the financing charges paid by revenue accounts to above the statutory minimum. Capital receipts could be used for debt repayment to a greater extent than legally required. The reduction in resources available for capital programmes will also save the council the future running costs of such schemes.
	Conversely, the council may decide that it will maximise its borrowing in order to maintain its capital programme. It will only repay the minimum amount of debt it is required to by government regulations.
Fees and charges	The fees and charges collected by councils are so numerous, that it is usually necessary to adopt a general strategy. Otherwise, each of the many cases has to be argued on its merits. Possible strategies are:
	— to increase by more than inflation, moving the burden of financing from tax-payers to service users (e.g. should a leisure centre be subsidised as part of the council's general expenditure, or should those choosing to use it meet more of the cost?);
	— to keep pace with some general indicator such as the RPI, or the average charge made by other councils for each service;
	— to reduce the burden on particular groups and clients (e.g. in the case of a leisure centre, local residents might pay a smaller charge than other users).
Council tax and precept targets	The council may have developed a plan to reduce its tax to the national average, or the standard set by the government. Conversely, it may be planning to increase its expenditure up to the maximum permissible. These overall policies on tax levels will dictate the total of resources to be distributed between services.
	In some councils, the requirement to match government spending assessments is even made service specific. This can lead to reallocations between committees. Suppose, for example, that education is not spending up to the level assumed by the government in calculating the council's *standard spending assessment (SSA)*. Social services, on the other hand, might be spending well above its SSA. Then a financial strategy of requiring services to spend at SSA levels will produce a local shift of resources from social services to education.

Table 2.2: continued

Other areas of financial strategy include:

— a policy of building up reserves, including capital receipts, so that the interest earned reduces the local taxation requirement;

— the extent to which balances, reserves and provisions are maintained above minimum levels.

An example of this is the balance maintained on the council's general fund. During any financial year, there are invariably unforeseen yet unavoidable items of expenditure. Ideally, a council could maintain balances or a contingency to cater for these. However, the tightness of government expenditure controls in recent years has led to balances being run down (or even eliminated) in many councils.

A restrictive financial strategy would thus be to draw funds in to balances and reserves. A looser one would be to direct some or all of existing balances out to service budgets. Some cynics might suggest this a cyclical process which has been followed since the time immemorial in step with municipal elections.

The annual budget process

If each council has its own unique budget process, there is still of course much common ground. Table 2.3 provides a summary of some of the main processes entailed.

Table 2.3: Budget processes

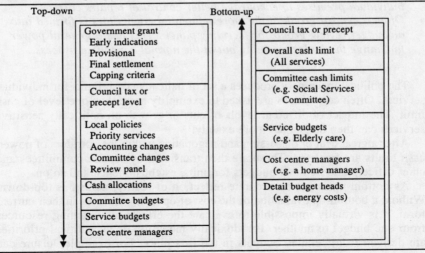

Top-down	Bottom-up
Government grant Early indications Provisional Final settlement Capping criteria	Council tax or precept
	Overall cash limit (All services)
Council tax or precept level	Committee cash limits (e.g. Social Services Committee)
Local policies Priority services Accounting changes Committee changes Review panel	Service budgets (e.g. Elderly care)
	Cost centre managers (e.g. a home manager)
Cash allocations	Detail budget heads (e.g. energy costs)
Committee budgets	
Service budgets	
Cost centre managers	

The two sides of this table represent two opposing schools of budgetary theory. Bottom-up views the budget calculation as beginning at the lowest level budgets are devised, say the energy budget for an elderly persons residential unit. All the different costs of the unit have their budget, and the first level of summarisation is to draw these together at home or cost centre level. Similarly, the budgets for all equivalent residential units are summarised in the council's residential care of the elderly budget. A further level of summarisation is to draw together all the different types of service offered to the elderly in a larger client group budget. All types of social services expenditure are summarised in a committee budget, which taken together with the cost of other council services is used to calculate the local tax demand.

Bottom-up is clearly a simplified view of reality. Without clear direction and rules set at the highest level, the accumulated budgetary demands of hundreds of individual cost centre managers might bear little relation to the resources available to the council, let alone politicians' views. Bottom-up does, however, demonstrate that any budget approach relies on the little building bricks of detailed budgets.

Top-down, on the other hand, starts from the perspective of the council's overall expenditure position. The current system of local government finance obliges councils to spend quite close to their government-determined SSA. Hence budgeting can begin as soon as the government has outlined its intentions towards the next financial year's council expenditure (usually in the Autumn Statement which covers public expenditure as a whole).

Once the likely maximum permissible level of expenditure is known, the political balancing act begins.

- *Councillors may want to give priority to one service over others.*
- *New accounting methods may be introduced to achieve policy objectives. Such a change would be to ask services to pay asset rents for the council property they use, in order to discourage wasteful use of office space. Centralised repairs and maintenance budgets might be delegated to individual premises to encourage better control of repairs costs.*
- *Often a central group of the more influential councillors is formed into a 'budget review group' or 'scrutiny panel'. This has a general power to change the budgets coming out of the normal committee process.*

The political machinery produces a set of indicative cash limits for individual services. Often committees are asked to exemplify more than one level of cash limit. The impact of different levels of cuts or growth on politically sensitive services can then be gauged more exactly.

After a great deal of discussion and negotiation within the corridors of power, cash limits are finalised. These are then translated by service committees and chief officers into detailed budgets for units, establishments, and so on.

As bottom-up is not an accurate reflection of reality, neither is top-down. Without a bottom-up evaluation of the cost of operating services in their current form, it is virtually impossible to evaluate the effects of switching resources from one budget to another. Paradoxically many top-down political priorities are derived from detailed budgets in the first place. For example, leisure can only be articulated as a political priority once it can be demonstrated that leisure centres will have to be closed unless allocated a bigger budget.

If all this theory seems a little abstract, it does at least provide us with some good pointers to keeping ahead in the budget game.

- It is essential to be aware of the policy decisions made at overall budget level, because it is surprisingly soon that these take effect in your own cost centre. Let's take our previous example of premises repair budgets being devolved to local managers. This may seem a fairly innocuous matter, but it could raise all sorts of problems in maintaining your repairs coverage.
  - —How will the central budget be distributed? This might be done on some rough guideline such as rateable value.
  - —Will the new budget be based on last year's expenditure? If so, you could suffer if your particular repairs spending was unusually low in that particular year.
  - —Do you know in any case the cost of providing repairs coverage?

  Overall policies are unlikely to be adjusted on the basis of an academic argument. If, however, you have prepared by calculating the specific effect on your service, you can develop a much stronger case.

- Take care to ensure that central guidelines on budget allocations have been correctly applied. If, for example, training budgets are to be based on the number of staff in post as of a certain date, then it makes sense to check the calculation. How many staff did you actually have? Finance department's figures are not invariably right. Sometimes significant errors are made. Often figures for moving budgets around are provided by the finance department to tight timescales. Moreover, to the finance department they are just that, figures. To you, they are real money, so check.

  This can sometimes prove a source of amusement. Accountants are not renowned for admitting their errors. Hence when faced with some inaccuracy in the way a budget has been calculated, they often resort to spontaneous complication to rationalise the erroneous figure. Usually this invalidates all of the figures that were, in fact, correct, and a form of ever more wobbly mental gymnastics ensues.

- A thorough knowledge of the basis of individual budget calculations always pays dividends. Councillors seem to have a happy knack of being able to choose the one area you're not briefed on as a starting point for any budget interrogation. To return to our premises example, if your knowledge is limited to knowing the total budget is £10,000, then you will be hard put to explain why you couldn't manage equally well with £5000. If, on the other hand, you can say that it includes £4000 for replacing dangerous electric wiring, and £3000 already committed under a previous year's contract, then you may excite a little more sympathy.

Preparing a budget

So far we have discussed budgets in general terms. Now we get down to more detail. As you will appreciate, budgets and accounts are essentially two sides of the same coin. This is shown diagrammatically in Table 2.4. All councils must by law operate a 1 April to 31 March financial year.

Table 2.4: The relationship between budgets and accounts

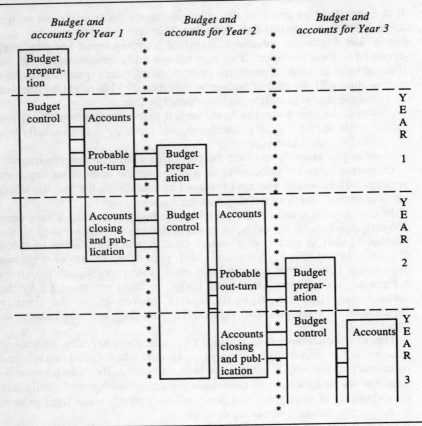

Starting in the top left-hand corner, we begin before the start of year 1 with preparing its budget. Once year 1 has begun, we use the accounts, to date, for year 1 to monitor progress against the budget. However, as you can see from the Table, before year 1 is complete, the time has come round for the preparation of year 2's budget.

However, the council chooses to prepare year 2's budget, one of the key factors is going to be how much will be spent on functions during year 1. Yet year 1's accounts are incomplete. This brings us to the concept of a probable out-turn. A *probable out-turn* is an estimate midway through the year of the total expenditure likely to be occurred for the year as a whole.

As underspending this year's budget is often the thin end of the reduction wedge for next year's budget, probable out-turns invariably show a remarkable propensity for services to spend at or near budget. You will note from the Table that, for much of the time, year 2's budget is in use for budgetary control, the

specialised function, but from which the financial ledger needs to get accounting information. These might include, for example, the system for paying housing benefits, the system for calculating pension entitlements, and so on. The transfer of accounting information from a feeder system in a form acceptable to the financial ledger is termed an *interface*. You will probably find your accountant colleagues take a masochistic delight in sorting out 'interface problems'.

Why operate feeder systems instead of incorporating their facilities in the financial ledger itself? The reason is that they are usually far too large in themselves, with accounting data being a small proportion of what they produce. So, for example, every time the payroll is run, the cost of salaries is charged out, via an interface into the financial ledger, to the relevant service accounts but, at the same time, the payroll system is updating numerous other files, such as an individual employee's tax details or any changes in employees' home addresses.

Table 2.5: Basis of council accounting systems

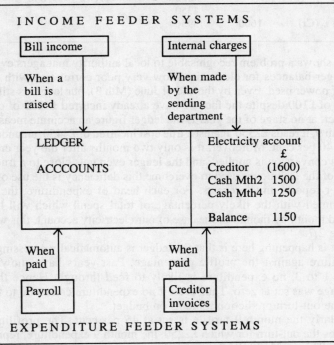

INCOME FEEDER SYSTEMS

Bill income — When a bill is raised

Internal charges — When made by the sending department

LEDGER ACCCOUNTS

Electricity account
£
Creditor   (1600)
Cash Mth2   1500
Cash Mth4   1250

Balance   1150

Payroll — When paid

Creditor invoices — When paid

EXPENDITURE FEEDER SYSTEMS

This method of collecting accounting information is not ideal for budgetary control. Items are charged in the financial ledger only when a transaction goes through one of the feeders. If a creditor is not paid promptly, the ledger is not updated promptly. This makes life a little difficult for managers who are required to deliver a result which will be calculated on an accruals basis.

Thus the ledger electricity account of our example in Table 2.4 is far from being a timely reflection of the value of power used, as the example in Table 2.6 shows.

Table 2.6: Comparison of financial ledger figures with actual costs incurred

	Financial ledger figures (Cr = creditor, I = payment)			Value of electricity used (by spreading invoices evenly)	
		Item £	Balance £	In month £	Balance £
MTH 1	(Cr)	(1600)	(1600)	MTH 1	410	410
MTH 2	(I)	1500	(100)	MTH 2	420	830
MTH 3		—	(100)	MTH 3	420	1250
MTH 4	(I)	1250	1150	MTH 4	460	1710
MTH 5		—	1150	MTH 5	470	2180
MTH 6		—	1150	MTH 6	470	2650
MTH 7	(I)	1400	2550	MTH 7	600	3250
MTH 8		—	2550	MTH 8	600	3850
MTH 9		—	2550	MTH 9	600	4450
MTH 10	(I)	1800	4350	MTH 10	530	4980
MTH 11		—	4350	MTH 11	530	5510
MTH 12		—	4350	MTH 12	540	6050
MTH 13		—	4350			
MTH 14	(Cr)	1600	5950			

This shows a problem recognisable to local authority managers everywhere. The ledger balances for electricity show very poor correlation with the actual value of power used. Even by the end of June (Mth 3), our ledger is still showing a credit of £100 despite the fact we have already incurred £1250 of cost.

In fact, at no stage of the year is the ledger figure an accurate measure. Even by month 9, it reads £2550 against a true cost incurred of £4450, an underestimate of over 40 per cent. Moreover, it is only two months after the year end that the accruals conversion is applied, and the ledger even gets close to a true figure.

One of the techniques used to overcome this deficiency is the use of *profiling* in ledger reports and forecasts. For each head of expenditure, the ledger is programmed with the likely percentage of total spend which will have been achieved month by month. In the case of our electricity account, this would read as Table 2.7.

What is happening here is that the ledger is automatically assessing reported expenditure against the profile percentage. Past years have shown that, in months 1 to 3, no expenditure is likely to feed through. Hence the profile percentage was set at zero. Thus even if no expenditure comes on to the ledger at all, the out-turn prediction remains on budget.

Similarly the month 9 profile is set at 45 per cent. The profiling system calculates the out-turn for which £2250, the month 9 expenditure, represents 45 per cent. This is £5670. Without profiling, it might have been assumed that 9/12 of the budget had been used at this stage. On that assumption, an out-turn of only £3000 would have been predicted (£2250 x 12/9).

Profiling is an extremely valuable facility, and it is well worth investigating whether it is available on your council's financial ledger system. Often managers fail to use profiling even when it is available; given our electricity example, avoid falling into the same trap.

Other methods of developing better financial monitoring information are standard costs, and commitment accounting.

Table 2.7: Example of ledger with profiling

Electricity budget reports (summary)
Budget allocation for year   £6500

Mth	Profile %	Budget to date £	Actual £	Budget for year £	Out- turn £	Variance £
01	0	0	(1600)	6500	6500	0
02	0	0	(100)	6500	6500	0
03	0	0	(100)	6500	6500	0
04	20	1300	1150	6500	5750	(750)
05	20	1300	1150	6500	5750	(750)
06	20	1300	1150	6500	5750	(750)
07	45	2600	2550	6500	5670	(830)
08	45	2600	2550	6500	5670	(830)
09	45	2600	2550	6500	5670	(830)
10	70	4550	4350	6500	6215	(285)
11	70	4550	4350	6500	6215	(285)
12	70	4550	4350	6500	6215	(285)

Standard costs

Standard costs work as the following example. A council building department needs to keep up-to-date accounts of its profit on a window replacement programme. Financial ledger costs are received too late, as the invoices paid to suppliers for new window frames take weeks to process. Only when invoices are paid do the costs feed into the financial ledger.

To overcome this problem, standard costs are calculated for all aspects of window replacement before the start of the contract. These might include £200 labour per window, £50 transport, and £1000 per frame. Using these standards, the department can measure its expenditure by simply multiplying the number of units replaced by the relevant standard costs. This can quickly be compared with the contract income.

A key aspect of the standard cost technique is to refine the standards with the benefit of experience. For example, the financial ledger eventually shows higher labour cost per unit than £200. This could be because wage rates are higher than assumed in preparing the standard (a *price variance*), or because it takes longer than assumed to actually do the work (a *quantity variance*).

Commitment accounting

Commitment accounting is an additional set of financial information available on many financial ledger systems. It enables managers to input commitments as, and when, goods are ordered. Financial reports show not only expenditure to date, but also the value of budget uncommitted.

Commitment accounting needs careful control:

- *Commitments have often (perfectly correctly) to be entered as estimates of costs. If these estimates are not promptly corrected for differences in*

actual costs, the commitment figures become unreliable.
- *orders not delivered by the year-end may be excluded from the financial accounts in accordance with accepted accounting practice. Budgets may thus technically be underspent, despite having been 100 per cent committed prior to the year-end.*

Revenue and capital

The revenue : capital distinction is one which, like the accruals basis we have just examined, has a fundamental importance for budgetary control. Table 2.8 summarises the distinctions between the two. For more detail on the management and control of capital expenditure, see Chapter 5.

Table 2.8: Revenue and capital

	Revenue	*Capital*
Examples of expenditure	Revenue expenditure is the ongoing cost of running the council, such as salaries, wages, energy, costs. Revenue income includes rents, charges for services, and interest earnings.	Capital expenditure represents the long-term assets of the council, such as buildings, land purchase, or road construction. Capital income (or receipts) includes land sales, or right to buy housing sales.
Basis of accounting	Revenue items are included in the reported costs of services for that year (the council's *summary revenue account*). They are adjusted at the year-end on an accruals basis. The debtors and creditors at the year-end appear in the council's balance sheet. Other revenue items in the balance sheet are provisions, and any unspent balances.	Capital items are normally financed by borrowing or by the use of capital receipts. If so, then they do not appear in the revenue account. They appear instead in the balance sheet as *fixed assets*. If the asset was loan financed, then the relevant revenue account must bear annual debt charges. As the debt is repaid over a number of years, the balance sheet value is reduced. The repaid debt deducted from the asset value is known as *capital discharged*.
Government controls	The government may set a limit to (or cap) the amount that an authority can draw from its *collection fund* (i.e. its council tax income). In order not to charge any item of expenditure to revenue, a	Councils are allowed to spend a proportion of their receipts on new capital schemes. They also receive an annual ration of *credit approvals*, which allows them to borrow for capital purposes. There is a statutory definition of

Table 2.8: (continued)

	council must be able to demonstrate the necessary borrowing or capital expenditure permission.	*expenditure for capital purposes.*
What is the overlap?	If capital expenditure is financed out of revenue instead of borrowing or capital receipts, then it may be charged to the summary revenue account.	Repairs and improvements are a grey area. Provided they have a significant element of improvement or enhancement, they may be charged to capital — resources permitting.
What is the period for which budgets are set?	Revenue is normally controlled by an annual revenue budget.	Councils operate a three-or five-year capital programme.

Overview of the budgetary process

So far we have looked in general terms at how the budget processes operate, and how the budget links into the council's accounting system. Next, we will consider the preparation of a budget in more detail, and how to use it for financial control during the year. Before we do so, check your knowledge so far.

- Find out and assess where your own council's budget process ranks as between a traditional method, cash limits, and a CCT-based or distributed approach.
- Establish the financial strategy followed by the council, and bear this in mind when framing any budget proposals.
- Budgeting is at once a bottom-up and top-down process. Be conversant with the overall rules set by the council, but try to gain a full understanding of what your detailed budgets cover.
- Remember that there is a constant interchange between budgets and accounts, and that this often involves more than a single financial year. A successful budget preparation entails not only predicting for the forthcoming year, but also managing this year's probable out-turn and last year's final accounts.
- Be aware of the deficiencies of council accounting systems, particularly in extrapolating mid-year expenditure to an out-turn prediction. Exploit the use of profiling or commitment accounting if available.
- Understand the revenue : capital distinction, and use it to open up budget options.
- We have also developed some general guides on approaching the budget.
  - There is no substitute for detailed knowledge of your budget and the underlying services and expenditure. If you need to justify these to a committee or to some other meeting and you are unsure, take somebody with you who isn't.
  - Don't take the accuracy of another department's calculations for

granted, especially as these could mean real service reductions to your budget.
— Be aware of the scope to use provisions and capitalisation as year-end adjusters.

Preparing a budget

The range of finance structures in different councils is very wide. In some, there continues to be a large central finance department which maintains an iron grip on all matters budgetary. In others, service departments have their own well-resourced finance function. They are thus largely responsible for their own budget calculations, subject to central guidance on cash limits and other general factors.

Our analysis is therefore more of a practical guide, rather than a technical analysis. In any case, experience demonstrates that many departmental managers need very little instruction in the art of beating the budget system.

Budget timetable and procedures

Unlike many local government tasks, the budget preparation deadlines are largely immovable. A council must set its council tax before the start of the financial year. Similarly, a precepting authority must set its precept early in March, so that the councils it has precepted on can prepare to collect this along with their own taxes.

Timing of the budget process will therefore run something like Table 2.9, though this may change from 94/5 onwards with the new Autumn Unified Budget.

Table 2.9: Budget timetables

Date	Stage
July—Sep	Provisional RSG settlement
Aug—Sep	The council sets its budget strategy, procedures and timetable.
Oct—Dec	Work continues in departments and by individual managers on detailed budgets.
Dec—Jan	Final RSG announcement.
Jan—Mar	Budgets are fine-tuned to match available resources.
Mar	Final budgets agreed/council tax or precept set.

Thus by the Autumn, or in time-honoured local government tradition 'after the summer holidays', finance department attention turns to defining the local budget timetable. (Before the summer holidays, accountants work on closing the previous year's accounts.) Timetables will usually include some of the following.

- *Standard formats to be used by all services for setting out the budget information, and reporting to council committees;*
- *deadlines for committee reports, or for information to be sent to finance department for checking;*

- *rules on dealing with the financial effects of various matters, such as:*
  - —inflation
  - —pay awards
  - —the revenue effects of capital programme bids
  - —new legislation
  - and so forth;
- *special information requirements, or budgetary rules which reflect that year's local policy flavour.*

More often than not, the work required to provide all this information by the deadlines set is considerable. There is every temptation to buy more time with some brinkmanship. However, the following need to be borne in mind.

- As the committee dates for budget reports are usually immovable, any time losses at the earlier stages of preparation will be reduplicated at the later stages. Say you have a month to set up a detailed budget, and a further month to prepare a committee report presenting your figures; if you let the first stage drift out to 6 weeks, then you will be scurrying around with only 2 weeks to do your report. That will show in its quality.
- Generally there is little mileage in not adhering to the agreed presentation and procedures, however burdensome it is to collect the information. Either you will be sent back to do it by your own committee/chief officer or, worse still, somebody else will do the figures for you. As they probably already have plenty of work of their own, they may not treat your budget as favourably as you would yourself.
- Councillors may not appreciate the complexities of getting your budget report together, and nothing creates a worse impression than being late with the information. If, for example, you are reduced to handing round late amendments actually at the committee, it doesn't sit comfortably with the notion that you have the department's finances under strict control.
- If you miss deadlines, this can create friction with finance department, who have the task of combining the submissions of different departments into reports on the council's overall budget. Given their power within the budget process, they are the last people to offend. They might even prepare what they think should be your budget if you don't produce one yourself.
- Particular problems arise when a budget has to be forced through committee as a set of general totals, with the detail to be added later. This may arguably fulfil the council's statutory requirement to set a budget, but creates serious budgetary control problems once the financial year begins. Without detailed budgets input to the financial ledger, the situation can deteriorate rapidly. When it comes to preparing next year's detailed budget, for example, you will have no idea of this year's detail, and no useful analysis of expenditure incurred to date.

Prior year figures, and the probable out-turn

Most budget presentations incorporate information on the current year's spend, and the last full financial year. Check these relationships in Table 2.4. For a single section, the information might appear as Table 2.10 in budget papers.

Table 2.10: Example budget presentation

1991/92 Actual £	1992/93 Probable Out-turn £	Item	1992/93 Budget £	1992/93 To date (Mth 6) £	1993/4 Budget (draft) £
26,240	30,920	Employees	36,000	14,290	38,000
10,010	5,050	Premises	8,470	3,500	9,500
(30,200)	(28,000)	Income	(24,000)	(16,000)	(27,000)
6,050	7,970	Total	20,470	1,790	20,500

Small wonder, given the complexity of such arrays of information, that many councils are moving away from consideration of the details of budgets. The pitfalls inherent in presenting such information are evident. Our Table after all has four separate figures which can be used to challenge the final right-hand column of the proposed budget. That means four potential banana skins for the credibility of your calculation.

Let's illustrate this with a few examples from the Table. On the face of it, the employees' budget for 1993/4 at £38,000 seems a reasonable increase on the 1992/93 figure of 36,000. Wait a minute though, how are we performing in 1992/93 in comparison to the budget? The probable out-turn shows just under £31,000 as our prediction. (Had we not been confined by having only spent £14,290 in the first six months of the year, we might have proposed a probable out-turn more in keeping with next year's budget demand.)

Worse still, we only managed to spend £26,240 in 1991/92. Our £38,000 demand now comes across as a 23 per cent increase on our own prediction of this year's spend, and a 45 per cent increase on last year's actual.

Check out the income figures in the Table. These are given as an example of trying to understate the true income potential of the activity.

If you are required to make this sort of presentation (or more significantly, prepare the relevant forecasts) some key points should be borne in mind.

- It stands out quite sharply if the probable out-turn is way in excess of expenditure achieved to date. Try to make the two reasonably compatible, or you are at risk of seeing next year's budget demand trimmed accordingly.
- Make sure you are comparing like with like. Services and structures are constantly changing, so how reliable is the last year's actual if the purpose of the budget has changed?
- Some expenditures do vary widely from year to year, such as premises costs. If last year's actual or the probable out-turn is particularly low, prepare a list of definite expenditure proposals to back up your increased budget demand.
- Try a dry run with a colleague playing devil's advocate.

In many councils, committees are concerning themselves less and less with the year-on-year fluctuations in detailed heads. Although this may mean an easier ride at your committee meetings, you will probably still need to justify your analysis to your higher level managers. Proper preparation is then even more important, as your colleagues will have a much better understanding of the realities of your service.

Detailed expenditure and income budgets

A key aspect of councils' budgetary and accounting procedures is their use of a *standard classification* of income and expenditure. This is published and updated from time to time by the CIPFA accounting body. Its purpose is to allow comparability between different councils' service costs.

It has both an *objective* and a *subjective* aspect.

Objective classification

There is a standard objective analysis of council functions. These are the separate services that should be shown in the council's summary revenue account. This structure is also used by the government in collecting expenditure data from councils (*revenue out-turn or RO forms*).

These would include, for example:

—Social services
—Highways
—Libraries
—Leisure

The objective analysis is pursued by forming divisions of service within each main service. In the case of social services this might include the different client groups such as children, elderly, and so on. At this *division of service* level, local choice often starts to break away from the CIPFA model.

This is because the local analysis of services into divisions, sub-divisions, and cost centres has to reflect the organisation of the relevant department. If, for example, all a council's sports facilities combine wet and dry sports, there is no point in having a separate division for each.

Another way to look at this is by examining the way council accounts are built up. All transactions, be they payments or income receipts, are coded to a ledger account. Codes, which may run to 12 characters or more, are usually set up in the way shown below. Let's consider, for example, code 0304010101564. We break this up into constituent elements as in Table 2.11.

Thus the code 0304010101564 signifies the ledger account for salaries at a specific children's home.

The subjective analysis

In our example (Table 2.11), we designated the central four digits to subjective analysis. This is a different way from the objective classification of analysing expenditure. It looks instead at the inputs required to provide services, and includes groups such as:

—Employees
—Premises

  —   Transport
  —   Supplies and services

These groupings are split down into sub-groups. For employees, these might be salaries, employer's national insurance contributions, agency staff, and so on.

Table 2.11: The CIPFA standard classification

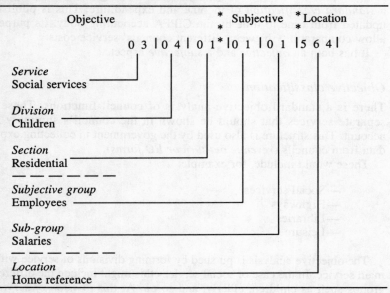

Analysis of accounting information

Financial ledger systems, amongst other things, are large number crunching databases. It is thus possible, exploiting the standard analysis, to extract numerous combinations of information depending on managers' needs. Common examples are:

- *all the budgets for a specific location or cost centre;*
- *all the costs charged to a specific subjective, such as the value of employer pension contributions right across the council;*
- *an **audit trail**, which is a detailed list of all the transactions on a particular code. This could be used to ensure there are no errors in what has been charged to that code.*

In some councils with highly devolved financial arrangements, budgets and accounts are often separated on local departmental systems. However, these are still required to be in harmony with the standard CIPFA form to enable data to be aggregated for the published statement of accounts.

Now that we have seen how budgets and accounts are built up on standard analyses and ledger codes, let's run through a few points on budgeting for the different heads of expenditure.

Employees

Wages and salary costs represent the majority of council expenditure. As a category, they are reasonably predictable. There are some points though that merit attention.

- Many councils operate an *establishment* system for posts. This is a plan of staff numbers, grades and functions department by department. Sometimes there is a rule that appointments may only be made to established posts, and a committee decision is required to vary the establishment. Unfortunately, establishments can quickly become out of date. Moreover, they often represent an ideal, rather than realistic, level of staffing. The employees' budget can then degenerate into a chaotic mixture of establishments, funded and unfunded posts, and actual staff in post.

  Try and square the circle by budgeting on actual staff requirements. Nothing is more debilitating than an esoteric argument between competing managers as to whose vacant posts are, or are not, funded, without any thought being given to the need or purpose of filling the disputed vacancies.
- It's well worth checking which staff salaries are being charged to your budgets. Coding allocations are usually changed only when managers let payroll know a change is needed. Are you still paying for somebody who has moved to a different department?
- Incorporate a realistic allowance for resignations, and the time taken to fill vacancies. Minimum percentages for budget purposes may be set centrally to prevent 'turnover' being used as a spurious financing measure.
- Even with large numbers of staff, it can be advantageous to draw up costings on an employee-by-employee basis. Local government grades may have a high value of increments between bottom and top. It can be misleading to assume all staff are paid at the middle point when budgeting.
- Allow an appropriate figure for employer's national insurance and pension contributions. Again, this may be done by using a centrally determined standard percentage.
- If some of your staff costs are to be met by recharging another section or department, make sure they have included this expenditure in their budget. It can be extremely difficult to resolve such disputes once two conflicting budgets have been agreed by the relevant committees.
- Staff costs may amount to 90 per cent or more of some sections' expenditure. Maintaining staffing levels at all costs can have a detrimental effect on other budgets as shown in Table 2.12. The gearing effect of protecting staff budgets will thus produce an exaggerated diminution in other budgets. If this means that staff cannot function effectively because of lack of equipment and support facilities, the approach will be self-defeating.

Running costs

The proportion of total budget devoted to running costs varies greatly from service to service. In a central professional department it can be 5 per cent or less, but in a service such as highways or housing it may represent over half the budget.

Table 2.12: How maintaining staffing levels at all costs may cause problems

A section's budget is 80 per cent salary costs:

Employees	72,000
Premises	4,500
Equipment	13,500
Total budget	90,000

Budget reductions of 5 per cent are required, but it is decided to maintain the employees' budget. This leads to the following:

Revised budget

% reduction		
Employees	72,000	Nil
Premises	3,375	25%
Equipment	10,125	25%
Total budget	85,500	5%

- Premises costs such as national non-domestic rates (business rates) or rents are reasonably easy to predict. Many councils now operate an asset rent system where services pay market rents over to a central property committee for their use of premises. If lease rentals are paid directly to an external landlord, remember to provide for rent reviews as and when these arise.
- Energy costs are often a fruitful area for cost reduction. There is a wide variety of literature available on energy saving techniques, which include adaptations to premises. Your council may have a specialist energy conservation unit, or a central fund earmarked for works which can demonstrate a quick pay-off in reduced energy bills. The utilities offer a range of different price tariffs for their supplies. It's well worth checking whether you are on the most cost-efficient tariff for your particular needs. Get specialist help to do this if your energy bills are significant. It's possible, for instance, to switch to a maximum demand electricity tariff. You then pay a sum on each bill for the highest wattage in use during the period. In return, the units of power consumed are much cheaper.
- Water charges are also worth review. Considerable cost savings can be made by opting to pay for a metered supply, instead of on rateable value.
- Repair and maintenance costs are notoriously difficult to control and predict. If you are responsible for a large maintenance budget, it pays to get technical help in assessing your needs and what the costs are likely to be. We discuss the control of housing repairs later in the chapter.

Recharges from other departments

Many councils now operate a system of service level agreements or SLAs to set the level of recharges from one department to another. A *recharge* is accounting terminology for an internal transfer between two different council departments. This might be for, say, architects' department work done for housing department, or legal department advice to the social services department. We discuss SLAs and recharges more fully in Chapter 7. However, here are a few key points to bear in mind in setting budgets.

- SLAs are often constructed to allow charge variations. If the provider department fails to deliver the agreed service, the price to you will be reduced. But if you, the client, do not keep your side of the SLA, you may end up having to pay higher charges. Take the case of an SLA with finance department which covers a payroll service for your staff. This may assume you provide all the necessary basic data to finance payroll section (correctly balanced of course!) within stipulated deadlines. Failure to do this may incur additional charges under the SLA. Budget on a realistic basis for your SLA charges.
- If your council has not developed SLAs, meet with departments who charge you to negotiate on the level of charges as far as possible.
- Recharges are often made as part of year-end accounts closing procedures. Remember this in predicting your out-turn. If there is no SLA system, maintain contact with the charging department to gain advance knowledge of any price variations. Nothing is worse than an unexpectedly high and unavoidable year-end charge which causes an overspend in an otherwise well-managed budget.
- If you are a major customer of another department, make sure your budgets for respective charge and recharge reconcile.

Relationships with finance department in preparing the budget

The finance function is operated in different ways in different councils. This affects the way the budget is prepared, as the more devolved the finance function, the less input central finance will have.

Finance is often accused, sometimes with justification, of having a 'best of both worlds' role in departmental budgets. If a budget is overspent, then the service managers alone usually take the blame. Yet, though finance disclaims accountability for budget results, it sets the rules for budget preparation and not infrequently insists on changes to what it considers unrealistic figures. Finance thus has power over service budgets, but no direct accountability.

This finance oversight is one of the facts of local government finance, so better to turn it to your advantage than try to beat the system.

- It's easy for finance to criticise your calculations from afar. Meet with them on any figures they don't agree, and get the basis of their calculations. It might be that your difficulties stem, say, from the central accounting system, and its lack of information. Try and get commitment to developments on finance's side to sort things out.
- Don't let antagonism towards finance drive you into championing an unrealistic budget. You will bear responsibility for any overspend, not finance. Strong finance opposition to your figures should set warning bells ringing; recheck all your assumptions and don't take any risks.

Collecting budget information

Before the budget can be assembled as a financial plan, there is a preliminary stage of collecting the basic information and figures. Just as a printed document has a certain authority, budget figures input to the financial ledger can seem to establish their own authority. In fact, the budget figures are only as accurate as the underlying information (or as you wish them to be!) We list some factors to consider when assembling your budget information.

- It does pay to discuss budget details fully with your section. You may be (unpleasantly?) surprised at their better knowledge of service practicalities. Remember those management meetings that grind to a halt for lack of information until the person that actually does the work is summoned to set the record straight?

  In a striking example of this principle, a finance management team was unable to agree what the department's practice was on accepting broker hospitality. This question was resolved, but not in the way expected. A summons was issued by the treasurer for the loans manager to come into the meeting. A few minutes later the message came back from his loans section colleagues. He could not be contacted as he was playing golf with brokers.

- Budget assumptions and supporting figures need to be analysed critically. You may intend to prepare a budget which is at variance from the basic data provided, but let it be you that does the varying. If, for example, a new item of expenditure proposed to you is to be funded by income generated, then there is every incentive for the proposer to err on the generous side. Tests which can be applied to income calculations include the following:

  —What is the physical quantity of sales or transactions underlying the value estimated? Examples might be the allowance for unused court sessions in predicting squash court receipts, or the level of void and unlet property assumed in assessing rent income.

  —Is there an allowance for the effect of fee increases on usage levels?

  —Has a suitable provision been made for non-collection and defaults?

  Expenditure predictions often fail to include all relevant costs. Try to think through all the associated costs of a proposal. If, for example, the item is purchase of computer equipment, then you may need to allow for any or all of maintenance agreements, installations, furniture, training, and so on.

- As far as possible, incorporate performance measures in your budget preparation. Figures make a lot more sense if supported by an idea of the volume, workload or quality that the budget is designed to achieve.

- It makes sense to compare and contrast rival information sources. Comparing, say, your payroll costing information with details from an independent personnel system can reveal some interesting anomalies. A colleague once explained how, for many years, he had complete faith in the figures supplied by an investment performance measurement company, until a combination of circumstances resulted in another company also providing this service to the council. The differences between the two companies' figures was more illuminating than the results themselves.

- Budget calculations are constantly revised and messed about before they are to everybody's liking. Try and use spreadsheets wherever possible, they save a lot of work.
- A dull but worthy piece of advice is to make sure you retain clear working papers or a computer file as to how figures were built up. We all enjoy deciphering one of those budget papers, always unsigned and undated, where the manuscript amendments outnumber the original typed figures. If you're later trying to justify your own budget which is seriously out of line, it's not always so funny.

Expenditure reductions

Local government is developing something of a siege mentality, but any budget synopsis needs to include the practicalities of achieving expenditure reductions.

One point to bear in mind is this: the longer reductions are delayed, the worse their impact will be. Say you need to cut your employees' budget by 5 per cent. If there are 5 per cent less staff in post at the start of the budget year, you will, by and large, achieve that reduction. If, however, your reductions will not come into operation until halfway through the year, then you will need to reduce by 10 per cent to achieve your cash limit. This is because you would then only get half the annual saving. Given notice periods, any reduction programme needs to start before the financial year in question in order to avoid unnecessarily large cuts.

Costs arising from redundancies must be provided for in budgets. These include pay in lieu of notice, and statutory redundancy pay. In some councils, these costs are charged to a central budget. Additionally, councils can secure permission from the Department of the Environment to treat redundancy costs as capital expenditure. These permissions are granted on a year-by-year basis, so make sure that your budget assumptions are up to date.

Budget presentation

We now move on to a brief discussion of the presentational aspects of budget preparation. This is not a lesson in public-speaking skills or case presentation; accountants are probably the last people you would turn to for such advice. Experience shows though that certain problems recur quite frequently, problems which concern the type of information provided to decision makers. Some observations are now given.

Accuracy

It may seem an obvious point, but it's surprising the number of times reports are presented with calculation errors. Certain councillors spend hours looking for addition mistakes in reports. It can be quite disconcerting to be confronted with such an error at the climax of your marvellous budget speech. Make sure figures are retotalled and checked in every way. Don't allow others to add appendices to your report without tallying any figures back to the main report. A small figure error can damage the credibility of any report.

Offer options

Managers and councillors like to be offered options for reaching a decision. If you offer a single method of achieving the cash limit, you may antagonise your audience. By all means offer a clear recommendation, but don't prejudge committee decisions too openly.

Over-information

Presenting a budget is a complex enough task without making a rod for your own back. You need to have information to back up your figures, but it can be a mistake to put too much detail down on paper. A question well answered on undocumented detail usually ends that line of enquiry. By putting all your answers down in print, you are merely redoubling the universe of potential enquiries.

Let's summarise what we have learned about budget preparation in a checklist.

- Get full details of your own council's budget timetable, and make every effort to adhere to it, in your own interests.
- Become conversant with, and use, the central rules and guidelines established for the budget preparation.
- Comparisons with previous year figures need careful explanation and justification.
- Get a copy of the CIPFA standard classification recommended for your service, and compare with the coding structure in use in your council.
- Avoid unnecessary complication in budgeting for employees by working on actual numbers rather than establishments.
- Running cost budgets offer considerable scope for value for money savings. Retain expert advice on these areas where relevant.
- Recharge budgets should be set at the level likely to be incurred. Check that the other side of the agreement has done the same.
- Your budget preparation will benefit from close liaison and co-operation with the finance department.
- Good background information is the key to assembling a reliable budget. Bring operational staff into the process, and keep clear records of how you calculate the various figures.
- If you are obliged to make a cuts programme, the sooner you put measures into effect the less the impact will be.
- When making a budget presentation, be well prepared for detail questions. Always check thoroughly that your figures are consistent.

Budgets for financial control

So far in this chapter we have examined budgets in general terms, and some hints on preparation and presentation. This is of course only part of the story, as we saw in Table 2.4. Once the financial year begins, you need to ensure your activities are operated within the financial resources provided. A key aspect of this is to establish a hierarchy of cost centre managers.

Cost centre managers

A cost centre is a focus for accounting measurement. It could be a housing neighbourhood, a residential unit, a professional division or a building department depot. Recall the coding structures set out in Table 2.11. Essentially, the financial ledger system can send expenditure and income to any combination of pigeon holes.

The principle of cost centre management is to match budgets and accounts for activities to the managers responsible for controlling them. So, if we take our example of a building depot, then the supervisor of that depot should have a clear budget for wages, materials, transport, and should know what income the depot needs to earn in work for other departments.

More importantly, the feedback on performance, the accounting results, should also be directed to that manager. It's no use setting a budget for a depot and expecting it to be achieved unless financial and management responsibilities are aligned. If the depot supervisor doesn't realise what results are expected, and all the financial information on the depot stays in the building department accounts section, success is unlikely.

According to cost centre management advocates, it is an ideal way to empower front line staff, and removes the need for lengthy management hierarchies. Table 2.13 compares cost centre management with a more traditional finance approach.

Table 2.13

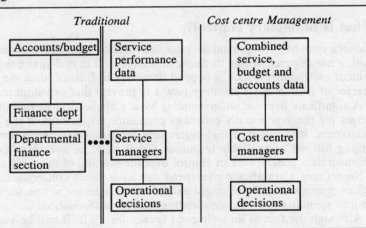

Even if you are not in a position to move to full cost centre management, it is very useful to set up a hierarchy of cost centres through which to operate budgetary control. In the case of a building department this might work as shown in Table 2.14.

Table 2.14: A hierarchy of cost centres

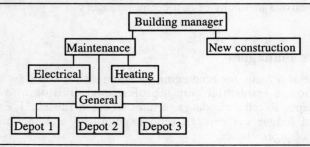

Note that the cost centre hierarchy is not simply a repeat of the organisational structure. Cost centres are tailored to fit the needs of the department. New construction might be ten times the size of Depot 3. But new construction is run as a single cost centre, with its manager as the cost centre manager. On the other hand, each maintenance depot has an accountable supervisor as its cost centre manager.

Budgetary control can be exercised through the cost centre hierarchy on the basis of exception reports. Let's take the example of the Month 3 building department budget reports on employee costs (Table 2.15 below).

In this case the exception threshold has been set at plus or minus 10 per cent, so the supervisor of Depot 3 would be required to explain the adverse variance to the general section manager, with plans to correct the overspend. The supervisors of Depots 1 and 2 are thus far on target so no action is necessary. This works on up the line, as demonstrated in the further reports shown.

What is budgetary control?

Budgetary control is important in councils at various levels. At the council-wide level, it must operate within its financial resources. If in mid-year it is proposing to incur expenditure which is beyond its ability to finance, then the council's director of finance has a statutory power to prevent that expenditure.

A significant over- or underspending by any major service committee on its budget for the year usually provokes councillor displeasure. If the budget is underspent, it is assumed that better services could have been provided by making full use of available resources. Conversely, an overspend is taken to demonstrate a general lack of control over the running of the service.

Sometimes a significant overspend can have direct consequences for the officer responsible. These might extend to disciplinary action for failure to monitor spending properly, or spending without authorisation.

Although the fact of an overspend speaks for itself, it will be viewed as a more serious matter if there is any element of recklessness. This is unlikely to be the case if reasonable steps have been taken during the year to control the budget.

Overspending or failure to achieve a required rate of return can have serious repercussions for a direct labour organisation whose work is subject to

Table 2.15: Budgeting control through the cost centre hiearchy

(a)	Centre	Budget to date	MTH 3	Variance exceeds 10 per cent
	Depot 1	50,000	57,000	*
	Depot 2	40,000	42,000	
	Depot 3	60,000	56,000	
	Total General	150,000	155,000	

Report to general manager

* Reason: Additional bonus payments to complete contract more quickly.
* Action: Recovered in agreed price increase.

(b)	Centre	Budget to date	MTH 3	Variance exceeds 10 per cent
	General	150,000	155,000	
	Electrical	66,000	65,000	
	Heating	30,000	15,000	*
	Total Maintenance	246,000	235,000	

Report to maintenance manager

* Reason: Unable to recruit trained staff.
* Action: Sub-contractors to be used to clear backlog.

(c)	Centre	Budget to date	MTH 3	Variance exceeds 10 per cent
	Maintenance	246,000	235,000	
	New build	300,000	332,000	*
	Total Department	546,000	567,000	

Report to building manager

* Reason: Contract underpriced in tender.
* Action: Need to make higher recovery on future work.

compulsory competition. If a trend of losses is seen over a number of financial years, then the government may instruct that the DLO is closed down.

As we saw earlier, these larger budgets are the combination of many individual cost centres. In some councils, there is a system of strict accountability for financial results at this level. In others the ups and down on individual cost centres are submerged in overall results.

Whatever the implications on your budget of under- or overspending, there are certain basic principles of budgetary control that can be applied (Table 2.16). Essentially they are means of constantly refining and improving your picture of service and financial results achieved to date. As the results move, action is needed to fine-tune services, bringing them back on target, a bit like driving a car along a twisty road (or more cynically, driving round and round the same loop of track).

Table 2.16: The basic principles of budgeting control

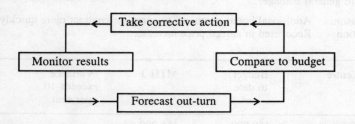

The budget must be known and understood

It will be difficult to achieve spending in line with budget unless managers know exactly what resources are available or, equally important, what service is to be provided out of a budget. Examples abound of failures to work to this principle.

Use all available information sources

It would be nice to have a single, authoritative source of budgetary control information, but financial ledgers are not always so reliable. Try and use any other sources, such as internal departmental records to refine your information base.

Financial results are usually related to the underlying service results

If your budget was set up systematically, you will have a plan of the service to be provided with the financial resources allocated. Conversely, service progress can be used to assemble or corroborate financial predictions. If, for example, your budget allows for 20 staff in a section and there are 22 in post, then you won't need accounting analysis to predict the likely overspend.

Check ongoing performance by unit costs

Many budgets are built up by assuming an average cost and applying this to the number of service units to be provided. Suppose the recruitment advertising budget is based on filling 50 posts at a cost of £1000 each. If an analysis shows the first 10 posts cost £1500 each, then the overall budget is clearly in question.

Use performance indicators

Performance indicators can draw attention to sections or functions not achieving planned results. This focuses budgetary control attention. Failure to achieve the desired indicator may stem from understaffing, and indicate a potential underspend.

Forecasting techniques

We saw in Table 2.7 the merits of profiling as a forecasting technique, rather than relying on simple expenditure processed to date. Other methods of developing forecasts include:

- *keeping a spreadsheet of individual staff salaries, start dates, increments, etc to maintain close control of employee budgets;*
- *setting out costed lists of proposed expenditure, such as planned training courses up to the year-end;*
- *using information directly from feeder systems. If, for example, your maintenance charges are updated quarterly by an interface between general ledger and a DLO system, you may be able to get the information you need more quickly from that source;*
- *if your budget includes regular payments to contractors, meeting with them to discuss their own out-turn expectations.*

Virement

Virement is the transfer of budget resources from an underspending area to an overspending one. The procedures for virement will be set out in your council's financial regulations.

Often it is acceptable to make small-scale virements without any external approval. Larger-scale transfers may need committee authorisation. Make sure it is clearly understood whether the virement is temporary (i.e. for that financial year only), or permanent.

Liaison with finance department

If there are difficulties in arriving at an out-turn forecast, it makes sense to liaise with finance and reach a joint prediction. You will need to set a clear agenda for such discussions, given the unerring capacity of finance staff to look on the gloomy side.

That then concludes our look at budgeting. Yet any list of techniques is really only part of the story. Never forget that budget preparation is usually a fight between competing demands for limited resources. Always look for the hidden agenda of participants from other departments in any budgetary exercise or discussion. A simple illustration will make the point.

A council was changing its method of controlling central departments to an SLA-type basis. Central department negotiators were pleasantly surprised to find ready acceptance by service departments of high charges. Some thought showed that this was only to be expected. The change to SLAs was to be accompanied by giving service departments an automatic budget for the first year's charges. The service departments were therefore keen to pay as much as possible, since that would provide them with resources which could be redirected to other purposes in later years. The message of satisfaction with the central charges was therefore utterly misleading.

Financial accounting

In much of our analysis of budgeting, we have been concerned with the council's accounts and accounting procedures. In this section of the chapter, we look briefly at the form of accounts used for accounting to the outside world. These published accounts are known as the statement of accounts. The stages in their production are set out in Table 2.17.

Table 2.17: Preparation of the statement of accounts

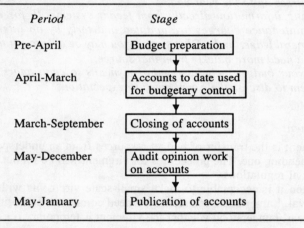

Period	Stage
Pre-April	Budget preparation
April-March	Accounts to date used for budgetary control
March-September	Closing of accounts
May-December	Audit opinion work on accounts
May-January	Publication of accounts

Closing of accounts

Closing of accounts is the process of converting and adding to the basic data used for monitoring expenditure during the year, to put it into the standard form prescribed for publication. Some of the work on closing accounts can start in advance of the financial year end, but the main effort is concentrated in the period from May onwards. A timetable for both finance and departmental work on closing accounts is normally issued by finance towards the year-end.

Accounts closing includes the following.

• Converting income and expenditure to an accruals basis (see page 41). Invoices which relate to the previous year may be coded to special year-end ledger runs: these are automatically converted to creditors. Invoices not received by then must be listed for conversion by *journal*. A journal is a method of making an adjustment between two financial ledger accounts, without any external transaction having taken place. So, for example, payroll costs normally feed into the financial ledger from the payroll system. But a journal might be made to provide in the accounts for a pay award whose date of coming into effect had passed, but which has not yet been finalised or paid. This award would not appear via the feeder system until paid, and thus a journal would be needed to include it in the accounts.

- Correcting coding errors in the accounts (on the assumption that this duty has not been religiously performed during the course of the financial year). There is usually a significant incidence of coding errors, arising from problems such as continued use of obsolete codes, or misunderstanding as to which budget is intended to cover a particular item of expense.
- Year-end stock figures for direct labour and trading organisations must be calculated (usually on the basis of a stockcheck in the department). This enables the cost of materials consumed in the year to be calculated, rather than using purchase figures which would include materials still in the stores. Stores are shown as a *current asset* in the balance sheet.
- Many council services are eligible for government subsidy. A year-end claim must be prepared, and the value of subsidy due shown as a debtor in the balance sheet. Often the calculation of subsidy is a laborious and highly technical task. The annual housing subsidy regulations, for example, usually run to over 100 pages of rules and formulae.
- Any revenue charges arising out of the capital programme and borrowing activities must be effected. This will include the statutory minimum revenue provision (see Chapter 5).
- Many elements of the accounts are only capable of being calculated once the financial year is finished. If, for example, the education committee has agreed to meet half of the cost of running a sports centre, then the accounts for the centre need to be finalised before an accurate charge may be made.
- Figures in the financial ledger for items such as housing rent income, or poll tax receipts must be reconciled with the prime records of those activities (usually a free-standing computer application). Ideally, this reconciliation would have been made regularly as the year progressed, simplifying the closing task.
- Central department costs (such as finance, legal, architects) must be effected by journals. Even if SLAs are not in force, accounting convention requires central costs to be recharged out to direct services.
- Provisions must be set up for any doubtful debts, or losses on collection.
- Statistical returns of the council's expenditure must be made to government departments, and to other bodies for use in national statistics.

Audit opinion work

Once the accounts are finished, and drawn up into the format required for a statement of accounts, then they must be signed by the director of finance and passed to the external auditors. There is a statutory requirement to have reached this stage by 30 September following the financial year. In practice, there are always a few councils whose closing runs past 30 September; their names are sometimes released as an Audit Commission rogues' gallery.

The purpose of opinion audit (see Chapter 3) is to attest that there is nothing so misleading in the accounts that it would give a false picture of the council's activities. As part of this process, auditors check the reliability of the accounting systems that provide the balance sheet figures. Say, for example, part of the year end debtors figure is derived from a computer billing system. The auditors will want to test the way the system works to ensure no debtors are overstated. (Errors such as this are more prevalent than might be supposed. They often arise from transactions that don't fit the normal pattern of events for which a system was designed. For instance, does the application have a facility to deal with the allocation of payments received which failed to state a debtor reference?) Opinion work of this nature can start before the financial year is actually finished.

Opinion work will also entail numerous detailed questions on the statement of accounts. Sometimes the statement of accounts will be changed by agreement with the auditors.

Publication of the accounts

The ideal situation is that accounts are published with an audit opinion. However, some councils are not prepared to wait for the opinion (often because they themselves have been late in providing the accounts for audit). They therefore publish subject to opinion. It is fairly unusual for audit to cause any significant changes in the accounts, so 'subject to opinion' accounts are reliable.

Many councils publish a combined report and accounts, similar in style to that of a PLC. The report section will provide details of council services, and perhaps statistics comparing council costs with other similar authorities.

There is no specific statutory requirement for councils to produce an annual report, though there is a 1980 code of practice covering their content. There is a requirement to publish the statement of accounts, though this may be limited to placing a few copies in local libraries and advertising its availability in a local newspaper.

Council accounts have a very different external readership from company accounts. There is no expert financial press waiting to pounce on the latest council figures, and make a buy or sell recommendation. Some of the purposes of council final accounts include:

- *independently audited information for government on subsidised services, enabling grant to be paid to councils;*
- *totals of expenditure on different local authority functions for statistical purposes;*
- *to check adherence to various limits and controls on expenditure (e.g. does total borrowing for capital purposes fall within available credit approvals?);*
- *to allow local residents the opportunity to raise questions on any financial matter with the external auditor.*

Few of these purposes require wide circulation or dissemination of published accounts. The author experienced this lack of interest at first hand when compiling a survey of local authority reports and accounts some years ago. In response to a treasurer questionnaire 'who are the main users of your published accounts', one wag truthfully admitted 'compilers of accounts surveys'.

Published accounts and the CIPFA Accounting Code of Practice

If (unlikely!) you were to compare a set of different councils' published accounts, you would find a very high degree of accounting standardisation. The reason for this is that, over the years, the CIPFA accounting body has assembled an ever-increasing and more comprehensive body of recommendations on council accounting practices.

During the early and mid-1980s, adherence to CIPFA rules began to fall into abeyance with some councils. Exploitation of accounting techniques to misrepresent council levels of expenditure was prevalent in this period of 'creative accounting'. At one stage, for example, councils paid grant penalties based on their expenditure. There was thus every incentive not to provide for doubtful debts, as to do so would cost a council grant penalties over and above the lost income.

To re-establish accounting integrity, CIPFA published, in 1987, a comprehensive accounting code of practice (ACOP). This consolidated many previous recommendations, and has since developed into a very detailed guideline on published accounts. It has some statutory force, as it is cited in legislation as defining proper accounting practice, provided it is not in conflict with legislative requirements. One of the main questions an auditor must answer in giving an opinion is whether the accounts reflect ACOP rules. If not, and the difference would affect the financial picture given by the accounts, then the accounts will be qualified. Table 2.18 sets out the main provisions of ACOP, and also the relationship between law and the ACOP rules.

Accounting concepts

ACOP defines four accounting concepts. These are a set of values by which any question as to the method of accounting for a particular transaction will be judged. Let's consider the four concepts, with practical examples.

Matching/accruals We have considered this in some detail already, particularly as it affects measuring the cost of supplies and services, but as well as bringing in a year-end creditor for unpaid goods, it might also mean deferring items paid for and not used. Thus if a quarter's rent were paid in advance on 1 March, the proportion covering April and May would be deducted from the year's expenditure and shown as a prepayment in the balance sheet.

The facility to defer expenditure was more widely used some years ago. It was used to spread the cost of items which were not capital over several financial years. This might include say the cost of developing a new computer system. A more recent example was the losses suffered by councils due to the closure of the BCCI bank. Debate continues amongst councils as to whether, under the 1989 Local Government and Housing Act, it is possible to defer expenditure without using a credit approval.

Consistency Common sense dictates that it would be difficult to make fair comparisons between a council's accounts for different years if its accounting methods kept changing. The consistency principle requires that any change

Table 2.18: ACOP and its relation to statutory requirements

Statutory rules

> *Format and presentation*
>
> Specifies which accounting statements are to be published (e.g. balance sheet, summary revenue account).
> When and where the accounts must be published.
> General procedure for audit of the accounts.
>
> *Accounting policies and principles*
>
> Some are set out in legislation (e.g. what costs can be charged to the housing revenue account, what expenditure may be treated as capital).
> In the absence of a statutory rule, the law requires councils to follow proper accounting practice as defined in ACOP.

Accounting code of practice

Company accounting standards if applicable

> *Financial statements*
>
> Guidance on what items should be disclosed in particular accounts (e.g. the balance sheet should include as a note a summary of all the council's land and property assets).
>
> *Accounting concepts*
>
> Broad principles which affect the way accounting figures are calculated (e.g. *consistency*: the same accounting methods should be used year-on-year to facilitate comparisons. The effect of any changes should be explained.
>
> *Accounting principles*
>
> Detailed guidance on the calculation of individual entries in the published accounts (e.g. the cost of central departments should be spread over direct public services).

should be disclosed, and its effect quantified. Sometimes there is every reason for a council to change its accounting method, if its existing practice does not accord with the ACOP rules.

An example of this might be a council which accounted for its superannuation (pension fund) transfers to and from other councils on a cash basis. If it changes to the preferred accruals basis, it will need to explain the effect of the change. Consider the following:

Year 1: Transfers paid cash £1,000,000, actual transfers due in year £800,000. (This means the council cleared some arrears of transfer values from earlier years.) It is the cash figure which appears in the accounts.

Year 2: Transfers paid cash £700,000, actual transfers due £900,000. It is the accrued figure (700,000) which appears in the accounts.

The two years' accounts compared would look as follows:

	Year 1 £	Year 2 £
Transfer values out	1,000,000	900,000

If it were not highlighted, the change in accounting policy would be misleading, as a reader would believe the value of transfers out was less in year 2 than year 1. The accounts would therefore be given a note as follows:

	Year 1 £	Year 2 £
Transfer values out	1,000,000 (*)	900,000

Note to the accounts
* In year 1 transfer values were accounted for on a cash basis. To accord with ACOP, transfer values are now accounted for on the accruals basis. Had the year 1 accounts been on an accruals basis, then transfer values would have been shown as 800,000.

Better still, the council could make what accountants term a *prior year adjustment*. When year 2's accounts are published, year 1's accounts are recalculated to show the figures that would have applied under the new accounting policy. This recalculation is for comparative purposes only, and would be shown as follows:

	Year 1 £	Year 2 £
Transfer values out	800,000 (*)	900,000

Note to the accounts
* In year 1 transfer values were accounted for on a cash basis. To accord with ACOP, transfer values are now accounted for on the accruals basis. Year 1 accounts have been adjusted to the new basis for comparative purposes.

A prior year adjustment is not always so easy to make, and is sometimes impossible. One can envisage the problems if the change in practice significantly affected the reported cost of finance department, which had been recharged across all departments.

Prudence

Put simply, prudence implies a reluctance to reflect income in the accounts until it is sure, but a determination to recognise every potential loss as early as possible. There are few hard and fast rules about exercising the prudence concept. Finance directors who see their role in life as keeping councillors' spending plans under restraint are constantly devising new items urgently in need of provisions. Examples of transactions meriting provisions might be:

- *expected losses on a DLO contract, even if the contract will not be completed for some years;*
- *writing off the value of any stocks that are very seldom called on, or are obsolete;*
- *any potential loss of subsidy when it is uncertain that a council's claim will be accepted in full.*

Substance over form

This concept was primarily developed for company accounts, where there is greater opportunity to misrepresent items. Say, for example, assets are being acquired under a finance lease (unlikely with a council as the assets would count as expenditure for capital purposes, and use up borrowing permissions). The legal provisions of the lease are that only when the last rental is paid does ownership of the assets pass to the council. This is the 'form'. The substance is that the council has acquired the assets by a 'loan', and hence the value of the asset should appear in the balance sheet, as well as the 'debt' outstanding.

Substance over form is usually cited by auditors in relation to any novel financing scheme, or device to maximise the council's position, but any serious doubts as to the validity of such schemes are usually tackled by an ultra vires challenge (see Chapter 3), which seeks to have the whole scheme deemed unlawful by the court.

Materiality

Materiality is a saving grace of the accountant's lot. It is the acceptance that all accounting measures have an element of estimation, and that:

- *auditors need not concern themselves with minor errors that do not change the overall message of the accounts;*
- *accounts can be presented in a summarised form, without the need to disclose trivial items. Thus if the effect of a change in accounting policy is negligible, it need not be reported.*

Accounting principles

ACOP lists 17 accounting principles, with examples of how they should be applied. Essentially, these are more detailed applications of the concepts we have already discussed. Let's look at two examples in more detail.

Cost of support services

The code requires that all *support services* are fully charged to the direct services that the council provides. Support services are those activities (such as legal advice, architects, or valuation) without which the council's main departments could not operate. Equally though, they are not an end in themselves.

Prior to 1981, many councils would publish a summary revenue account essentially as follows:

Summary revenue account	£'000
Education	10,230
Highways	5,633
Leisure	2,005
Finance	1,376
Town Clerk's Dept	560
Cost of services	19,804

Note that the costs of central departments effectively appear as a service in their own right. This is misleading, not least because:

- *the central departments are part of the resources used to provide direct services, just as the various supplies and services charged directly in the Education accounts. Depending on whether professional services are purchased externally or internally, the reported cost of education would differ;*
- *some councils allocated central costs out to services, others did not. This variation in accounting practice made it difficult to compare costs between one authority and another.*

The effect of the CIPFA recommendation would be to increase the reported cost of services, including their use of central department work. The only costs which CIPFA recommend should not be allocated are those for corporate management. Corporate management includes:

- *the chief executive's costs;*
- *preparing the published accounts, and work on overall budget strategy;*
- *the cost of local elections, and some of the allowances paid to members.*

The summary revenue account would then appear as follows:

Summary revenue account	£'000
Education	11,306
Highways	6,221
Leisure	2,211
Corporate management	66
Cost of services	19,804

Note to the accounts

Central department costs are fully allocated to services in accordance with CIPFA recommendations. The basis of allocation is the expenditure incurred by services. The only costs not allocated are those relating to the corporate management of the council.

Capital financing

In Chapter 5 we discuss the system of capital controls in force for local authorities. This requires councils to charge to their revenue account each year both the interest payable on loans and a *minimum revenue provision*. This is a fixed percentage of their capital debt (2 per cent housing, 4 per cent non-housing). There are, in practice, a number of accounting methods to fulfil this requirement, and these are spelt out in the Code:

Consolidated loans pool

This is a long standing accounting method which works as follows:

- *Borrowing needs of individual services are treated as assets of the loans pool. These are usually known as advances to borrowing accounts.*
- *The combined borrowing needs are raised by the loans pool, and the debt is managed on a council-wide basis. This means, in practice, that specific external loans cannot be matched to specific service borrowing from the loans pool. Some of the borrowing needs may be met by temporary use of internal funds, such as the balance on the general fund.*
- *Rules are made for the period of advances, and how these are to be repaid. For instance, the principal advanced might be repayable in equal annual instalments over the life of the loan.*

The loans pool is a survival from earlier legislation, where, instead of a minimum revenue provision, there was a general requirement to provide for repayment over the lifetime of a loan.

Under the loans pool system, the sums charged to borrowing accounts may be greater or lesser than the minimum revenue provision. If lesser, they must be adjusted upwards to the statutory minimum. This is explained in Table 2.19.

Table 2.19: The loans pool system

Asset type	Period of advance (years)	% of debt repaid each year	MRP needed %	Change %
Housing land	60	1.67	2.00	+0.33
Plant for DLO	10	10.00	4.00	none

Under the loans pool system, the charges in the revenue accounts for assets acquired by borrowing reflect the notional loan repayments made to the consolidated loans pool.

Consolidated advances and borrowing pool

The consolidated advances and borrowing pool (CABP) is a method which carries on the principle of the loans pool, but reflects the new control system. Under the system, there is a limit on council capital borrowing known as the *credit ceiling*. In the CABP system, the total of advances to borrowing accounts is exactly this credit ceiling.

In the loans pool system, the total of advances to borrowing accounts would be unlikely to agree with the statutory credit ceiling for a number of reasons.

- *Some borrowings before 1 April 1990 were not recognised in the new opening credit ceilings.*
- *When councils sell capital assets, a **reserved element** may arise. This must be used eventually for debt repayment. It is immediately deducted from the credit ceiling so, in the CABP method, the value of advances will be reduced by any reserved receipts. Under the loans pool system, advances would only be reduced when external debt was actually repaid.*

The CABP is thus a better system for monitoring adherence to the statutory controls. Moreover, charges to borrowing accounts will be at the level of the statutory minimum revenue provision, but perhaps we can also see that depending on the method chosen, loans pool or CABP, the reported cost of services will differ. Were this not complicated enough, a third method is also permissible, *the central loans and investment account*.

Central loans and investment account (CLIA)

The CLIA is a break with the principle of charging borrowing costs to individual services for their capital borrowing needs. It relies on the fact that the need to make a minimum revenue provision is not service specific. This statutory requirement can be fulfilled by a single charge in the summary revenue account for all services.

In an extreme version, the CLIA method might appear as follows:

Summary revenue account	£'000
Education	9,832
Highways	5,023
Leisure	1,991
Capital financing costs	2,958
Cost of services	19,804

This would not afford a very sensible view of council services. As we saw earlier for central costs, capital financing costs are not an end in themselves.

Councils using a CLIA method usually replace the direct charges made under the loans pool or CABP system by some form of asset rent or economic charge. This reallocates the total of CLIA costs to services using some form of market rental or asset rent. However, the reported cost of a service could then differ quite significantly from the charge under loans pool or CABP methods.

The financial statements

So far we have looked at how accounting figures are calculated under ACOP rules. ACOP and legislation also specify what separate accounts must be published. These are as follows:

- *a general or county fund summary revenue account;*
- *a consolidate balance sheet;*
- *a statement of revenue and capital movements;*
- *(housing authorities only) a housing revenue account;*
- *(tax collecting authorities only) a collection fund;*
- *a summary DSO revenue and appropriation account;*
- *(for superannuation authorities) a superannuation revenue account and net assets statement.*

All the statements should include comparative figures for the previous financial year, and relevant notes.

There should also be a statement of the accounting policies used in preparing the accounts, and an explanatory foreword by the council's finance director.

Some examples of accounts

We now have a panoply of accounting rules and regulations with which to assess examples of published accounts. Let's take the example of a district council, which is thus not responsible for administering the superannuation function (see Chapter 6).

Before looking at accounts in detail, we consider the relationship between the council's main accounts and the collection fund (Table 2.20).

Table 2.20: Collection fund accounts

The position under poll tax

```
┌────────────────┐              ┌────────────────┐
│   Government   │              │   Local taxes  │
└────────────────┘              └────────────────┘
        ┌───────────────────────────────────┐
        │          Collection fund          │
        └───────────────────────────────────┘
┌────────────────┐              ┌────────────────┐
│  District needs │              │  County needs  │
└────────────────┘              └────────────────┘
```

The position under poll tax

The collection fund operates as a link or buffer between the income needs of districts and counties, and the demands made to local taxpayers. Any surplus on collection (if actual collection performance is better than budgeted for) must be held in the fund as a deduction in calculating next year's demands. It is the demand on the collection fund that is used in assessing capping limits.

The position under council tax

Under the council tax, the practice of paying government support into the collection fund has been discontinued, and the scheme will be as shown in Table 2.21.

Table 2.21: The position under council tax

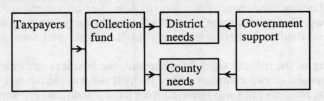

Government support paid to councils includes revenue support grant (RSG) and redistribution of non-domestic rates from a central pool (NNDR).

Example of a collection fund account (Table 2.22) (poll tax basis)

Table 2.22: A collection fund account

Expenditure			£'000	£'000
1. Demands	— County council		40,635	
2.	— Own purposes		4,335	
3.	— Parish councils		566	
			45,536	
4. Interest (net)			80	
5. Provision for non-collection (poll tax)			587	
			46,203	
Income				
6. Business rates (incl. from national pool)				17,525
7. Poll tax payers			20,067	
8. less	— Benefits granted		(2,050)	
9.	— Transitional relief		(494)	
				17,523
10. Community charge benefit				2,050
11. Interest (net)				92
12. Government grants (incl transitional relief)				8,673
13. Balance carried forward 31 March				340
				46,203

There are a number of points worth noting in this account. First, of the total income demanded, the district's own requirements are (lines 1 to 3) less than

10 per cent. Small wonder there is a certain coolness between districts and shires on the matter of who is responsible for the local resident's headline tax bill.

Line 5, the making of a provision for bad debts, is an example of the application of the prudence concept. This provision does not mean the council has abandoned recovery of that value of poll tax, rather that, of the total outstanding at the year-end, it expected to realise just over 55 per cent (see collection fund balance sheet (Table 2.23). The ability to charge such a provision in the collection fund directly spreads the liabilities of non-payers over those who do pay. This caused some dissatisfaction in the early stages of the poll tax, being described as 'other adjustments' in the prescribed form of poll tax demand.

Turning to the income side of the account, the business rates element (line 6) is composed of two elements. When the poll tax was introduced, the power to set local business rates was removed from local authorities. The same national multiplier is applied to all ratable values in the country. The pool of income collected is then redistributed to councils in direct proportion to their adult population, or so much per head.

In our example, the total due to the collection fund from the national pool was £17.525m. Of this, £9.2m had already been collected locally. The figure in the account therefore includes just over £8.3m transferred over from the government.

Actual demands on poll tax payers amount to £17.523m. This figure allows for two reliefs: community charge benefit to the lower paid, and a special transitional relief which was introduced to limit the increase suffered by an individual payer in moving from rates to poll tax. These reliefs are reimbursed to the council via government grants.

As we see from our example, the expenditure of the collection fund has exceeded its income by £340,000. (Remember this is on an accruals basis, and is not the difference between payments or transfers out and the money collected in.) The fund's balance sheet is shown in Table 2.23.

Table 2.23

Current assets		£'000	£'000
Debtors	— poll tax payers	1,344	
	— less provision for bad debts (36%)	(587)	
			757
	— business rates	385	
	— less provision for bad debts (18%)	(70)	
			315
			1,072
Deficit on fund			340
			1,412
Current liabilities			
Creditors			129
Cash overdrawn			1,283
			1,412

The summary revenue account

The summary revenue account reports the costs of council services, and is thus the most important of the various items in the statement of accounts. Look at the example in Table 2.24.

Table 2.24: Example of a district council summary revenue account

	1990/91			1989/90
	Gross Expenditure £'000	Income £'000	Net expenditure £'000	Net expenditure £'000
Environmental health	660	74	586	472
Leisure	1,126	147	979	851
Planning and development	1,454	952	502	286
Rate collection	45	40	5	437
Poll tax collection	765	120	645	174
Business rate collection	148	65	83	42
Poll tax/rate rebates	2,211	2,054	157	129
Registration of electors	125	1	124	78
Waste collection	953	154	799	900
Housing (private sector)	1,953	1,674	279	250
Civil defence	33	30	3	(1)
Car parking	120	80	40	45
Miscellaneous	692	398	294	265
Net expenditure on services	10,285	5,789	4,496	3,928

Principal repayments on notional debt	(302)	—
Appropriation of interest to general services reserve	707	—
Contribution to/(from) housing revenue account	55	(1,039)
Rate income adjustment re-1989/90	7	—
Contribution to general services reserve fund	—	1,000
Direct revenue financing of capital schemes	627	—
Interest and investment income	(1,308)	(942)
Net expenditure	4,282	2,947
Government block grant	—	(979)
Demand on collection fund	(4,335)	—
Ratepayers	—	(2,172)
Surplus for the year	(53)	(204)

General fund working balance

Balance at beginning of year	1,502	1,298
Surplus for the year	53	204
Transfer of balances on special rate accounts	16	—
	1,571	1,502

Our example immediately illustrates the problems inherent in council financial reporting: what is the non-expert to make of such an array of figures? The development of standard council performance indicators by the Audit Commission is partly an effort to side step the accounts themselves. For instance, in the first line, we are told the council's expenditure on environmental health, but unless we know more data about the service, the number of premises visited, the population served, etc., the expenditure in itself is of little significance. We are unable to judge whether it is too high, too low or about right.

Some of the expenditure figures in this account give interesting perspectives on council finances though. Note how, in 1990/91, the cost of poll tax collection (£645,000) amounts to nearly 15 per cent of the council's net expenditure, or, returning to our example of the collection fund in Table 2.23, some 3.5 per cent of the £17.5m billed for county and the district's own purposes. Much greater economy is expected in collecting the council tax.

Councils have an increasing role as distributors of government backed benefits, or *transfer payments*. Of the council's £10.285m gross expenditure, £2.211m was in poll tax benefits (largely reimbursed by government subsidy) and a further £1.953m (described as private sector housing) in rate rebates to private sector tenants was similarly covered by government subsidy. These transfer payments accounted for almost 40 per cent of gross expenditure.

The council is a housing authority, but the costs of council housing are shown in a separate statutory account, the housing revenue account, universally known as the HRA. Under legislation which took effect in 1990/91, the HRA is *ring-fenced*. This means that it is not allowed to be subsidised by other council services.

The account does seem to incorporate a number of large adjustments and transfers in moving from service expenditure to net expenditure. The £0.707m 'appropriation of interest to general services reserve' is basically an addition to general fund balances. Note that the equivalent 1989/90 figure is a transfer of £1m to a general services reserve *fund*. Prior to 1 April 1990, councils had wide powers to establish funds for purposes including 'service preservation'. Now the only funds a district may operate (indeed must operate) are its general fund and collection fund.

Why were councils so keen to operate funds? Because, under the block grant system of central government grant to councils, grant could be affected by the level of a council's expenditure. Contributions into funds ranked as 'expenditure', whereas expenditure out of funds didn't. Funds were thus a very useful way of changing the incidence of expenditure from one year to another. Under the present grant system, entitlement to RSG is not dependent on a council's expenditure level.

The position now is that money is held in reserve as an earmarked part of the general fund balance, rather than being in separate funds. However, in looking through a council's statement of accounts, you may be surprised at all the different little reserves and balances that have accumulated. As we saw in Table 2.2, the level of reserves and balances is a key aspect of financial strategy.

The comparison in financing of net expenditure between 1989/90 and 1990/91 shows the effect of the collection fund's introduction. In the more recent year, it is not possible to determine from the summary revenue account the mixture of central/local funding, as this information appears in the collection fund.

Before we move on to the housing revenue account, let's just check our knowledge on summary revenue accounts.

- A summary revenue account provides an overview of expenditure on services, but excludes most aspects of the housing function.
- The cost of council services to local residents is expressed as a demand on the collection fund. Council tax or poll tax income is not shown directly in the summary revenue account.
- The account should also show the amount of money transferred into reserve, or retained as balances.
- The true level of local expenditure may be masked by the high level of government-subsidised transfer payments included in reported gross expenditure.
- Without supporting statistics on the level of service demand, it's difficult to gauge from the summary revenue account the adequacy of council expenditure in specific areas.

The housing revenue account

The housing revenue account is ring-fenced, which means that it must rely on adjustments in housing rents to finance its expenditure. Consider the structure in Table 2.25.

Table 2.25: The ring fenced housing account

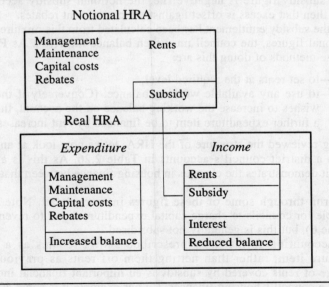

Table 2.25 is split into a notional and real HRA to reflect the method used to calculate housing subsidy, but let us examine first the real HRA. On the

expenditure side, we have the costs of housing management: rent collection, letting property, and so forth, and maintenance (primarily repairs). The two other large items will be the cost of interest payments on housing capital borrowings, and the value of rent rebates allowed to council tenants.

On the income side, we have interest (earned on any balance on the HRA) or from mortgages advanced to tenants so that they may exercise their right to buy. Another large contributor to HRA income is government housing subsidy. But here, life starts to get more complicated.

The subsidy is based not on the actual costs incurred in the HRA but on a mixture of real and notional amounts. So, for example, the subsidy on capital interest payments is based on the true interest rate paid by the council, but that interest rate is not applied to all the council's housing borrowings.

The subsidy figure for management and maintenance is based not on the actual costs incurred but on a notional cost per HRA dwelling. A base for this figure was set when the present subsidy arrangements came into force on 1 April 1990.

Finally, on the expenditure side of our notional subsidy account, we have the cost of housing benefits actually paid with a number of reductions. The government will not subsidise rents set above a certain level; this is particularly relevant where the council adds to its housing stock by leasing property that becomes available on the open market.

On the income side of the subsidy calculation, the rents assumed to be charged are set down in government regulations. They are likely to differ from actual rents charged, because councils' actual HRA costs exceed the notional subsidy figures. As the account must balance, they are therefore obliged to charge higher rents to finance the non-subsidised expenditure.

If the subsidy figure is negative (i.e. the notional subsidy account is in surplus), then that excess is offset against the cost of rent rebates.

Once the subsidy entitlement has been calculated from this mixture of actual and notional figures, the council must then balance the HRA. As Figure 2.6 shows, the methods of doing this are:

—to set rents at the required level;
—to use any available working balance. (Conversely if the council wishes to increase the working balance on the account, this will be a further expenditure item to be financed by rent increases.)

Having reviewed the structure of the HRA, let us now look at an example based on a district council's accounts in Table 2.26. As this is a 1990/91 account, it demonstrates the changes in housing finance between that year and 1989/90.

Let's run through some of these figures in more detail. Note that it is permissible for councils to charge capital expenditure direct to revenue in the HRA (line 6), but this is generally not subsidised.

The accounting format now prescribed shows rebates as a separate expenditure item, rather than netting them off rents as previously. The percentage of rents covered by subsidy is an important financial indicator in assessing a council's housing finances. (In our example it is some 40 per cent of the benefits paid (line 7) as a proportion of the rents charged (line 10).) Remember the government is meeting the cost of benefits virtually 100 per cent.

Table 2.26: Housing revenue account example

	1989/90 £'000	1990/91 £'000
Expenditure		
1. Supervision and management		
2. — general	1,484	1,685
3. — specific	1,333	1,137
4. Repairs and maintenance	2,101	2,297
Capital		
5. — financing costs	12,619	5,271
6. — charged to revenue	612	1,100
7. Rent rebates	—	4,131
8. General fund contribution	561	—
9. Provision for bad debts	70	25
Total	18,780	15,646
Income		
Rents		
10. — dwellings	5,362	10,575
11. — shops	114	117
12. Housing subsidy	8,795	4,543
13. General fund contribution	129	28
14. Investment income	3,025	103
15. Mortgage interest	216	238
16. Other	73	54
Total	17,714	15,658
17. Deficit/(surplus) for year	1,066	(12)
18. Balance brought forward 1 April	2,073	1,007
19. Balance carried forward 31 March	1,007	1,019

It is also possible to compare actual entries with the notional figures used in the 1990/91 housing subsidy calculations as follows:

	Notional	Actual
Management and maintenance costs	4,402	5,119
Capital costs	5,263	6,371
Net rents (rents less benefits)	(5,086)	(6,444)
Other income and expenditure	(36)	(503)
Subsidy	4,543	4,543

Paradoxically, it is only the subsidy figure, based on the notional account, that is the same in both sets of figures.

So the more the council can maximise the take-up of benefits by tenants, the less the impact of rents on the HRA.

If, for example, a tenant is not receiving benefit to which he or she is eligible, then the arrears on that property may start to rise with all the consequent housing management problems for the council. If that tenant can be brought into the benefit net, then the required rent will be guaranteed to the council in the form of government housing subsidy.

Note in line 8 that the council made a transfer in 1989/90 of income from the HRA into its general fund. This it can still do under the new system in certain circumstances, but it cannot move funds the other way.

A further change between 1989/90 and 1990/91 in housing finance is the treatment of interest on housing receipts. Prior to 1 April 1990, such interest could be credited to the HRA. But from 1 April 1990 the interest is credited to the general fund. The reason for this approach is set out below.

- Housing subsidy for capital borrowing costs is based on the council's housing credit ceiling (broadly the sum of its past capital borrowings).
- When a capital receipt arises, the housing credit ceiling is normally reduced (though between 31.11.92 and 31.12.93 there is no deduction for new receipts).
- The subsidy entitlement is calculated by applying the interest rate actually paid on borrowings to the reduced ceiling.
- The net effect is that the subsidy is reduced to reflect the income earned on receipts, and that the HRA will have to recoup the lost subsidy by higher rents.

Note also that in 1989/90 our example shows a deficit for the year being financed out of the working balances.

The consolidated balance sheet

Council balance sheets are very different from their corporate equivalents. This is not surprising given the different aims of the two types of organisation. So what are the distinctions?

- The values shown in a council balance sheet for fixed assets (land, buildings, infrastructure) usually bear little relation to their market value.
- Figures for *net current liabilities* are not a worthwhile measure of the council's financial strength. Net current liabilities is the difference between easily realisable assets (cash, stocks, debts due to be paid within a year) and liabilities due to be met within a year (creditors for supplies and services, short term loans). For a company, this ratio may predict future cashflow problems. This is not relevant to a council, which has a completely different financial structure.

In the past, councils were required to keep separate balance sheets for revenue transactions and capital. This was abandoned some years ago, but the present combined revenue and capital balance sheet can give a false impression of a council's finances. That is because local government law prevents capital resources being used for revenue purposes. So, for example, in Table 2.27 the net assets of £127m (line 14) are shown as financed by borrowing, provisions and reserves, but the long-term borrowing may only legally be used to finance fixed, not current assets. Similarly, a figure of nil reserves might comprise £5m of capital receipts (which could not be used for revenue purposes) and a deficit on the general fund of £5m.

There is considerable debate within local government finance as to how local authority balance sheets might be improved. Suggestions include bringing in fixed assets at their market value, or at a depreciated figure, but the balance sheets are a reflection of current local authority financing mechanisms, and cannot reasonably be looked to to provide information that is not part of a council's role and objectives. CIPFA is currently reviewing the system of council capital accounting.

Table 2.27: Example of shire county balance sheet

	£'000	£'000	£'000
1. Fixed assets, land and buildings, infrastructure, vehicles, plant furniture and equipment			137,010
2. Long-term investments			3
3. Long-term debtors			11,647
4. Total long-term assets			148,660
Current assets			
5. Stocks and work in progress	2,277		
6. Payments in advance	7,693		
7. Debtors	21,677		
8. Short-term investments	620		
		32,267	
Current liabilities			
9. Creditors	(29,673)		
10. Income in advance	(1,263)		
11. Short-term loans	(11,298)		
12. Cash overdrawn	(11,988)		
		(54,222)	
13. Net current liabilities			(21,955)
14. Net assets			126,705
Financed by			
15. Long-term borrowing			97,300
16. Provisions			1,696
17. Provision for credit liabilities			772
Reserves			
18. Usable capital receipts	5,807		
19. Revenue balance	4,634		
20. Other reserves	16,496		
			26,937
			126,705

Housing

We conclude our review of accounting and service finance by looking briefly at some of the main council services. Housing certainly ranks as one of these: councils have some 4 million units of housing under their direct management. In 1991/92, they spent some £6 billion on revenue account, and £1.5 billion on capital in order to operate the housing service. So what are the key financial factors in relation to housing?

Subsidy

As we saw earlier, government housing subsidy is a predominant factor in councils' housing activities. The housing revenue account is ring-fenced, so unsubsidised expenditure must be financed from increased rents. In considering any aspect of the housing function, treasurers will always keep in mind the likely subsidy effect.

As with many local government finance matters, subsidy rules are far from user-friendly. This is often borne out when it comes to the audit of the accounts. One often used to see the housing accountant explaining, over many hours, the subsidy rules to the auditor, who would then proceed to 'audit' the very same accountant's subsidy claim. So much for audit independence.

Given the complexity of the rules, correct interpretation and accounting presentation of activities can pay large dividends in maximising subsidy entitlement. Developing the necessary accounting expertise can take some years, but the quality of specialist housing finance advice is a good test of any treasurer's department.

Trends in the housing service

Recent years have seen large changes in government housing policy, and particularly towards council housing. The early 1980s saw the introduction of the right to buy, which offered discounts dependent on the number of years' tenancy. Right to buy has depleted the stocks of council properties, as resources available for new investment have not kept pace with the rate of diminution. More concerningly for councils, right to buy has naturally been more popular for attractive, well-maintained properties. In some councils, this has led to a reduction in the average quality of homes available for rent, as the pleasant houses have been sold to tenants, but the problematic high-rise developments remain.

At the same time, the role of housing associations has been advancing. These are clearly viewed by government as more effective providers of rented accommodation than monolithic council housing departments. (Though it should be noted that many housing associations are now very large landlords in their own right.) Associations can secure subsidy from the government-backed Housing Corporation, and can borrow with less of the rigid controls which apply to councils. They also have greater flexibility to combine housing for rent with housing for sale in the same development. Unlike councils, they have long had

100 per cent usability of any receipts generated! Even more in their favour, their rented housing stays in their stock as there is no right to buy for most association tenants.

Indeed, some of the current council capital regulations favour association development at the expense of council provision. *Nomination rights* are a good example. It is customary for associations to give councils the right to choose the tenants for a certain proportion of association development in the council's area. However, if the council supports the association's programme by, say, selling it land at a low price, then the association may reciprocate by increasing the number of its rented properties where the council can choose the tenant from its own council waiting list.

Thus there are often cases where the cheapest way for a council to develop its housing land is to sell it to an association at a low price. The proactive image of associations as developers, compared with the typical council as a jealous hoarder of sites it is unwilling to develop, owes something to the financial rules of the two sectors, rather than to any fundamental difference in housing management capability.

The role of the council in rented housing is thus more and more that of enabling others to achieve development, be they associations or private companies. Certain councils have taken this to an extreme position and sold their entire housing stock to associations. No more housing management problems for them.

Housing management

But if the trend of government policy is to phase out councils as landlords, what of the 4 million properties still under council control? The government announced recently that council housing management itself would become subject to compulsory competitive tendering (CCT). This would mean that the in-house housing department would be obliged to compete with outside agencies (such as housing associations) for the right to manage the council's own housing stock. It is likely that the housing management function to be tendered will include:

- *allocating and letting property;*
- *tenant management, such as resolving disputes under tenancy agreements, or involving tenants in the service through tenants' associations and liaison meetings;*
- *collecting rents and service charges;*
- *organising repairs and maintenance;*
- *reletting empty property.*

Tenderers would be expected to supply a specified standard of service in these areas in return for a fixed fee.

Increasingly, housing departments are organising themselves on a neighbourhood basis. This means that tenants are able to find most of the services they require at a small, local office rather than needing to find their way through a central bureaucracy. This devolution of functions down to neighbourhoods is usually reliant on networked computer systems for dealing with rents, housing benefits and repairs.

Under the CCT proposals, it would be possible to tender the management of individual neighbourhoods or areas separately.

Rents

Setting the level of housing rents is usually a major stage of the annual budget round, though ring-fencing means that the decision is not made in competition with the demands of other services. There is always a difficult balancing act between minimising the headline increase, and providing sufficient income to provide a satisfactory service.

Councils have a statutory duty to set rents which will bring the HRA into balance. During the financial year they must keep their rent income assumptions under review, and make appropriate increases if a deficit appears probable.

Always a key factor in setting rents are collection assumptions. There is quite a wide variation between authorities as to the percentage of rents charged actually collected. To some extent this reflects how tough the council gets with families that fall into arrears; eviction is usually the ultimate sanction. Councils with lower collection rates can often point to the difficult social conditions on problem estates; after all, high-rise flats with a record of crime and vandalism aren't the easiest place to follow-up rent arrears.

Rent income achievement and benefits are inextricably linked, as we have seen earlier. Often, tenants in arrears are eligible for housing benefits, in which case government subsidy may eliminate the arrears.

Housing rents are not always accountants' favourite topic, as part of the year-end closing procedures is to balance the total of individual tenants' rent records with the accounting entries in the financial ledger. Unless there have been interim reconciliations during the year, this can be a daunting task.

Voids and unauthorised occupation

A key performance indicator for housing management is the proportion of empty or *void* properties. There is a penalty implicit in the subsidy calculation for an excessive level of voids. Whilst some properties are capable of an immediate relet, others can require substantial repairs to put them back into lettable condition. A further difficulty in some councils is the prevalence of squatting in recently vacated units. This means that prompt security measures need to be taken once the legitimate tenants leave, including security grilles to windows and doors.

A more insidious problem is the level of *unauthorised occupation* prevalent in some authorities. This is where official tenants pass on their tenancy to others without the council's knowledge, thus depriving the next families on the waiting list. Often the property is being relet at a profit. In some councils this malpractice has reached quite high levels, and again is prevalent in areas where problem estates intensify the normal difficulties of housing management.

Thus we see that renting the stock is not perhaps as straightforward as might be imagined. Similarly, the management of repairs is far from simple.

Control of housing repairs

Various independent surveys have confirmed the huge value of maintenance work necessary to bring council housing stock up to a satisfactory state of repair. Let alone the limited capital resources available to councils, many of the rapid post-war developments now show serious design deficiencies.

As we saw earlier, some repairs (essentially major renovations) may be capitalised. The rest must be financed out of the HRA. Repairs are often a fertile ground for audit enquiries, and review of budgetary control procedures.

Social services

Social services is a council function with high political sensitivity. Its service clients are by implication usually from the most disadvantaged groups in society, and a strong case is usually made in the annual budget round for some sort of special dispensation.

Good financial management in social services is important because of the large sums of money spent on the function. At the same time, the pattern of service delivery is changing rapidly, and great care will need to be exercised by councils in order to operate within their social services budgets over the next few years.

At a practical level, there is often an interesting split within the departmental management between those with a perspective oriented to care and service delivery, and the more financially attuned. Councils can suffer considerable loss of credibility for any major deficiency in care standards, as recent episodes have shown, let alone the much more important factor of damage to clients. In social services, finance can thus never be considered as an issue in isolation.

Recent legislation changing the pattern of service provision is the Children Act 1989, the NHS and Community Care Act 1990, and the Criminal Justice Act 1991. Treasurers, who are used by now to one or more new pieces of council finance legislation a year, may take some comfort that other services suffer the same degree of parliamentary activity. The main service impact of the first two of these items is as follows.

Children Act 1989

- The Act introduced various reforms, and provided a clear statement of the law which was previously based on a variety of precedents and earlier statutes.
- In most councils the Act led to some reorganisation and review of departmental functions.
- Main features of the Act include:
  —emphasis on the child's welfare in any decisions of the court, with the participation of the child in any discussions as far as possible;
  —that children should remain with their family wherever possible, but that they should be safe, and protected by intervention if in danger;
  —families should be assisted by councils to bring up children in need. (Need is defined as disability, or the likelihood of not achieving reasonable health and development.)

- Council services thus range from investigation (and potentially a care or supervision order) through to running pre-school facilities for children in need, fostering arrangements, and the registration of child minders.

The NHS and Community Care Act 1990

The emphasis of council responsibilities has moved from direct care provision to one of:

- *assessing individuals' needs in consultation with other agencies;*
- *integrating the services of the various health care providers and organising or purchasing care from them: councils themselves, health authorities, and the independent sector (private homes and voluntary agencies, including housing associations);*
- *increased inspection duties for residential establishments.*

Under previous legislation, the DSS met the cost of residential care for many people in private homes through income support. Now councils will meet these costs, and government funds have been transferred to them accordingly.

Clients assessed for residential care will have a right of choice as to their accommodation. If their particular choice is beyond the reasonable cost accepted by the council, then a third party must agree to meet the extra cost.

Councils' increased responsibilities will be funded by a special transitional grant and additions to the social services SSA under which English councils will receive:

£400m in 1993/94
£1050m in 1994/95
£1570m in 1995/96

In later years the transfer will become part of the normal RSG and SSA calculations. (Part of the reason that the amount transferred rises over the three years is that many existing residents of homes have 'preserved rights' to continue to receive higher level income support.)

Councils became fully responsible for their new functions on 1 April 1993, but there are two conditions attached to the grant.

- *Councils must have agreed strategies with local health authorities on placing people in nursing homes, and how hospital discharge arrangements will be integrated with council assessment procedures.*
- *At least 75 per cent of the grant must be spent in the independent sector.*

The new community care responsibilities will have a big influence on financial management in social services departments. Certainly, many councils have welcomed the rationalisation of community care. Under previous arrangements, the various care providers (or in the case of the DSS, care financers) concentrated on their own direct service operations. Each had its own criteria for granting admission or assistance, and inconsistencies in the quality of services secured by different individuals abounded.

If councils welcome their new role, however, they might have more doubts about the financing of the transfer and the management of the new arrangements. An administrative problem, which ought not to be underestimated, is that in much of the country there is no common set of boundaries for health and local authorities. This threatens a proliferation of liaison arrangements, as one council deals with several health districts and one health district with several councils.

The funding arrangements have an element of coercion on councils to exercise their functions in the manner intended by government. During the political debate as to how community care was to be financed, concerns were expressed as to how councils would use the funds transferred with their new duties.

If money previously spent by the DSS on residential care were simply added to councils' SSAs, then that would have given councils freedom to spend the money as they wished, and not necessarily to that degree on community care. Although each council's SSA is the summation of calculated spending needs on a service by service basis, the consequent revenue support grant to councils is unhypothecated.

Conversely, councils might have been required to keep a separate, ring-fenced account for community care. This would have made the level of government subsidy for the function explicit, and thus perhaps fuelled a different type of debate.

The compromise reached was to operate for the first three years of the new system on a mixture of SSA increases and a specific transitional grant, following which the funding would be entirely submerged in the social services SSA. With candour, the joint government/local authority association group formed to set the basis of allocating the transitional grant is termed 'the algebra group' in government circulars.

Special transitional grant for community care

The grant will be paid in 1993/94, 1994/95, and 1995/96. It will also be paid in 1996/97, though at a reduced level as it is phased out. Funding will then pass entirely through the normal RSG system.

The system will work so that one year's special transitional grant becomes the addition to next year's SSAs (though it will not necessarily work out this way at the individual council level). (See Table 2.28.)

Table 2.28

Year	Transitional grant £m	SSA element £m
93—94	399	—
94—95	651	399
95—96	518	1050
96—97	?	1568

A further 140m will be distributed in 1993/94 to cover authorities costs in setting up their new functions.

The grant will be distributed partly in accordance with past DSS expenditure in council areas, and the balance according to SSA-type factors.

Social services budgets prior to 1993/94 were of course meeting many of the costs that councils will incur under their community care powers, such as their own establishments, day centres and so forth.

The number of elderly people needing residential care is rising quickly, though for other groups residential care is becoming a less favoured option. Councils will have doubts in the longer term as to whether an SSA-based spending ability will enable them to meet the needs of all their clients. If, for example, the district health authority is having to close geriatric facilities for budget reasons, and the local council too is forced to cut social services spending because of general pressure on its SSA, might it not be the clients who lose out?

The care assessment and purchasing process requires much more detailed costing information about clients and payments to agencies than has previously been the case.

Financial information requirements for community care

Individuals' care arrangements will need to be costed, so that the overall care budget can be kept under control, and charges recovered according to clients' financial resources. Where the cost of a chosen care package exceeds the council's accepted limits, recovery must be made from a third party.

Councils will need to manage care contracts with the same caution as any other type of contract. This will require:

- *internal reorganisation to split the care commissioning and the care providing sections of the social services department;*
- *effective procedures to validate charges made under contracts. Most payments will be made directly to homes, and it will be necessary to ensure that residency continued for the full periods claimed. Some payment systems operate on an exception basis, so that, once a payment is established at a fixed weekly rate, it continues until there is some intervention. Particular attention will need to be paid in these circumstances to avoid excessive expenditure.*

The social services budget is often difficult to prepare, because of the diverse client groups and the range of services provided by councils. The trend of legislation, which obliges councils to develop clearer strategies for allocating resources, should help to clarify both service and financial objectives but the main concern for councils over the next few years may well be whether they will have sufficient funding available to cope with ever rising service demands.

Education

Education still accounts for nearly half of councils' expenditure, though local government is rapidly losing elements of the function. Even for those schools and colleges remaining under council control, the power and influence of the education committee has become significantly reduced. Indeed, under a bill introduced in late 1992, the government has set the framework for the eventual elimination of councils' financial responsibility for schools.

As readers will be able to judge, the constant revision of structures and functions during the last few years has created a healthy market for acronyms.

Higher and further education

Councils had, for many years, run the polytechnics and other colleges offering higher education, with degree and HND courses which were more industrially or commercially oriented than the rival universities. In 1990, the polytechnics and colleges were taken out of local government control, and started to be funded by the Polytechnics and Colleges Funding Council (PCFC).

In 1992, these institutions were allowed to apply for the right to call themselves universities, and given wider freedom to award degrees. Hence the recent proliferation of hitherto unknown universities advertising their degree courses. At the same time, funding decisions on both the 'new' universities and the longer-established ones were transferred to the Higher Education Funding Council (HEFC).

Despite the loss of their higher education institutions in 1990, councils still retained many colleges providing further education (essentially full-time GCSE or A-level courses, and part-time vocational courses for those aged over 16). In many councils, a policy had been followed for some years of transferring 16+ academic studies out of school sixth forms and into the colleges.

From 1 April 1993, these further education colleges too were split off from council control, and set up as further education corporations. They will derive their funding from the new Further Education Funding Council (FEFC).

Further education will continue to be provided in schools, but it is no longer a duty, simply a power, for councils to provide full-time education to 16 to 18 year-olds. Thus before expanding this type of provision at a school, councils must gain FEFC consent to the changes.

The 1993/94 RSG settlement dealt with the transfer of further education funding to the FEFC. In particular, year-on-year comparisons of council budgets were based on notional budgets for 1992/93. These were government estimates of what councils would have spent in that year, had they been responsible for further education.

Not surprisingly, councils felt the Secretary of State was unusually generous in his assessment of what it had cost councils to run these functions, money that would now go to the FEFC. Many were able to gain SSA increases by demonstrating what their actual expenditure levels had been.

Schools

The pattern of state school education had proceeded relatively unchanged for some years, with councils as local education authorities (LEAs) maintaining two categories of school (county and voluntary). (The latter set, for example Church of England schools, differ from mainstream schools in that they were independently established, but the council had now become responsible for their maintenance. In some cases, the school governors continue to bear some responsibility for premises costs from the relevant charity's own funds.)

In 1990, following on from the 1988 Education Reform Act, councils were required to begin schemes to devolve control of school finances down to school governing bodies. (In London, a further two years were allowed to enable councils to cope with the upheaval following the abolition of the Inner London Education Authority (ILEA)).

Although not all schools' expenditure falls under governing body control (see Table 2.29), the majority does. Each LEA council must establish a resource allocation formula, rather like a mini-SSA system.

Table 2.29: Calculation of schools budgets

Councils set their *general schools budget (GSB)* This is essentially the total cost of providing primary, middle and secondary school education.

Certain items are excepted from devolution. These include:
— capital expenditure and financing costs;
— home to school transport;
— cost of the school meals service.

The budget left after deducting these excepted items is known as the *potential schools budget (PSB)*.

The total of budgets devolved to schools is termed the aggregated schools budget (ASB). The ASB must be at least 85 per cent of the PSB.

80 per cent of the ASB must be shared out according to the numbers and ages of pupils at the schools.

Under the 1992 Education Bill, the degree of budgetary devolution to schools will increase yet further.

Grant maintained schools

From 1990, schools have been able to opt out of council control entirely, provided a simple majority of the parents have voted in favour. In that case, the government takes over the funding of the school, and the governing body becomes accountable to the government. There is no role for the LEA.

However, the rate of opt-outs has been lower than government intentions and the government now plans to drive the process along rapidly. These changes include the following.

• A new *funding agency for schools (FAS)*. Once 10 per cent of the pupils in an LEA area are in grant-maintained schools, the council will cease to be in sole control of education in its maintained schools. All decisions on provision must then be made jointly between the council and the agency. Once the percentage of pupils in grant-maintained schools reaches 75 per cent, the FAS will have sole responsibility in that area.

- The funding for grant-maintained schools will be based on the council's SSA calculation. This will be shared out to schools under a *common funding formula (CFF)*.
- Where councils believe schools are at risk because delegation and LMS budgeting is not working, they can step in and bring the school back under full LEA control, but if the council fails to turn the school's fortunes round, a regional *education association* will take over the school and prepare it for grant-maintained status.
- Councils will be stopped from spending significant sums on promoting opposition to opt-outs.

In view of the above, a review of councils' education finance is liable to develop into something of an obituary, yet the service obviously needs to be run efficiently during the present transitional period. We thus look briefly at some of the key financial issues affecting the service.

Recoupment

Increasing parental choice has meant that more and more pupils are resident in one council's area but go to school in another's. The cost of education is allowed for in the SSA of the authority in which the pupil lives, so it makes sense to provide for financial compensation to the council actually paying for his or her education.

Because of the high financial value associated with each pupil, councils need to ensure that all relevant cases are picked up. Schools complete a form based on class details on a particular day of the year. It is to be hoped teachers and secretaries are fully briefed as to the significance of this particular missive from what they often fondly refer to as 'the office'.

Good local knowledge is useful in correctly charging for pupils resident in streets where the council boundary runs down the middle. Councils need to bill sending authorities within 18 months of the end of the financial year.

School capacity

The elimination of surplus school capacity has long been a source of potential cost savings. Various Audit Commission reviews have looked at the scope for savings.

Politically, the closure of a school is likely to be a contentious issue, and involve a long-winded process that can drag on for many years, but under the 1992 Education Bill, the secretary of state would be able to take a much more active role in promoting closures. It is estimated there are some 1.5 million surplus places in local schools.

Part of the development strategy for any council's education service should cover the rationalisation of premises, as the financial gain from eliminating unnecessary schools could be very significant. However, the capacity analysis is based on localities, and it could well prove that overprovision in one area exists at the same time as there is overcrowding in another.

Awards

A major item in council's budgets is the payment of awards to students. These are paid by the council in whose area the student is normally resident, and councils recover the cost of *mandatory awards* through a specific grant from the Department for Education. These are usually awards for a first degree, or for teacher training.

Awards include payment of college fees, and a maintenance grant. *Discretionary awards* are made either to send students, who do not meet the mandatory criteria on degree courses, or to students undertaking lower level studies.

Financial controls need to be strong in the awards area, as for any function where high value payments are made directly to individuals. In London recently, there was evidence of organised attempts to defraud councils on a large scale, involving the use of forged documents such as examination certificates.

Devolved budgets

In the mid-1980s, a small number of county councils began development of devolved budgets for schools. Even these first steps were hailed as being somewhat revolutionary, as traditionally the council's education office had kept a tight rein on school spending. In one now defunct authority, this entailed school secretaries making voluminous expenditure returns to central finance. The items of expenditure which had to be recorded separately included 'cutting of new keys' and 'teachers' bus fares to training courses'. Precisely how that information was used for service planning was never clear.

As an antidote to excessive bureaucracy, and council interference, the Education Reform Act 1988 introduced a statutory requirement for local management of schools. Early problems with devolution included resolving the high incremental costs of more experienced and qualified teachers. Should schools with a predominance of such staff receive a higher budget allocation, or were they already getting better value for money due to the services of those more costly teachers? In most councils, the latter argument won the day.

In reality, the financial opportunities presented by LMS are something less than entrepreneurial. The greater part of a school budget is staff costs and, prior to LMS, most schools already received a capitation allowance for teaching materials, books and so forth. With inescapable premises costs to pay, newly powerful parent governors may have found their financial options limited.

Whilst schools have control of their budgets, they still rely on central accounting and financial management processes. Although responsible for staff appointments, for example, governing bodies do not actually take over the technical process of payroll, nor would doing so afford them greater control over the staff budget. An issue not fully resolved in many councils is the integration of schools' localised accounting systems and procedures into the council's overall financial information system.

Whatever the technical problems, LMS seems not to have effected the degree of change in schools its advocates intended. Certainly, government thinking seems to have moved more on to the lines of universal grant-maintained status.

Perhaps in a few years the LMS phase will come to be regarded as little more than a brief interlude in the process of transferring school finances out of local authority control entirely.

Summary

In this chapter we have covered in some detail the budgetary and accounting procedures used by councils, including a brief analysis of some of their published accounting statements. We have also considered some of the finance issues in three major services: housing, social services and education. Because of the many government policy initiatives on council services, council finances are in a transitional phase. The major council services will probably look very different in the late 1990s from their present structure. That is if they remain council functions at all.

At least the knowledge gained from this chapter should enable you to contribute more effectively to budgeting and accounting for your own services, under this difficult scenario, and to develop a deeper understanding of your council's finances as a whole.

3 Audit

It has been said that one of the great lies in the world is 'I am the auditor, I've come to help you'. Past actions, which were the best you could do at the time, can take on a different light under the cold light of audit scrutiny. As anybody whose activities have been the subject of a detailed audit or management inquiry will confirm, being audited is not the nicest thing that can happen to you. Perhaps this is nothing more than human nature. Most people resent others criticising the way they have done their job, however constructively the criticisms are expressed.

Councils, as public bodies, have no shortage of auditors. Not only will the Finance Department have an internal audit section, but the council will have external auditors as well. The purpose of this chapter is to show you how to get the most out of being audited, and to dispel some of the fears people have of auditors' gestapo tactics.

To do this, we look at how auditors work and what their duties entail. After all, however unwelcome, they're only trying to do their job. We also look at the Audit Commission. The Commission is well known for its public pronouncements on whether councils are giving the country good value for money, but it also oversees all council external audits. Most importantly, we look at how you can deal with being audited. This will enable you to keep control of the situation, and avoid unnecessary disputes over audit results. If you can keep on terms with your auditors, it is often possible to direct part of their efforts towards a problem area which you would like investigated.

Being audited is never going to be a pleasure, but with the right preparation it shouldn't be an ordeal.

Two types of audit

As Table 3.1 shows, there are two separate sets of auditors for any council: the external auditors (usually district audit, but sometimes a firm of accountants) and the treasurer's internal audit section. Some of the work they do is similar, but in other respects their activities are very different. Both spend time looking at whether the council's financial systems are up to scratch. But the external auditors spend up to half their time checking the council's year-end accounts, which is an area the internal auditors seldom look at. Conversely, the internal auditors investigate any frauds which arise in the council; only if it were a very major case would external auditors make detailed fraud investigations.

Although the two sets of auditors have different jobs to do, there should always be a great deal of liaison between them. They should plan their programmes of systems audits to avoid both looking at the same thing at the same time. If the external auditors detect a fraud, they will often ask internal audit to carry out the detailed investigation.

Table 3.1: External and internal audit

Internal	External
Staff, are usually council employees although a few councils use outside firms.	The district audit service (70% of councils), or a major firm of accountants.
Under the accounts and audit regulations 1983, Treasurers must ensure councils have 'adequate and effective' internal audit.	The auditor has statutory powers and duties under the Local Government Act 1982.
Audit powers, etc will be set out in the council's financial regulations. Councils may choose to adopt CIPFA and/or APB guidelines.	Auditors must adhere to the Audit Commission's Code of Audit Practice.
Type of work/(percentage of workload)	*Type of work/(percentage of workload)*
Systems audit (50%/60%)	Systems audit (10%)
Fraud investigations (5%/15%)	Fraud investigations (1%/2%)
No final accounts work	Checking the final accounts and giving an opinion (50%).
Value for money, efficiency (35%)	Value for money, management arrangements (30%/40%)
	Hearing objections to the accounts (5% or less)
	Court applications, certifying sums due (rare, only happens in a few audits)
Issue audit reports to Chief Officers responsible for the particular service	Reports to the public (certifying published accounts, or emphasising major problems in running the council). Also reports on lesser issues to the Council and its chief officers.
Accountable to the treasurer	The district auditor derives his/her personal authority from local government law, though he/she will, in practice, follow Audit Commission guidance on many issues.

Internal audit

You are likely to have a great deal more contact with internal audit than with the external auditors. In the sections which follow, we therefore go into some detail about internal audit. We look at what its purpose is, and how it goes about its work. Then we deal with all the practical problems that can arise for you, the auditee, and how to overcome them. Armed with this knowledge, you should have no difficulty dealing with your next audit.

CIPFA, which has a long history of developing the (science?) of internal audit, has defined the purpose of internal audit as

> 'An independent appraisal function within an organisation, for the review of activities as a service to all levels of management. It is a control which measures, evaluates and reports upon the effectiveness of internal controls, financial and other, as a contribution to the effective use of resources within an organisation.' (*Statements on Internal Audit Practice — Public Sector*)

This rather grandiose definition contains the three key ingredients of internal audit, which may, or may not, be present in any one council's audit section. These are that it should be independent, that it is interested in checking *internal control*, and that its purpose in life is to help the council achieve better services. Does the audit section you deal with measure up to them?

The purpose of internal audit

Independence

Audit should be at arms' length from any routine functions. If it is involved itself in running a service (e.g. issuing receipt books, or routinely checking payments), how could it audit that service objectively?

Audit should be free to report its findings to the highest level, and its investigations should not be influenced. Some commentators suggest audit should therefore be outside the treasurer's control, but until the relevant law which makes the treasurer responsible is changed, this is unlikely.

Internal control

Auditors' stock in trade is internal control. Internal control means all the methods used to regulate, manage, and monitor the council's activities. This is a very wide-ranging field, enabling auditors to investigate just about anything they have a mind to. Aspects of internal control that auditors are likely to concentrate their attentions on include:

— the physical security of stocks, materials and cash;
— whether there is enough division of duties. Is a single person able to deal with every aspect of a transaction (e.g. both sending out accounts and collecting in money)? Such an arrangement will often prevent the detection of mistakes or even provide the opportunity for fraud.

Audit's contribution

Audit should not be an end in itself. The auditors reviewing your activities are themselves a significant cost to the council. Unless their findings and recommendations enable the council to operate more efficiently, they are really not up to the job. You, the auditee, have every right to challenge the results of an audit as to their correctness and relevance. How long did the audit take? Is there evidence to support all the findings? Are the recommendations realistic and practical. In short, the auditors need to prove their worth just as much as you must account for your activities to them.

Professional standards for internal audit

Internal audit has been part of councils' finance function for many years. However, the first real codification of audit's objectives and the way it should work was provided in a booklet issued by CIPFA in 1979. 'Statements on Internal Audit Practice — Public Sector' covered 12 areas of audit activity (see Table 3.3). Many councils still work (or claim to work) in accordance with these statements.

However, as CIPFA sought to establish its place in the wider accountancy profession, its internal audit statements became subsumed in the pronouncements of an umbrella group, the APC (Auditing Practices Committee). This published its own guideline in 1990 'Guidance for Internal Auditors' (differences from the earlier CIPFA guide are shown in Table 3.2).

One of the main areas where the APC (later reformed as the APB) guideline is likely to differ from your own council's practice is on the matter of fraud. APC plays down the importance of fraud in audit's workload, regarding its investigation more as a job for management. Most council auditors like nothing better than the excitement of delving into suspicious circumstances, and tackle frauds (real or imagined) with great relish. You have been warned!

If one considers the CIPFA and APC requirements (Table 3.2), many of them seem little better than common sense. Auditors should be properly trained. Who would expect them to show anything less than due care in carrying out their work? But, if you want a handy checklist to assess the performance of your council's auditors, you may find either the CIPFA statements or the APC guideline extremely useful. After all, if the auditors can't live up to their own statements, you are entitled to take their prognostications with a pinch of salt.

Types of audit

So far in this chapter we have looked at what auditors' overall aims are, the difference between internal auditors and external auditors, and what are the professional standards internal auditors are expected to achieve. To get down to the practicalitites of dealing with the pleasure of being audited by our friendly internal auditors, we now need to learn about how individual audits are carried out. These audits fall into three main categories:

—system reviews;
—value for money;
—fraud.

There are a few other specialised areas such as computer audit and contract audit which we will also touch on very briefly.

Table 3.2: Audit standards

CIPFA

General standards

Independence	Audit must be sufficiently independent to produce effective and impartial recommendations.
Due professsional care	This is defined by CIPFA (not very specifically) as 'the application of that measure of skill and care which might reasonably be expected of a competent auditor relative to the specific duties undertaken'.

The scope of internal audit

Internal control	Audit must review the soundness, adequacy and application of financial controls, both financial and otherwise.
Irregularities and fraud	The CIPFA standard expects auditors to detect any system weakness which might allow fraud to be perpetrated, informing management of any suspicions. In practice, the auditor's role in relation to fraud is much more comprehensive.

Internal audit management

Planning and control	Work must be properly planned and controlled.
Supervision	Staff must be properly supervised at all stages of the audit. Work should be monitored against standards. Many benefits flow from codifying procedures in an audit manual.
Training	Auditors need adequate training in both general and specialised audit techniques. Senior staff need to develop appropriate management skills.

Reporting

Evidence	The need to interview all relevant persons is stressed, as is the importance of maintaining properly organised working papers.
Reporting	Audit findings must be conveyed promptly to management, and any recommendations followed-up.

Table 3.2: (continued)

Audit relationships

External auditors	It is advantageous to the two groups of auditors if there is as much co-operation and exchange of information as possible.
Client departments	CIPFA believes this should be based on 'mutual confidence and understanding'. We examine this view later in the chapter.
Other review agencies	Many councils have other quasi-audit sections, such as a management services or internal consultancy section. Again, auditors are advised to achieve 'mutual confidence' though they are warned not to compromise their independence in so doing.

APC (where significantly different from CIPFA)

Scope of internal audit	The guidance states quite categorically that it is management (i.e. the service department's, not internal audit's) who are responsible for 'the prevention and detection of fraud and other illegal acts'.
Reporting	The head of internal audit should have direct reporting access to chief officers, the chief executive, and any audit committee.

Systems audit

Modern audit thinking relies on the idea of a systems audit. This is a type of audit that can be applied to any part of the council's operations, ranging from the way that incoming cheques are processed in the mail room to the entire system for collecting the council tax. The main stages of a systems audit are shown in Table 3.3.

The aim of a systems audit is to recommend improvements in the way a section operates, or a service is provided. It is difficult to understand this in abstract, and Table 3.4 gives some examples of the sort of results that might be produced.

What the auditors are looking for are lapses in internal control. Types of internal control are listed in Table 3.3, though this is by no means exhaustive.

In theory, an experienced auditor should be able to use experience and judgement to spot any weaknesses or deficiencies in the way the system operates. This should enable appropriate action to be taken. In practice, a systems audit can prove to be a very costly exercise which produces very little in the way of practical recommendations. Why is this so often the case?

Auditors often spend a great deal of time on the first stage of documenting the system. If they are unfamiliar with your department or with the particular area being investigated, they will doubtless wish to interview all the different staff involved. They may also decide to produce a schematic diagram or flowchart of how documents move from section to section and how various

Table 3.3: Elements of a systems audit

Stage 1   Documenting the system

Interviewing staff, checking office manuals, and collecting any available information in order to prepare a record of the system. This could be in the form of audit notes, or shown diagrammatically as a flow chart.

Stage 2   Walk through tests

The auditors then check the accuracy of what they understand the system to be. This is done by following a small sample of items right through from the start to finish. Any mistakes made in recording the system can thus be corrected.

Stage 3   Evaluate the controls

Using their expertise, the auditors look for any weaknesses in the system as it is supposed to be operated. This could range from a relatively minor point (e.g. a document should be retained on file rather than destroyed), to a major deficiency (a computer program that is badly written and miscalculates large sums of income due to the council).

Stage 4   Compliance testing

This stage entails checking that staff are actually operating the system as it should be run, using a sample of transactions. Human nature being what it is, staff remote from senior management often change procedures to suit their own convenience. An example might be the sharing of passwords for a computer system. The security of such a system might rely on the assumption that staff can only access their own data, using their own password. The compliance tests are also used to demonstrate, with actual examples, how the system weaknesses identified can cause losses or inefficiency.

Stage 5   Recommendations and report

EXAMPLES OF INTERNAL CONTROLS

Division of duties   Systems should be organised so that no one person is responsible for all stages of the work, thus avoiding the scope for fraud or manipulation.

Audit trail   There should be a record maintained for checking purposes of all the justification and authorisations for a transaction.

Management information   Managers responsible for a function should be provided with all the management information necessary to control the activity.

Security   Stocks and cash should be physically secure. Access to computer systems should be restricted.

Table 3.4: Systems audit — examples of results

Audit background	Audit results
Audit are called in by the housing benefits manager who is concerned that large, back-dated claims are being paid without sufficient checks.	Audit documented the system, and found that — there were no special rules for checking large payments; — the case officer who first interviewed the client could also release a payment to the client. Audits recommendations (which were agreed by management) were that any payment over £500 had to be countersigned by the benefits manager, and that the input of case details should be done by a separate section from the one releasing the payments.
A systems audit of a computerised payment system was carried out as part of the annual audit plan.	Audit found that there were insufficient controls over the creation of new creditor numbers. This meant that a single supplier could be input as a creditor more than once, each with a different creditor number and with a slightly different description (e.g. creditor 100962, Smith Builders; creditor 107321, B. Smith (Bldg)). There was a real risk of duplicate payments, as the same invoice could be input on the two creditor numbers. Audit recommendations included: — changes to the system software to exception report not only identical creditor descriptions with different numbers, but largely similar descriptions too. — exception reports to be produced of different payments to the same creditor for identical amounts.

computer systems relate to each other. How can an auditee avoid unnecessary audit time (and cost), let alone the disruption to day-to-day work?

- *Provide the auditors with copies of any procedure notes, system specifications, and staff instructions that have been issued.*
- *Tell the auditors who are the best people to see in order to build up an understanding of how the system operates.*
- *Ask to see the auditors' work when it is completed. This will enable you to check its accuracy, and may also be of future use as a record of procedures.*

Auditors often lack the expertise to grapple with the sorts of problems that managers would like help with. If we take the example of a systems audit of how the council's suppliers are paid, auditors are usually more than able to spot traditional faults such as staff failing to initial invoices that prices have been checked, or goods supplied without an official order being placed. Auditors are less active with the more intractable problems that exercise managers' minds. Why does it take so many weeks for paid invoices to be reflected in the financial information system which is used for budgetary control? How can the response time of the computerised payments system be speeded up? There are a number of ways to try and stop auditors concentrating on their own pet areas, and avoiding the real problems.

- *Make sure you get the auditors to include the problems you want resolving in their terms of reference. Don't be brushed off by responses such as 'that isn't really part of our audit', or 'you need to deal with a different section of the finance department'.*
- *Practise some lateral thinking, and invite audit to participate in the design of a new system as a member of the project team. They should appreciate the chance to get their suggestions built into the system, rather than bringing forward expensive corrections once the system is already up and running.*
- *If you find the auditors lack the experience or expertise necessary to deal with the complexities of your service or systems, point this out (diplomatically!) to their manager.*

That then is a very brief guide to systems audit. To be fair to auditors, it isn't always quite as easy as it might seem. I well remember, as a trainee internal auditor in a northern borough, being sent with a colleague to document the stores system. Although this was partly computerised, many of the controls depended on duplicate, triplicate, or more multitudinous copies of documents being sent to various sections for different stages of the stores issue process. The different copies were printed on different coloured paper for convenience: red for the store, yellow for accounts, and so on. After many hours of trailing round glum storekeepers and the accounts office, we finally thought we had made a faithful record of the system.

However, when checking a few sample transactions, we were totally flummoxed to come across a large file of yellow dockets. On each of these had been carefully written the legend 'THIS IS *NOT* A PINK DOCKET!'. What was the purpose of going to such great pains to state the obvious? Clearly, this was some subtlety in the internal control process that had escaped our notice.

Our enquiries were greeted with scorn by the storekeeper. Wasn't it obvious? Some time ago, the supply of pink dockets had run low, and had run out before the new supply had arrived. To keep the stores running, yellow dockets had been used as substitutes for the pink dockets, each overwritten 'THIS IS A PINK DOCKET'. Once a new supply of pink dockets had arrived, the yellow dockets (now used solely as yellow dockets) might still have been assumed to be pink. Hence each was carefully overwritten to remind the recipient it was not pink. With the inexorable logic of this explanation, it was impossible to argue.

Value for money (VFM) audit

Value for money came into audit popularity in the late 1970s and early 1980s. The aim of a value for money (or VFM) audit is to discover ways in which a service or function could be operated more cheaply or more effectively. This has often been split into the three es: economy, efficiency and effectiveness.

Let us use our payments example again (see Table 3.5) to see how a vfm audit differs from a routine systems audit. Economy, the cost of resources used in carrying out the functions, is examined for the two main costs of the system, staff and computing. In a systems audit, the auditors would have been more interested in making sure that no single member of staff could beat the system and create a false creditor, or that the same invoice couldn't be paid twice. In a vfm review, the emphasis is on looking at ways to save money, whilst still delivering the function.

How do auditors carry out a value for money exercise? In practice, there is no standard, universal procedure. There are, however, a number of techniques which are frequently used.

Table 3.5: Example of a value for money audit

An audit was carried out to recommend changes in the council's payments procedures which would offer better value-for-money. The following recommendations were made.

Area examined	Suggested improvements
Economy	
Staffing	The number of staff in post was 50 per cent higher than necessary, and could be reduced without any detriment to the service provided.
Computing	The system as currently operating can access on-line records of the past 3 years' payments, though the audit showed that only the most recent year is consulted with any frequency. Full access to the system is available on over 200 terminals throughout the council. This is expensive because of the high demand for mainframe time, and the audit showed that some terminals are hardly ever used. Recommendations were to cut the period for which records could be accessed on-line to 1 year (earlier records are to be retained on microfiche). It was also recommended to cut the number of terminals with access to 100.
Efficiency	
Payment method	It was found that the major utilities (water, gas, electric) were rendering accounts for individual properties, and that these were paid by cheque through the system. It was recommended that the utilities should in future be paid by BACS, the system whereby a computer tape from the utility is run by the council's bank to transfer funds directly to the utilities. This would save bank charges, and avoid threats of disconnection for the inevitable late payment on some of the council's many properties.
Effectiveness	
Discounts	The system was found to be ineffective in securing the maximum possible prompt payment discounts for the council. Recommendations to improve the council's cash flow included better operator training in the identification of discount opportunities, and negotiations with major suppliers not offering prompt payment discounts to achieve these.

Value for money techniques

Cost comparisons

There are a whole range of published comparative statistics. These list a whole range of service costs for every council (e.g. cost per tonne of refuse collected, cost per pupil educated). These can be used to highlight areas of potential value for money improvements.

Best practice guides

Information on new ideas, and examples of good management practice are published by the professional institutes and trade organisations.

Audit Commission studies

The Commission publishes several studies a year which take a comprehensive look at the way a particular service is provided. Although these are often used by councils' external auditors the next year for audit work, they can at the same time be used internally. They are also often worth returning to some years later.

Other local authorities

Unlike the private sector, councils are happy to exchange ideas on good practice, and many useful ideas can be picked up from this source. The Audit Commission runs a quality exchange using this approach.

Value for money audit sounds like a good idea, but again the results can prove disappointing. What are some of the main problems you will encounter?

Imprecise recommendations

Once auditors get off the safe ground of systems work, it becomes more difficult to make clear and categorical recommendations. Beware of vague generalisations such as 'managers should receive better management information'. To be of any use to you, the recommendation needs to tell you precisely what information is needed and why. You also need to know how it can be provided, and what will be the additional cost.

Lack of realism

There is a limit to the rate at which existing procedures can be modified. Be suspicious of sweeping reorganisations, or completely new approaches. Auditors should recognise the realities of council life, not bring forward ideal solutions which have little chance of ever being implemented.

Fraud investigations

Fraud is the auditor's traditional stock in trade, though in most councils it is likely to actually form a only small proportion of audit activity. Most councils' financial regulations include a requirement that audit is informed of any suspected fraud or irregularity. Unfortunately, fraud is more prevalent in council activities than might be supposed. The Audit Commission publishes an analysis of frauds exceeding £500 each year, but these figures (see Table 3.6) rely on councils disclosing the necessary information to the local auditors.

The level of frauds actually perpetrated is clearly higher than these figures. Many frauds are never discovered. There are also many cases of employees who are under suspicion being persuaded to resign from the council. Often, no further action is considered appropriate in such circumstances, and the extent of the fraud is never established. Certainly what the fraud statistics demonstrate is that it would be a naive manager who ran a section on the assumption 'it could never happen with any of my staff'.

Table 3.6: Frauds reported by the Audit Commission

The ten most common methods

Method	Number of cases	Value £
False claims	183	2,840,073
Cash retention	248	2,314,796
False invoices	66	1,481,574
False records	63	856,513
Forging receipts	20	668,866
Cheque theft	80	584,523
Theft of stores	46	468,348
Theft	80	403,791
Falsifying work done	9	344,518
False accounting	58	355,421

The ten most likely perpetrators

Perpetrator	Percentage of value
Outsider	30.5
Officer	26.2
Ticket attendant	12.8
Supervisor/chargehand	6.6
Accountant/solicitor	4.1
Clerk	3.6
Manual worker	2.9
Teacher/lecturer	2.7
Cashier/collector	2.5
Unknown	2.1

Source: Audit Commission fraud data 1983/84 to 1990/91.

Frauds (or more accurately fraud allegations) come to audit's attention in two main ways:

—they are detected by departmental management;
—information or tip-offs, often anonymous, from fellow employees, councillors or the public.

Surprisingly, it is quite unusual for a fraud to first come to light during a routine audit. Conversely, there are a myriad of potentially fraudulent opportunities for all types of council staff. Whilst you shouldn't be oversuspicious of your staff, all those rules and procedures were put there for a reason.

Examples of potential fraud areas

Staff engaged in awarding or managing contracts

Manipulating the tender process to make sure one contractor is successful.
Directing more than the fair share of work to one contractor.
Letting contractors get away with sub-standard work.
Receiving hospitality or gifts from contractors.
Letting contractors overcharge the council.
(These are problems with council staff, let alone with the contractors!)

Staff collecting cash or income

Stealing money paid to the council.
Substituting cheques to cover for borrowed cash.
Suppressing information which would lead to arrears action against family or friends.
Deliberate undercharging of contractors.
'Moonlighting' in council time using council materials.

Staff making payments

Paying fake or forged invoices.
Stealing council cheques.
Unauthorised borrowing from petty cash.
Creating false records of casual staff to cover payments to themselves.

These few examples from a potentially endless list show the potential that exists for fraud. Given this catalogue of human frailty, what are the sorts of circumstances which might incline you to look more closely at a section or member of staff and perhaps call in audit? Let's look at a few examples (table 3.7). These demonstrate a number of the reasons why it is preferable to involve audit, rather than try to go it alone with your own detective work.

- Audit will have a great deal more experience of investigating such matters, and are more likely to bring any investigation to a successful conclusion.
- You can continue with your routine work. Such investigations are often extremely time-consuming; audit have the staffing resources to cope.
- If you are to be part of any future disciplinary panel, it is better to be able to rely on the independent evidence of the audit investigation when hearing the case. If you conduct both the inquiry and hear the disciplinary, you could reasonably be accused of acting as both judge and jury.

Table 3.7: Examples of suspected frauds referred to audit

Circumstances	*Management/audit action*
The building manager has received a number of allegations that a surveyor is being bribed by a contractor to direct work to him. The surveyor has been with the department for many years and is a well-liked member of staff. The building manager therefore considers that an investigation by building staff is unlikely to be effective.	The building manager contacted internal audit. An analysis of work orders showed that an undue proportion of work had been placed with contractor A, even though other, cheaper contractors were available. This was in clear contravention of the council's contract standing orders. The surveyor was interviewed by audit, but was unable to give a satisfactory explanation of the anomaly. The police were informed of the facts of the case, but were not interested in taking the matter further as there was no firm evidence of corruption. The surveyor was suspended from duty under the council's disciplinary procedures, charged with gross misconduct. The surveyor resigned before the disciplinary hearing took place.
The car parks manager is concerned at the low level of takings from one of the council's multi-storey car parks, at which attendants collect cash from leaving motorists. A spot check carried out by management showed cash takings balanced to the ticket machine records. Audit were asked to investigate.	Auditors, working in pairs, kept the car park under observation for two whole working days, keeping accurate records of cars entering and leaving. It was found that the attendants had devised a way to interfere with the ticket machine and raise the barrier. The attendants were interviewed and confessed, at which time they were cautioned. They were disciplined under council procedures, and dismissed from the council. New, tamper-proof automatic ticket equipment was installed.

How do auditors investigate a fraud? Basically, by collecting as much information and evidence about the alleged activities as possible. This will include examining relevant files, records and correspondence. Often the auditors will insist on taking away key files and documents. This is only reasonable as evidence could quickly be destroyed by the perpetrators of the fraud, once it is realised an audit is under way. No evidence, no case. If you need continued use of the documents, ask audit to provide photocopies.

In serious cases, auditors may advise you to suspend the officer(s) under investigation, to allow greater freedom to pursue the audit and avoid any interference with records. As audits often take longer than expected, you should first consider temporarily transferring the officer to a different section or type of work. If the officer is ultimately exonerated, you will have caused the council a great deal of unnecessary cost if they were paid a full salary to sit at home for several months. If audit insist on a suspension, be equally insistent on defining a tight deadline for completion of the investigation.

An investigation will also involve numerous interviews. These will initially be of a fact-finding, informal nature. Later, more formal interviews will be carried out. Two auditors are always present (one recording all that is said). The interviewee is usually entitled to be accompanied by a trade union representative or friend, in an observer capacity, not to answer questions!

If evidence gained from an audit interview is ultimately to be used in a court, it would need to be collected in accordance with the Police and Criminal Evidence Act 1984. This would entail cautioning the suspect, and taking various measures to demonstrate that no duress was applied. In practice, most fraud inquiries culminate in internal disciplinary procedures, and PACE does not therefore apply. Moreover, even in cases that do come to court, the police will inevitably re-interview the person charged, whatever audit have done previously. Auditors will err on the side of safety, and generally caution an interviewee who is confessing to involvement in a fraud.

The report of a fraud investigation needs to be able to stand up to a very rigorous appraisal. In receiving such a report, you should ask questions such as the following.

- Have all relevant staff and outside persons who could shed light on the matter been interviewed?
- Is evidence provided to support all the conclusions?
- If the conclusions are based on a sample of transactions, was the sample sufficiently representative?
- Will the report survive the sort of scrutiny it is likely to receive from the defence's representative during a disciplinary hearing?

As somebody's job may well hang on the conclusions of such a report, it is only fair to check and double check all the sections of the report and the supporting working papers.

Even fraud investigations are not without their lighter moments. Again as a trainee, I was sent with an audit manager to observe the activities of a cashier in the cafeteria of a college. She was suspected of not ringing all her takings into the till. In order to observe as closely as possible, we purchased a meal and took our seats at the table closest to the till. We were ridiculously conspicuous as the only two 'students' dressed in sober grey suits.

However, this threat to the secrecy of our surveillance was redoubled by a most unfortunate circumstance. As the cafeteria was becoming crowded, two women students took the seats on the other side of our table, virtually blocking our view of the suspect. In order to maintain our observation, we were thus driven to some fairly curious gyrations to maintain sight of the cashier.

These actions were not well received by our table companions, and in the altercation that ensued my boss was forced to exonerate himself by explaining he was 'the county auditor'. The import of his remarks was not lost on the cashier, and on our later checking the till, it balanced to the penny.

Computer and contract audit reviews

In addition to the three main areas of audit activity, two specialised areas of audit coverage are worth a brief mention. The development of computer systems and their operation is a highly technical area. Although all auditors should be capable of dealing with the review of a computer-based system, there are certain aspects which merit special attention. These are:

- the purchasing and procurement of computer equipment and software;
- security of the computer installation and the council's computerised systems;
- procedures for the development of new systems, and the amendment and enhancement of new systems;
- the cost of computer facilities and operations, and the scope for cost savings;
- the council's information technology strategy;
- resolving technical deficiencies in the operation of systems.

Contract audit reviews

Similarly, there are various aspects of the audit of capital or construction contracts where considerable benefit is derived from specialist investigation. Although very important results may stem from these areas of investigation, they are not likely to form a major element of audit activity:

- evaluating the need and justification for new capital projects;
- the propriety of the tendering process;
- the operation of any approved list of contractors;
- site visits to check work claimed for by contractors;
- detailed checking of the contractor's final account;
- investigating claims by contractors for increased costs.

Audit planning

Thus far we have looked at the role of internal audit, and the professional standards that the audit section should be working to. We have also examined the three main areas of audit work: systems, value for money, fraud. In each case, we have looked at examples of the sort of work that is done and typical audit results. However, even if we have a better understanding of what audit is about, there still remain the much more practical questions.

- *Who decides which audits are carried out?*
- *Once an audit begins, what control does the section being audited (the auditee) have over the work done and the final report?*

In a large organisation such as a local authority, there are innumerable potential areas for audit activity. Virtually all audit sections have developed some form of planning to decide which audits have priority.

The extent to which departments are able to influence the choice of topics in the plan varies from council to council. In some, treasurers make much of the point that it is their statutory responsibility (see Table 3.1) to run audit. Little regard is taken of departmental views. In others, where the principle of internal markets or service level agreements is well established, departments are able largely to choose which audits they are prepared to pay for. (The Treasurer usually continues to provide a non-negotiable core audit to fulfil the statutory requirement.)

The trend towards negotiability is likely to continue. Internal audit is categorised as 'highly suitable for competition' in the recent DOE white paper on compulsory competition for council white-collar work. It is not clear yet whether, under these proposals, the client specifying the audit service would be the service departments, or the treasurer.

Table 3.8 sets out some of the main considerations in preparing an audit plan. Some of these are fairly self-evident, and would relate to any type of plan, such as staff availability. What is perhaps more interesting to departments and managers is why particular parts of their domain are chosen in preference to others. Often, audit plans are not prepared with the same thoroughness that auditors apply to their audits. Any reasonable audit manager should be prepared to discuss the contents of the plan as it affects your areas of responsibility. This may lead to changes in the plan once auditors have a better understanding of the relative significance of particular activities, or become aware of long-running problems managers would like auditing. Certainly, in meetings with auditors, you should sometimes take the initiative by asking them to report on their actual performance against your particular part of the plan.

Before we move on to how far an auditee can control audit work, it is worth noting that there are a whole series of *performance indicators* for audit work. These are summarised in Table 3.9. If you have concerns about the audit service you are receiving, why not ask about the section's results using these indicators?

Contributing to the audit and its recommendations

Audit is a substantial cost in any council, so managers are under an obligation to ensure audits are not a waste of money. Unfortunately, it is not always possible to rely on auditors to achieve this. There are a number of steps which you can take to avoid problems arising.

Before the audit

We have already seen the importance of contributing to the planning process, preventing auditors wasting resources on insignificant functions or activities.

Ask to see the terms of reference of the audit, and respond promptly with any suggested changes. Get the agreed terms of reference confirmed in writing. This will prove invaluable in evaluating the final report.

Steer the auditors away from carrying out audits at peak demand periods. It's not a good idea, for example, to have an audit of the education grants section in September, when all staff are more than fully occupied in issuing cheques to the students who have just gained college places.

Try and establish an understanding with audit that you will be informed before any audit or visit takes place. It is best to find out what the audit is about before it is very far developed, and brief staff accordingly. In only a few instances is a surprise element essential to the success of the audit. Exceptions are a surprise cash check, or fraud investigations.

During the audit work

If you are interviewed by audit, keep a note of the main points discussed. Retain copies of any documents provided. Ask audit to sign for any files removed, etc.

Table 3.8: How an audit plan is prepared

Duration	A long term plan is prepared to cover all the main audits over a three- or perhaps five-year cycle. If a major system is left unaudited for longer than this, audit coverage is arguably inadequate. This long-term plan is then translated into a one-year *operational plan*. This sets out in some detail the actual audits to be carried out in the financial year.
Scope	The plan should cover: — all the main financial systems; — all services or activities having significant income and expenditure or use of the council's assets; — (optional) an allowance for establishment visits or audits; — reviews of major computer systems; — reviews of large contracts (construction or for services); — value for money reviews of services likely to have scope for major cost savings; — an allowance for fraud investigations (the precise subjects obviously as yet being unknown!).
Resources	A number of auditor days should be allocated to each audit. If possible, the time should be split over the different grades of auditor (e.g. manager, assistant). The plan should be based on a realistic assessment of the likely budgets for audit, and staff numbers.
Priorities	Various factors are used to prioritise audits. Sometimes these are combined in a risk index calculation: — the scale of the budget for a service (usually the gross total of income and expenditure); — past problems, and audit judgement as to the general financial health of a particular area; — the time that has lapsed since the last audit; — whether external auditors plan to look at the same area.
Monitoring	Most sections operate a time-recording system to charge auditor time to projects. In some councils, there is an annual (or perhaps more frequent) report of audit activities to a council committee. See Table 3.9 for other audit performance indicators.

There is nothing more infuriating than being unable to prove that a lost file was taken by audit. If you are businesslike in your approach to documents, etc audit, in turn, will treat your files more carefully.

If you are interviewed formally, exercise your right to be accompanied. You or your colleague should keep a careful record of everything that is said. Stick to facts and explanations of which you have genuine knowledge and clear recollection.

If the audit is a lengthy one, set up regular meetings with the responsible audit manager to progress check. Try to get a view on what the recommendations are likely to be. The earlier you can correct any misconceptions or errors, the better.

Table 3.9: Audit performance indicators

Area of performance	Examples of indicators
Time	What percentage of audit time is spent directly on audits (i.e. how much is devoted to training, administration, etc)?
	What is the time planned audit-by-audit against time actually taken?
	Were audits delivered on time?
Cost	Has the section kept to its budget? What is the cost of a day's audit? How much did each audit cost?
Plans	Have all the planned audits been achieved?
Recommendations	How many have been: • made; • accepted; • implemented?
Staff and skills	Are the planned number of staff in post?
	What percentage of the section are qualified accountants or qualified internal auditors?
Quality	Are auditees surveyed for their opinions as to their satisfaction with each report issued? Is there a strong internal review process within the audit section to check working papers, etc?

The audit report

Having endured the audit, the tables are now turned when it comes to the report. If an audit has taken 20 days' work, the report you receive will represent an investment of perhaps £5000 (allowing for all the costs of running the audit section). Try to judge it in the light of its cost. What you are buying is £5000 worth of improved systems, clear recommendations, or in-depth investigation. The following are danger signals in relation to an audit report.

• Beware of padding such as long introductions explaining the scope of the service, etc. As the manager, you already know all this much better than the auditors.

- Bad presentation, unclear expression, even a minor failing such as sloppy wordprocessing or typing: all these are indicative of a general lack of attention to the quality of the audit.
- Any fundamental or basic misunderstanding as to how the section operates or the services provided. This almost invariably demonstrates that the auditors have not put in the amount of work necessary to carry out a proper and thorough review.
- All the findings must be supported by clear evidence. Look out for vague assertions such as 'most payments are made on time'. This only leads you to ask a great many unanswered questions. What percentage were late? What was the range of delays found? Did it matter that the payments were late, financially or otherwise? And so on. In case of doubt, always ask to see working papers, statistics, etc.
- Long delays in producing the report are again symptomatic of a poor audit. Most good auditors would agree that 80 per cent of audit results are usually achieved in the first 20 per cent of the audit. If the auditors are not able to achieve the relatively simple management exercise of completing their assignment roughly to time, it damages their credibility to assess the more complex management issues of operating your service.
- Recommendations should be conducive to action. Suggestions such as 'the payments system should be reviewed' are mere buck-passing. Expert recommendations should consist of a specific piece of action, how it is to be achieved, by whom, and when. So, in the case of our payments example, this might read: 'the assistant director should form a project team to effect the following enhancements to the system (listed). These should be in place for the financial year 1993/94. The development costs are provided for in the finance department's budget.'

Follow-up and implementation

Auditors, whatever their failings, do share certain human qualities with the rest of us. This includes being more interested in starting something new than finishing off properly the tedious exercise that has just been completed. Hence once an audit report is issued (unless it confirms a course of action already being actively pursued by management) it often remains unimplemented however important and worthwhile its recommendations.

A little thought will show that the proportion of audit recommendations which are actually put into practice is probably the single most effective measure of audit success. If the percentage of recommendations actually implemented is (say) only 20 per cent, then the cost of performing the wasted 80 per cent of audits becomes a big overhead. Our previous example of a 20-day audit costing £5000 has now increased to a worrying £25,000 if we use the more realistic approach of cost per useful audit.

The responsibility for following up and implementing audit recommendations is a shared one between you and the auditor. It is worth doing the job properly, as a persistent inability on your part to action audit findings is going to undermine your negotiating position on audit issues. Try to adopt approaches and procedures which meet the guidelines set out in Table 3.10.

Table 3.10: Implementing audit recommendations

Stage	Action
Report	Set out in writing which points you agree with and which you don't. Organise a meeting to resolve the differences. Where appropriate, circulate the report to other staff for their views/comments. Many councils have a rule that the report is sent, in the first instance, to the departmental chief officer. Ask your chief officer if you can see the report once you know it has been issued. Some sections issue draft reports, in which case any agreed changes should be reflected in the final version.
Action plan	Agree a plan with audit, recommendation by recommendation, as to who is responsible for implementing agreed recommendations, and when. Send a copy to all your relevant staff. Don't accept recommendations merely to placate auditors if you know there is no realistic chance of their being implemented. If this is the case, say so.
Follow-up	The first question at the next audit will be: 'have previous recommendations been implemented?' Avoid problems by doing a quarterly exercise yourself to progress chase. Inform audit of any delays, which may be for reasons outside your control (e.g. budget restrictions mean a lack of finance for a better computer system). Many audit sections have their own follow-up routines; suggest doing this as a joint exercise. Aim to action the report and its recommendations as quickly as possible, so that you can finish with it. Better to spend time sorting out the problems once and for all than explaining to audit over and over again why nothing has happened.

Internal audit – a summary

Internal audit is an inescapable part of the finance function, if only because it is a statutory requirement. At its best, it can perform a very useful function, resolving systems problems or dealing with sensitive investigations which are unsuitable for managers to handle directly. It is certainly a very costly service, and therefore the onus is on the client or auditee to demand a high-quality product. It is hoped that, in this brief account of how internal audit operates, enough pointers have been provided to enable you to look more critically at the audits you receive. The following checklist of eight key points may be of use in this direction. And, if it wasn't enough of a nuisance to have to deal with internal auditors, we now turn our attention to a second set of inquisitors, the external auditors.

- Get a copy of audit's scope and objectives and compare to the CIPFA/APC standards. Raise any concerns with your audit manager.
- Get a copy of the audit plan, particularly as it relates to your department/

services. Make sure the priorities were established logically, and reflect a genuine need for audits to take place.

- Find out the scope for any form of service level agreement as regards audit services, and what influence you can have over the plan.
- Try and get the right to comment on the terms of reference for an audit before it starts. Make a strong case for any additions or deletions you believe are necessary. Make sure a clear deadline is set for delivery of the report.
- Monitor the progress of the audit carefully, and try to correct audit misconceptions as they arise. Let audit management know immediately if you are dissatisfied with the expertise or general approach of a particular auditor.
- Assess the report thoroughly, having regard to the cost of the exercise. Make sure it is clear precisely what action is going to arise from the report.
- Make sure that any agreed recommendations are confirmed in writing, and that an action plan is established. Follow this up relentlessly until it is complete, so that the audit can be concluded.
- Always alert audit if you have an informed suspicion about malpractice by your staff, or indeed any other party or person dealing for, or with, the council.

External auditors and the Audit Commission

In the remainder of this chapter, we consider the external audit of councils. Service managers are unlikely to be dealing with external auditors nearly as often as their internal audit counterparts. However, the powers of an external auditor are considerable, so it is worth having a broad understanding of what these are. Moreover, the Audit Commission, the central body controlling the appointment of external auditors and the standard of their work, is a high profile organisation. Its pronouncements on the efficiency (or inefficiency) of council services often hit the headlines. Accordingly, we look briefly at its precise powers and duties.

External auditors and surcharge

Council external audit has a very long history, stretching back to the poor law days of the eighteenth and nineteenth centuries. In those days, the main duty of councils was to collect a poor rate and distribute poor relief. As there were few records or accounts of this process, it was not unknown for the person in charge of distributing poor relief to retain a healthy percentage for his own pocket.

The role of the external auditor was to add up the evidence for genuine payments, and compare this with the amount of the poor rate that had been collected in. If the difference proved to be too remarkable, the auditor had the power to charge or 'surcharge' the culprits with making good the difference. This power has continued, in a different form, to the present day. Hence the threat of surcharge is often spoken of by council staff in relation to some loss or question of legality.

In fact, the threat of surcharge to a council officer or councillor is extremely remote, provided they have acted responsibly. As we will now show, the potential for surcharge would arise when the council had either incurred unlawful expenditure, or unnecessary losses or failure to bring sums into account had occurred.

Duties of auditors re unlawful expenditure

- Councils must make annual accounts and all associated vouchers available for public inspection. Any elector may object to the auditor if an item of account appears unlawful.
- Auditors can seek a declaration from the court that any expenditure is unlawful.
- Having decided any expenditure is unlawful, the court may decide those responsible for incurring any loss must repay it. If councillors are responsible, they may be banned from office.
- If the auditor decides:
    —sums have not properly been brought into account;
    —that losses have been caused by wilful misconduct;
    the auditor may certify sums due from the person(s) responsible. There is a right of appeal to the court against certification. Councillors causing losses exceeding £2000 may be banned from office for five years.
- Auditors suspecting a council is about to:
    —incur unlawful expenditure;
    —take unlawful action which would cause a loss;
    —enter an unlawful item of account;
    may issue a prohibition order. The proposed action is then rendered immediately unlawful for the council concerned until either:
    —the auditor lifts the order;
    —the council successfully appeals to the court.

In the case of unlawful (or ultra vires) expenditure, the auditor would first have to secure a declaration from the court that the precise item of expenditure was beyond the many powers of councils which are set out in local government legislation. Even if successful in this, the auditor would further have to seek a declaration that the persons causing the loss had done so recklessly. In legal parlance, the test is that of 'wilful misconduct', which can loosely be described as acting in the face of all advice, without regard to the consequences.

Similarly, in the case of losses (which are certified directly by the auditor), the standard of wilful misconduct still applies. Again, any person so charged may appeal to the court.

Thus, although there are various precedents for expenditure being declared ultra vires, there are only a few of these which also resulted in the surcharging of the officers concerned. Recent cases of ultra vires expenditure are the Hammersmith & Fulham swaps case (all such transactions were held unlawful by the House of Lords in 1991), and the South Tyneside case on redundancy payments where it was held in March 1992 that councils could only pay the minimum level of compensation set out in local government law. Yet in both these cases, no officer or councillor was held to be surchargeable, nor did the auditors seek such an application despite the huge sums of money involved.

Examples where surcharge was applied are the councillors of Liverpool and Lambeth in the mid-1980s where a deliberate delay in setting a rate caused losses to these councils. This happened during the first years in which the government took powers to limit individual councils' tax levels. These are obviously a very different type of case, where (no doubt for genuinely held personal convictions) the persons concerned were determined to go against the law, whatever the consequences.

Ultra vires

Ultra vires, or 'beyond the powers' also relates back to the law of previous centuries. It is the legal principle that a council may do only that which is expressly set out in local government legislation, and that any contract entered into outside such powers is null and void.

In one sense, the doctrine of ultra vires seems eminently sensible. If Parliament in its wisdom has chosen to restrict council activities by its legislation, why should individual councils be able to succeed in going beyond these limits? However, a little thought shows that ultra vires has its drawbacks as well. First, a person who enters into a contract with a council in good faith has no remedy if the council is eventually proved to have acted ultra vires. Hence, in the swaps case mentioned earlier, the banks could not require councils to perform their contracts, only to seek restitution of any money paid over.

The second and more invidious aspect of ultra vires is that it is far from clear, in many instances, how far council powers extend. Officers trying to show initiative or innovation can thus find themselves in a dangerous grey area between the traditional method of providing a function and illegality. At the time of writing, such an example is the question of whether it is lawful for councils to tender for work with a neighbouring council (termed cross-boundary tendering). Many council managers see this as a commonsense way of using any spare capacity that happens to be available. Auditors incline more to the view that the practice is too close to trading for profit, which is definitely out for councils. In-between, managers trying to run perhaps a building department or a maintenance unit to tight financial limits are left to try and reach their own decisions.

Cases on the ultra vires principle are often determined on the court's view of Section 111 of the Local Government Act 1972. This states that, where a council has a statutory power, it may do anything to 'facilitate, or which is conducive or incidental to the function'. S111 does not override any specific statutory limitation. Legal precedents on S111 vary from generous to extremely severe, as in the Hammersmith case where it was held swaps were nothing to do with borrowing. This notion would seem a little curious to many a corporate treasurer.

Since 1988, auditors have had the power to issue a stop order if it is felt a council is about to enter into unlawful expenditure. The council is then prohibited from proceeding until either the auditor lifts the order, or the council appeals successfully to the court. Unfortunately, these powers, which would fast-track court decisions on illegality, are seldom (if ever) used.

A final point on the ultra vires principle is the view, not least in the 1992 report of the Bank of England sponsored Alexander Committee, that it were better abolished altogether. Any council would then have the same legal status as an individual in contractual terms. Provided a counterparty reasonably believed the council was empowered, and made sure officers acting for the council were duly authorised, contracts would be enforceable.

But this is some way in the future, and we end this section on surcharge and ultra vires with a few key points to remember should you ever become involved in such problems. We then turn to the more mundane audit duties of checking the accounts, and carrying out value for money reviews.

Dealing with ultra vires issues

- If an action is called into question, the first thing the auditors will check is your personal authorisation for taking such an action. This means tracing the line from the relevant legislation, down through council and committee decisions or standing orders, and through delegation of powers to chief officers and below. Even if you are not involved in a sensitive area, it's worth checking your personal authority for activities such as entering into contracts, or authorising expenditure. Try and play devil's advocate and check your authority is really as clear cut as you would like to think it is. Wide generalisations such as 'The director may enter into all relevant contracts . . .' are sometimes rejected by auditors or the courts as too vague to be meaningful.
- Most people like to work on their own initiative some of the time, particularly if a new or novel approach is their particular idea. However, if you are at all worried or concerned about the validity of an action, practise some upward delegation and consult your manager or chief officer. It is better to take on opposition to a new idea at this stage, rather than face a later inquiry without any internal support.
- In potential areas of illegality, always keep your own legal department fully informed of what you plan to do, and give very full consideration to their advice. They may, in turn, seek Counsel's opinion. As an external audit colleague once ruefully admitted to me, 'properly formulated counsel's opinion is a very good defence'.
- Check your actions with auditors in advance. This does not mean that you must ultimately defer to their view, but in any future inquiry it might seem a little odd not to have discussed things with them at all. They will never, being auditors, commit themselves to confirming in writing that a particular course of action is lawful. You will be able to gauge, though, from off-the-record discussions and from the general nature of their reaction how strongly they feel on the issue. If you start getting lots of faxes from Audit Commission headquarters, be careful!

- A final, if self-evident point, is to keep a record of key conversations, meetings and correspondence. At the time, you may be decision making at a rapid pace. The auditors may not even enquire into the matter until years later, by which time you may find it hard to recall the precise reason for doing things a certain way. Try to exercise good judgement in destroying old files. Keep key items such as legal advice, approvals from senior management, and notes of meetings where important decisions were made.

Opinion audit

Fortunately, instances of ultra vires or surcharge are very rare. External auditors' main duties are to give an opinion on the council's published accounts, and to carry out value for money reviews. The form of opinion given is to certify that the accounts 'present fairly'. The emphasis is very much that the accounts should not give a misleading view of the authority's finances. Given the scale of council expenditures, and the summarised nature of the financial statements, it is usually quite a major item that leads the auditor to qualify an audit opinion. This might be a major contract which is potentially ultra vires, or that the financial records supporting a figure had broken down and could not be reconciled (e.g. a housing rents system that didn't calculate tenants' arrears properly).

Auditors must carry out their work in accordance with the 'Code of audit practice' issued by the Audit Commission. This prescribes various forms of opinion (see Table 3.11), with subtle variations to reflect varying degrees of audit dissatisfaction. Whether these ever reach the awareness of council residents is another matter.

Most queries on the accounts are resolved in discussions between auditors and council finance staff. These may resolve around long lists of figures, and such momentous issues as 'there are no working papers to support the balance of £523.16 shown on ledger code Z39927629'. If you are not part of the finance department, you are most likely to become involved in opinion audit if your department's records are the basis of one of the balance sheet figures. This would happen, for example, in the case of a highways stores, where the stock figure would appear as part of the council's current assets in the balance sheet.

As an illustration that all is not plain sailing for auditors, I have it on good authority from a former county treasurer that there used to be no better accounting ruse than a stock of road salt. If the highways budget was overspent, this was explained by the fact that a large stock of salt had accumulated. Conversely, if the budget was underspent, one must add in the very serious depletion of the salt.

This lack of accounting purity aggrieved one auditor who spent many a summer day searching through the county for piles of salt in lay-bys, which he set about measuring. Having calculated his results with much use of trigonometry and logarithmic tables (pre-electronic calculator days), he was just about to disprove the 31 March balance sheet figure when an early autumn cold spell sent out the gritters and destroyed his evidence. What a pity.

Table 3.11: Audit opinions — Audit Commision code

Key issues
- *Accounts must comply with CIPFA 'code of practice on local authority accounting', unless impractical or to do so would give a misleading view.*
- *Figures must not be materially wrong.*
- *Entries must not be misleadingly described.*
- *Statutory accounting requirements must be met.*
- *All material items must be disclosed.*
- *The accounts must be suitably analysed and presented.*

Form of opinion
- Must certify audit carried out in accordance with legislation. 'Presents fairly' opinion.

Qualification of opinion
- Opinion is unqualified except for:
  — uncertainty (e.g. major litigation in progress);
  — disagreement (the auditor doesn't agree with how an item is treated in the accounts).

Value for money and the management letter

A fundamental difference between the external audit of councils and that of other organisations is the high priority given to value-for-money work. Auditors have a statutory duty to satisfy themselves that the council has 'made proper arrangements for securing economy, efficiency and effectiveness in its use of resources'. This work is mainly a local interpretation of national studies published by the Audit Commission. Here are examples of topics tackled in recent years.

Recent Audit Commission value-for-money reports

'Towards a healthier environment: managing environmental health services'

The £350m spent on this service could be used more effectively. Each council should develop a corporate policy for the service, assemble information on local environmental health needs, and target resources accordingly

'Healthy housing: the role of environmental health services'

The study found 50 per cent of housing in multiple occupation needed work to meet health and safety standards, but that, at the current rate of improvement, it would take councils 20 years to bring about the improvements. The report recognised the lack of capital investment in private housing, but pointed out that, if less productive authorities performed as well as the top 25 per cent, the number of statutory enforcement actions could increase by 75 per cent with no additional staff costs.

'Fine lines: improving the traffic warden service'

The report states sagely 'there is little popular pressure for a more active approach to enforcement' (surprise). It notes the wide range of productivity from council to council, and the high proportion of warden time spent travelling to and from beats. It has no firm view on whether the service should be managed by councils or the police.

Findings from value for money reviews (along with significant findings on the accounts) are usually summarised in a management letter sent to the Council. Under new legislation, this has become a public document, which must be publicised and debated by the council in open session. It therefore will repay managers to examine any report on their service extremely thoroughly, preferably at draft stage. It is often the case that the accountants carrying out the study are not fully conversant with the practical management issues of a service. Any misconceptions should be pointed out, and corrections sought, before the report enters the public domain.

Role of the Audit Commission and performance indicators

We conclude the chapter by looking very briefly at the role of the Audit Commission itself. One of its main responsibilities is to appoint the auditors to individual councils. Two-thirds of these are provided by the commission's own District Audit Service, the rest by major firms of chartered accountants.

Members are appointed by the Secretary of State, after consultation with the local authority associations, the accountancy bodies and other interested parties.

The Audit Commission:

- *appoints the auditors to individual councils, either from the district audit service (70 per cent of audits) or accountancy firms;*
- *issues and maintains a code of audit practice which is followed by auditors in carrying out their work;*
- *sets and collects audit fees;*
- *can direct an emergency (extraordinary) audit of any council;*
- *carries out efficiency studies into council services generally;*
- *may also research the impact of particular legislation or ministerial action on local government.*

In practice, the Commission works closely with individual auditors, via its code of audit practice, but also in a constant stream of guidance notes that emanate from its Vincent Square headquarters. Although it is individual auditors who bear the statutory responsibilities outlined on page 97, their decisions are usually determined by advice from Vincent square.

Finally, the Audit Commission is currently preparing a set of performance indicators for use by councils in accordance with the citizen's charter. The requirements for this new development are as follows.

- The Commission determines what information councils should publish which will 'facilitate the making of appropriate comparisons' between:
    —the standards of performance achieved by different councils;
    —any one council's performance from one year to another.

- The criteria for assessing performance are cost, efficiency, economy, and effectiveness.
- Councils will be told next financial year's performance indicators the previous December (after appropriate consultation by the Commission).
- Councils must ensure their published information is 'accurate and complete'.
- The information will be audited, and the Commission itself may publish league tables of best and worst performing councils.

Thus, although external audit is less frequently encountered than internal audit, it is clear that their powers are extremely wide ranging. Managers should be aware of these powers, and treat any external audit investigation or enquiries with due care.

Summary

We have dealt with the two types of audit: internal and external, at some length. Armed with this knowledge, you should have little difficulty in operating on equal terms with your friendly auditors. It is essential to remember that they too should be accountable for their performance; if you are dissatisfied with any aspect of the service they provide, draw the matter to their attention. Bad audit is a waste of money, but good audit might even make your own job easier.

Further reading

CIPFA publish a wide range of publications on internal audit.

'Internal audit in the public sector' by Buttery and Simpson explains the technical requirements of internal audit.

'Local Government Audit Law' by Reginald Jones is an excellent and comprehensive review of local authority external audit, including summaries of relevant court cases and a history of the district audit service.

The Audit Commission produces not only its audit code of practice but also numerous reviews of particular council services, as well as its annual report which gives a good summary of current issues.

There is frequent coverage of audit matters in all the accountancy journals (*PFA*, *Accountancy Age*), and local government journals such as *LGC*.

4 Financing

In this chapter, we look at how councils finance their expenditure, including grants from central government and the locally raised council tax which replaced the poll tax from 1 April 1993. We also consider the benefit system which is administered by councils.

Revenue support grant

Before examining the details of the main government grant paid to councils, we look at the methodology behind the government's use of SSAs or *standard spending assessments*. It is fair to say that this mechanism has long been a source of dissatisfaction amongst councils. Equally, it would take the wisdom of Solomon to devise a method of distributing grant to councils which met with universal acclaim. After all, the grant total is fixed and one council's gain is another's loss.

If we run through a little mathematics, this may explain the derivation of some of the SSA. Consider first Fig. 4.1 which shows a simple relationship between, say, the speed of a car and petrol consumption. Point A represents the minimum rate of consumption. If we connected speed to consumption by a mathematical formula, then we could use a technique (calculus) to find the minimum point mathematically.

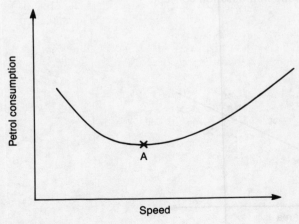

Fig. 4.1

Look now at Fig. 4.2. This represents a plot of council expenditure on (say) members' expenses against geographical area. Each point represents the expenditure/area statistic for a particular council.

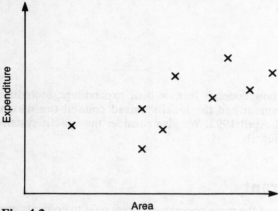

Fig. 4.2

Suppose we wished to establish a formula to allocate funds for members' expenses to councils on a reasonable basis. This might be done on a simple rule such as so much per head of population, or a percentage grant of whatever a council actually spends. We might wish to be more sophisticated though, and we see from table 4.2 that there appears to be a rough correlation between expenditure and area. Most of the small area councils have low expenditure, and vice versa.

If we want a formula to distribute grant based partly on council areas, one approach would be to fit a straight line through the data, making as close a match as possible. This straight line would provide a mathematical equation to distribute the grant (Fig. 4.3). In order to decide exactly which straight line best fits our data, we return to the minimisation concept.

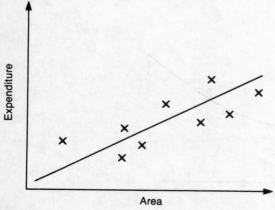

Fig. 4.3

Fig. 4.4 isolates the expenditure statistic for a single council, and we wish to measure how close it is to our chosen formula line. Point J is the actual expenditure/area point, and K is the nearest point on our formula line.

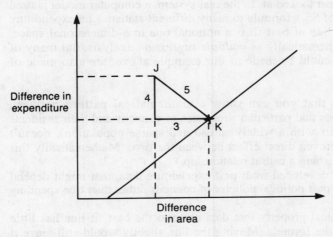

Difference in expenditure

4

5

3

K

J

Difference in area

Fig. 4.4

The distance can be analysed into the components due to:

- *the variation in actual council expenditure from the point on the formula line*
- *the variation in actual council area from the point on the formula line.*

In Fig. 4.4, this unit difference is part of the little 3, 4, 5 triangle. Put mathematically:

Square of total variation =   Square of area variation + Square of expenditure
                                                                variation

or in our case:

25 (5 squared) = 16 (4 squared) plus 9 (3 squared).

Imagine this process repeated for all the data in Fig. 4.2. For any formula line this will give a total, or sum of squares, calculated from all the actual points. To get the line of best fit, we simply minimise this sum of squares. This is sometimes known mathematically as the method of least squares.

All we know, having found our formula, is that it is the best fit to the available information on council spending. It might be:

Standard council spending on members' allowances =	Basic amount for any council	+	Council area × a factor
or	£6000	+	33 per cent of council area

127

We don't really know that the area is a fair basis on which to work out how much councils should be spending on members' allowances, but simply that it happens to fit some data from a past year.

Much of the SSA system relies on calculations which follow the type of principle we have just looked at. In the real system, a computer model is used to find the best fit of SSA formula to many different statistics on expenditure patterns. Thus the line of best fit is a notional one in n-dimensional space. This is known mathematically as *multiple regression* analysis, but many of the criticisms that could be made of our example above, are also made of SSAs.

- The mere fact that you can show a mathematical pattern between expenditure needs and particular properties of councils and their residents (such as councils with a widely spread and sparse population), doesn't demonstrate a proven direct effect between the two. (Mathematically this is termed establishing a causal relationship.)
- If the SSA was developed from past expenditure data, that might depend significantly on past political policies of councils rather than true spending need.
- It's a mathematical property that data close to the best fit line has little contribution to the formula. Moving the line slightly would still leave it fitting this data well. On the other hand, data a long way from the line adds significantly to the distance function that is being minimised. These unusual figures thus have a much larger effect on the formula line than the average data.
- The formula line is the result of a mathematical process. Without access to the model, it is extremely difficult for an individual council to comment on the adequacy of that solution, or to isolate the effect of one particular factor in the calculation as a whole. These types of exercise are often undertaken by the local authority associations, but they are usually more interested in whether their members as a whole gain or lose.

It's probably fair to say that the SSA system is not exactly user-friendly. As we see later in this chapter, though, the SSA is by far the most important factor in deciding how much an individual council can spend each year. Before we look at how individual councils are affected by their SSA determination, we consider briefly the national process of planning local government expenditure.

The annual RSG settlement

The timetable for announcing the RSG settlement has been changed for financial year 1994/5, as government adopts an Autumn Unified Budget. In earlier years, councils could often pick up hints in March of their likely treatment in the detailed Autumn Statement.

There is, in existence, a consultative machinery for developing the RSG settlement, though there is a degree of cynicism amongst councils as to the scope for local government to affect the ultimate results. The snappily titled

Consultative Committee for Local Government Finance (CCLGF) is the medium for these discussions.

Well in advance of the financial year in question, CCLGF working groups begin to assess councils' likely spending needs. In the last few years, the continuing change in council functions has complicated this task, and it has involved much more than simply updating previous years' budgets for inflation as used to be the case. For 1993/94, for example, further education colleges were transferred out of local authority control, and councils gained increased social services responsibilities under community care legislation.

As we have commented earlier, the local government view of councils' expenditure needs is usually very different from central government's. But as well as the size of the overall settlement, the working groups look at changes to the SSA formula. These changes would probably appear fairly innocuous or even esoteric to the outside world, but can have the result of moving large amounts of spending power from one set of councils to another.

In 1991, for example, the groups looked amongst other changes at how the SSA for 'other services' (which includes leisure, refuse collection, and many of the services under district council control), could be made to reflect more accurately the effect on service demand of large numbers of visitors into a council's area. It has long been recognised in grant calculations that permanent population is not always a reliable guide to the demand for council services. An inner London borough will have to provide all the services required by the thousands of commuters who work in the borough during the day. A tourist resort might have several times its normal population during the season.

The population used to calculate the other services SSA prior to 1991 was increased by 25 per cent of the daily inflow of commuters, and 50 per cent of the number of overnight visitors (excluding foreigners). As the visitor-nights figure was found to be based on a 1970s survey, one option was to scrap the allowance altogether. This would have favoured the majority of councils at the expense of some coastal resorts and a few inner London authorities.

Other options were to use more up-to-date survey information, and to include an allowance for foreign visitors. Under this last option the resorts and inner London would have gained significantly. Such a debate underlines the uncertainties in the whole SSA process. Most of the indicators (See RSG Settlement box) seem to have some relation to the cost of council services. How exactly that relationship should be reflected in the SSA formula is another matter.

The working groups report back to the CCLGF, and then await the DOE's autumn announcement as to the basic structure and level of the RSG settlement. Once the total level of grant is known, work is done to establish a formula for distributing that money to councils. Having considered these proposals, the DoE issue a consultative version of the final settlement. This is usually finalised before Christmas so that each council knows precisely what its SSA will be, and can set its revenue budget accordingly.

A key element of the settlement is the announcement of capping criteria. The secretary of state has powers to limit the expenditure of councils, and the reason that the capping criteria are announced well in advance of the financial year is so that councils can adjust their budgets, hence avoiding the need to be actually capped.

Under past capping rules, a council might only discover after setting its budget, and even after issuing tax demands, that it had fallen foul of that year's criteria. Large costs would then be incurred in rebilling residents at the new, lower tax rate.

Basically, it is pointless under the present advance notice system for a council to set a budget which breaches the capping limits, as it will eventually be forced to reduce its expenditure back to the capped limit. There is a right of appeal against designation for capping, but an appealing authority could find its budget cut instead of increased.

Details are set out of the SSA calculation for 1993/94, with some figures on the overall settlement. Details of the capping criteria set, are also provided.

The settlement also covers what the national poundage will be for non-domestic rates. Before 1990, businesses paid the local rate set by their council. As part of the poll tax system, the power to determine local business rates was withdrawn from councils. Instead, the rate poundage is set by the government. The proceeds of this tax are collected by councils and paid over to a central pool. The pool is redistributed in the form of an allowance to councils of about £200 per head of population.

Details of 1993/94 RSG settlement and SSA calculation

SSAs are built up from seven blocks. The box below shows what these are, and the national planning totals of expenditure on the various services.

	£m	£m
Education		
Primary	6,524	
Secondary	7,146	
Post-16	1,052	
Under 5	903	
Other	906	
		16,531
Social services		
Children	1,681	
Elderly	2,201	
Other	1,020	
		4,902
Police		2,788
Fire and civil defence		1,139
Highways maintenance		1,736
All other services		7,006
Capital financing		2,520
Total		36,622

Each council has a total SSA falling into the above blocks (assuming it is responsible for that function), but it is at the council's discretion how it spends its total resources, and this need not follow the breakdown of its SSA.

The SSA blocks for individual councils are calculated by complex formulae. These use *indicators* relating to the council (see box below, for example). The local calculations are then multiplied by a *scaling factor* which brings the sum of individual councils' SSAs back to the national planning total.

The sub-block for other social services is calculated from:

Resident population aged 18 to 64

x

(£22.86 + (£1.84 × All ages social index))

x

the area cost adjustment for social services

x

the scaling factor for the other social services block.

As if this formula were not complicated enough in itself, the *all ages social index* is used in the formula as defined as:

The proportion of people living in non-self contained accommodation, *minus* 0.0082, and then divided by 0.0132

plus

the proportion of people in private households without exclusive use of a bath or inside WC, *minus* 0.0322, *divided by* 0.0188

plus further similar factors for single parent families, overcrowded households, and heads of household born in the new Commonwealth or Pakistan.

Readers may make their own judgements about the sense of controlling council expenditures on this sort of basis.

The government expected that 6 million single adult households would receive the relevant 25 per cent discount on the council tax, and that 3 million households on income support would pay nothing at all.

Local government expenditure was estimated to account for 26 per cent of general government expenditure, and was claimed to have increased by 3.6 per cent a year over the last two years in real terms. The secretary of state warned that it was 'unreasonable to expect such growth to continue'.

Total council expenditure in England was expected to be 41 billion, with central government funding £36 billion of that total.

Capping criteria

The criteria for designating a budget excessive are shown in the box.

Percentage by which 1993/94 budget exceeds SSA	Maximum percentage increase allowed 1992/3 to 1993/4
12.5 or more	any budget excessive
10 to 12.5	0.5
5 to 10	1
1 to 5	1.75
0 to 1	2
Below SSA	any increase allowed

The effect of this type of tariff is to drive councils into a funnel which brings all budgets closer to SSA over the years. This is because the cash increases permitted are below the actual year on year rise in SSAs. Thus it is virtually impossible for a council to increase its budget relative to the SSA (unless it is already below SSA). The only way is down. This process is exemplified in the box below.

To understand this process, run down the column for council A. As its 1992/93 budget is already 10.5% over the 1993 SSA of £100m, any increase on that budget will put it in the 'over 10 per cent' category of the previous box. The maximum year on year cash increase is thus 0.5 per cent, or a cash 1993/94 budget of £111m.

The cash figure of £111m is only worth £107.8m in real terms, however, when deflated for the general 3 per cent rise in SSAs, so the capping criteria have reduced the council's budget excess down to less than 8 per cent over SSA.

The process starts again in 1994/95. Now the 1993 cash budget can be increased by more, 1 per cent, because the excess over SSA (the real terms figure of 7.8 per cent) will now come in the 5 to 10 per cent category of the previous box, so the 1994/95 cash figure will be £112.0m. In real terms this will be only £105.6m, however, and moving inexorably closer to SSA as the excess is only just over 5 per cent.

Similarly, for councils B and C, capable of higher year-on-year cash increases owing to starting the process nearer to SSA, they still cannot move further above the SSA than they started in 1992, even with maximum permissible budget increases.

Having looked at RSG in overall terms, let's look at the impact on individual councils. Table 4.1 is taken from the RSG announcement for 1993/94 made in November 1992. (Some of these figures later changed marginally, but the Table serves to illustrate some of the main principles.)

	Council A	Council B	Council C
Increase in cash SSAs 1992 to 1993, and 1993 to 1994 (rounded) is 3 per cent			
Assume standard SSA is £100m for 1993/94.			
Assume 1993 capping criteria will also apply for 1994.			
1992/93 budget (cash)	110.5	107.0	103.0
Maximum increase avoiding capping (%)	0.5	1.0	1.75
1993/94 budget (cash)	111.0	108.0	104.75
1993/94 budget (real terms)	107.8	104.8	101.7
Maximum increase avoiding capping	1.0	1.0	1.75
1994/95 budget (cash)	112.0	109.0	106.5
1994/95 budget (real terms)	105.6	102.7	100.5

By working through the figures, we can see the underlying principle of the system which is that if a council spends at SSA, the amount of grant and redistributed NNDR it receives will enable it to set a council tax at the national standard rate.

Total budget at SSA level = Revenue support grant
+
Share of non-domestic rates from national pool
+
Proceeds of setting the national standard council tax (i.e. the rate for a band D property)

Table 4.1: 1993/94 RSG settlement for sample of London authorities

Item	Hackney	Harrow	Westminster
1. Resident population	183,569	201,543	182,462
2. Taxbase	64,498	81,144	112,884
3. SSA (£million)	258.194	136.023	220.768
4. Standard tax income (£m)	21.642	28.867	37.877
5. Business rate income (£m)	39.060	42.884	38.824
6. RSG (£m)	197.493	64.27‡	144.067
7. Special grants (£m)	1.329	—	1.492
8. Total external support (£m) (lines 5 to 7)	237.881	107.155	184.383
9. SSA per head of population (£) ((3)/(1))	1,407	675	1,210
10. Number of residents per band D tax payer equivalent ((1)/(2))	2.85	2.48	1.6
11. Business rate received per head of population (£) ((5)/(1))	213	213	213
12. Percentage of expenditure met by council tax payers ((4)/(3)).	8.4	21.2	17.2
13. Percentage of expenditure met by share of business rates ((5)/(3))	15.1	31.5	17.6

Although the figures in Table 4.1 are government assumptions, which are probably different from councils' actual budgets, there are some striking differences between the three London Boroughs chosen. Whatever the deficiencies of the SSA, it certainly recognises a huge difference in spending need between Hackney and Harrow: over £1400 for every resident in Hackney, against less that £700 in Harrow.

At the same time, Hackney has a weak council tax base. On government assumptions, an average of 2.85 residents will produce the tax income of one bank 'D' property, whereas in Westminster, with its high tax base, 1.6 residents produce the income of a 'D' property.

Thus Hackney, with a combination of high spending need and low tax base, needs to fund less than 10 per cent of its expenditure locally. That low figure is before the further reduction, because of the benefits system, on what local residents actually pay. For many of them, their bills will be reduced by council tax benefit which is administered by councils but funded by the government.

In such a position, where only a fraction of funding is actually collected locally, the need for any form of local taxation seems questionable.

Harrow's low SSA, £675 a head, makes the standard £213 a head share of nationally set business rates it receives a significant element of its funding (over 30 per cent), but basically it doesn't make a great difference to a council whether government aid comes in the form of redistributed business rates or RSG because the central support is adjusted to provide the difference between the SSA and standard tax income.

Problems may arise for an individual council because, as the SSA, RSG and NNDR payout are fixed, the small percentage of expenditure funded by council tax is liable to a powerful gearing effect. (As shown in Table 1.1 of Chapter 1, a small percentage variation in the fixed element requires a disproportionate compensation in the small variable element.)

Changes which may cause council tax levels to exceed greatly the standard government level include the following.

- A much lower collection rate may be achieved in practice than is assumed by the government. Those areas with high SSAs, and thus the highest gearing, are usually those of the greatest deprivation. They therefore suffer more from losses in collection than more prosperous areas which in any case have a higher local tax base. Councils base their budgets on local estimates of the collection rate that will be achieved, not the government standard.
- The council's budget may be higher than the SSA, in which case all the additional expenditure will need to be financed locally. To take the example from Table 4.1 above of a council with 8 per cent local funding, a 1 per cent increase in the total budget would require a 12 per cent increase in the council tax.

The two effects could be combined as follows:	£
Assumed council tax for SSA spending level, given 98 per cent collection rate	400
Effect of 90 per cent collection assumption	36
Effect of 1 per cent total expenditure increase, given 10 per cent of expenditure funded locally	44
Actual council tax requirement	480

Also, if the council's performance in collecting NNDR is below government minimum standards, or it if has to borrow because of slow collection of the council tax, those costs too may fall on the council.

So far we have looked at the government funding side of financing council services. We now turn to the local aspect of tax collection. Before we do so, we include a checklist on revenue support grant.

- The total level of council expenditure is largely determined as part of the government's overall spending plans, which are announced in the Autumn.
- Councils are set a standard spending assessment or SSA. They will be capped for exceeding the SSA by more than a small amount, so the SSA is the most important factor in a council's budget.
- SSAs are calculated by a complex mathematical process which seeks to relate council spending needs to various factors such as age profile of the local population, the number of single parent families, and the sparsity or density of population in the council's area.
- General government assistance to councils takes the form of revenue support grant and payments out of the national business rates pool. The system operates so that, if a council sets the government-assumed council tax for a band D property, then it will receive just sufficient RSG and NNDR money to enable it to spend at its SSA.
- Capping criteria are announced well in advance, so that councils can tailor their budgets accordingly. Few councils actually confront the government by setting a budget in excess of the capping criteria.

The council tax and poll tax

Thus far in this chapter we have looked at the RSG system of grant to councils, and how the annual settlement is the dominant factor in setting a council's budget. Now we look in more detail at the local taxation which balances council budgets.

The poll tax experiment

The poll tax, always referred to as the community charge by government ministers, first took effect in 1990. The government had long been committed to reform of the rating system. Poll tax was chosen in preference to other options such as local income tax, local sales tax, or indeed the abolition of local taxation altogether.

Table 4.2 compares the poll tax with the old rates system. Clearly there were some major changes between the two, and the new tax was widely opposed from its first announcement by council treasurers. Particular problems were seen to be the greater difficulty of collection, and that an individual's liability was not related to ability to pay (except if the individual had such a low income that he or she was eligible for community charge benefit). Experience in Scotland, where the tax was introduced a year earlier, did not bode well for England and Wales.

Thought the poll tax was always likely to be expensive to collect, and known to increase the tax burden of the less wealthy, it was surprising how quickly the tax was abandoned and plans announced for its successor. Only some future review with a historical perspective will establish the degree of injustice inherent in the tax; certainly, during its brief life, much of the opposition to it was claimed to be on moral grounds.

A more pragmatic approach was taken by an individual who claimed to have an ancient Cornish charter exempting anybody who would subscribe to membership from Westminster taxation. This soon went the way of most council creative accounting schemes.

Table 4.2: Rates, poll tax and council tax compared

Rates	Poll tax	Council tax
Who is liable to pay?		
Property occupier	Adults resident in the council's area.	Householders in the council's area
How is the tax liability calculated?		
A fixed rate poundage was applied to the property's *ratable value*. The ratable value was calculated from a mixture of rental evidence, and statutory rules.	A flat rate *personal community charge*.	Houses are valued in 8 bands, ranging from band A (up to £40,000) up to band H (over £320,00). The council sets its band D council tax, and the council tax for other bands is a standard percentage above or below the band D charge.
What about businesses?		
Pays the local rate set by the council	The business rate poundage was set nationally, though the local council was responsible for collection.	As for poll tax.
What discounts are available for individuals?		
No discounts available to individuals, though those on low incomes could get up to 100 per cent rate rebates.	No need for individual discounts, as adults living alone paid less than families with more than one adult. Benefits scheme limited rebate to 80 per cent of charge.	25 per cent discount on the tax for single adult households.
What is the relationship in the shire areas between the districts that collect the tax, and the counties who have much larger expenditure per head?		
Counties precepted for their needs on the districts who levied rates. A domestic rate relief grant (a standard rate poundage) was paid to districts. Additionally councils	Charging authorities (i.e. the districts) were required to maintain an independent *collection fund*. Into this was paid poll tax income, and revenue support grant for both district and county	The collection fund continues, but county shares of *revenue support grant* and the NNDR redistribution are received directly.

received *block grant* depending on their local spending level in comparison to the government's grant related expenditure assessment, and compensating them (where necessary) for a lower than average rateable value per head of population.

authorities. The billing authority was only allowed to draw from the collection fund its predetermined budget requirement, and to pay over the precept demanded by the county. The collection fund also received business rates collected, and effected any payment or redistribution to the national pool.

Who are the gainers and losers under the system?

Gainers: families with several adults living in a single property. Those living in properties where the ratable value was disproportionately low compared to the capital value.

Losers: persons living alone in high ratable value properties.

Gainers: those living in properties with a high rateable value. Single adult families. People living in a council area with a strong base of rate income, because the new grant system no longer equalised tax resources.

Losers: families with several adults in a single household. Those on the lowest incomes, who were required to pay 20 per cent of the tax. People living in poorer areas, as no equalisation of tax base in RSG system.

Gainers: those living in property with a low capital value. Those on very low incomes who are now eligible for 100 per cent rebates. People living in council areas with low average property values, as the government grant system compensates councils with a low tax base.

Losers: people living in very high value property. Those living in council areas with high average property values.

The council tax

As the poll tax is now abolished, its main interest to councils is their ability to collect in the outstanding arrears. We now look in more detail at the operation of the council tax. The government has sought to redress some of the main deficiencies apparent in the poll tax, and in particular:

- *the tax, being based on the value of properties, ought to bear some relation to individuals' ability to pay. Those on the lowest incomes will be eligible for 100 per cent rebates.*
- *the government grant system now pays less money to councils with a strong tax base, and more to those with a weak one.*
- *there ought to be a clearer understanding by local residents of how their tax bill is arrived at, because it is directly related to property value.*
- *most importantly from councils' point of view, the new tax should be much easier and less costly to collect.*

Despite its claimed improvements over the poll tax, council tax has already hit a few teething problems. Using the more transparent tax basis of property value has proved to be a mixed blessing. Much of the valuation work was contracted out by the Inland Revenue, and some political capital was gained by opponents of the tax when it was demonstrated that the cost per property of these expert assessments was less than that of well-known chocolate bar.

More unsatisfactorily, the tax levied on 1 April 1993 banded property according to its 1 April 1991 value. UK property prices had fallen significantly during that period. Taxpayers could thus easily find their property legitimately assessed into a higher band than its current market value. A more subtle effect claimed by some commentators is the acceptance by householders of an unreasonably high banding, on the grounds that this might support an unrealistic selling price demanded for the property.

London is likely to fare worse than the rest of the country under council tax, because of the high average value of properties. If the grant process and council budgets worked according to government intentions, then a London resident in a Band D property would be paying the same council tax as a Band D resident elsewhere in the country. However, high property prices in London mean that fewer residents are in the lower valuation bands. The bottom line, the average local tax bill, is thus much higher. During the legislative process, there was a strong lobby for a separate banding scheme to apply to London. Although, in the short term, the effect of the change will be masked by a transitional relief scheme, this London factor could prove a long-term source of dissatisfaction with the council tax.

The council tax

Properties are valued into eight bands (see box). The valuations are carried out by the Inland revenue, who must appoint a listing officer (who may be a partner in a firm of surveyors) for each council area.
The valuation bands are as follows:

A	£40,000 or less
B	Over £40,000 but not over £52,000
C	Over £52,000 but not over £68,000
D	Over £68,000 but not over £88,000
E	Over £88,000 but not over £120,000
F	Over £120,000 but not over £160,000
G	Over £160,000 but not over £320,000
H	Over £320,000

Band D is highlighted as it has special significance.

- *It is used as the headline council tax figure (e.g. Anyborough sets £500 council tax means that that is the charge on a band D property*
- *It plays a special role in the way government grant is shared out. The*

tax base of a council is calculated as a number of band D equivalent properties.

(In Wales, all the limits of the individual bands are 25 per cent lower, so that for example band H is £320,000 less 25 per cent and covers properties valued over £240,000.)

The tax actually charged to a householder is increased according to the valuation band. (In legislation this is explained by the mystical sequence 6 : 7 : 8 : 9 : 11 : 13 : 15 : 18.) This means, say, that the taxes for a band A property and a band H property should be in the ration 6 to 18 (or 1 to 3). The relationship between the tax levels is shown in the box, with an example of how the tax levels would compare to a £450 band D charge.

Band	Number	Tax as % of D	Charge
A	6	67%	£300
B	7	78%	£350
C	8	89%	£400
D	9	100%	£450
E	11	122%	£550
F	13	144%	£650
G	15	167%	£750
H	18	200%	£900

There are two levels of discount available: 25 per cent and 50 per cent. This works as follows:

Various categories of individual have been scheduled (see box). If *all* the adults who live in a property fall into some part of the schedule, the council tax for that property is reduced by 50 per cent. Also, scheduled individuals are disregarded in working out whether a lower, 25 per cent single occupant discount is available. So, for example, if a household consisted of two adults, one scheduled and one not, then that household would be eligible for the 25 per cent discount.

If only one adult occupies a property, there is an automatic right to a 25 per cent discount. Finally, there is a 50 per cent discount if the property is unoccupied, or if all the residents are under 18.

Scheduled persons (examples)
School children aged over 18
School leavers under 20 for the first 6 months after leaving school
Full-time students, apprentices, trainees and student nurses
Any person living in a hospital, nursing home or residential care
Certain care workers, and some carers for the disabled (not a spouse or parent)

The introduction of these discounts caused some consternation amongst finance practitioners. After all, one of the reasons the poll tax was so expensive to collect in comparison to rates was the need for councils to maintain a register of residents. (Under the old rates system, all councils had to keep was a valuation list of properties; there was no need to know who lived there other than the name of the occupier or owner for billing purposes. Rebates could be dealt with under a separate system, and relied on positive action by claimants.) Hopes of avoiding such a register on returning to the property-based council tax, were undermined by the need to maintain details such as how many adults live at a property, and to verify whether they fall under the various scheduled categories.

There is a transitional relief scheme, which limits the increase a household can suffer in the change from poll tax to council tax. This scheme will be paid for by government grant to councils, and then passed on to households in their council tax bills. The government announced that the maximum increase would be as follows:

Band				
	A	£1.75 a week	or	£91 a year
	B	£2.00		£104
	C	£2.25		£117
	D	£2.50		£130
	E	£2.75		£143
	F	£3.00		£156
	G	£3.25		£169
	H	£3.50		£182

However, as with most things in local government finance, the scheme is not as simple as it might appear.

- Anybody moving house automatically loses the protection of the scheme. This is administrative sense. For somebody moving within the same council area, the benchmark poll tax figure against which protection is given would be fixed in the calculation. However much council tax liability increased by moving to a more expensive and higher-banded property, the government would be funding most of the increase. (Perhaps a way of reviving the property market?)
- The council tax used to assess the transitional relief is not the actual council tax charged by the council! Instead, the council must calculate a *scheme council tax* for itself. Under the relevant regulations, this assumes, amongst other things, that a 98 per cent collection rate is achieved. As we have seen earlier, any downgrading of that assumption can produce a large increase in the council tax actually set because of the gearing effect (see box).

Consider a single adult household whose 1992/93 poll tax was £300. The property is in band H, and the scheme council tax for the council is £400 (Band D). However, because the council has budgeted for a 90 per cent collection rate, the actual band D tax set is £435. The band H tax is thus £870 (band H tax is twice the rate of band D). Transitional relief is calculated as follows:

	£
Scheme council tax (band H)	800
Less 25 per cent single householder discount	(200)
	600
Less 1992 poll tax liability	300
Extra cost	300
Maximum permissible increase under relief scheme	182
Transitional relief	118

But the actual council tax bill will be:

	£
Band H liability	870
Less 25 per cent discount	218
	652
Less transitional relief	(118)
Council tax liability	534
Poll tax liability in 1992	300
Increased cost	234
Maximum increase provided for under government scheme	182
'Excess' increase	52

Certain property is exempt from the council tax.

- *A dwelling which is unoccupied and unfurnished is exempt for 6 months.*
- *A dwelling which has just been substantially improved, and remains unfurnished will be exempt for 6 months if it remains unoccupied.*
- *The homes of people in residential care, hospital, or prison (provided no other adult is living in the property) are exempt.*
- *If all the residents are students, the property is exempt.*

Again, one can imagine the complexities of controlling exemptions claimed under the last two categories.

Appeals and changes in valuation are allowed for under the legislation. Unless a fundamental error was made in the valuation, the main circumstances in which a valuation will be altered are if the property is extended or partially demolished (an extreme way to save council tax?).

Disability relief is available for properties which are the sole or main residence of somebody who is substantially and permanently disabled. This relief is granted by the method of allocating the property into the next lowest band, thus if the property is already valued in band A, no relief is available. During the legislative process, various concerns were raised about the valuation of properties adapted for use by the disabled. In particular, valuable works to facilitate its use by a disabled person could push the property up into a higher value band. The method of relief, if complex administratively, is no doubt intended to assuage these concerns.

How is the council tax calculated?

As we saw earlier on p. 133, the council tax system works so that, if a council levies the government-assumed tax, this plus government grants should enable it to provide a standard level of service. We have also seen how local differences from government plans can change the council tax level which must be demanded from residents.

- *The collection rate that is predicted by the council can vary (what proportion of the tax due will actually be collected).*
- *The council might increase or decrease its demand on the collection fund depending on whether it is building up or reducing its financial reserves.*
- *If the council has a surplus or deficit on its collection fund from the poll tax system, that could affect its 1993/94 budget. As a special provision for 1993/94, any such surplus or deficit is carried to the general fund of the council operating the collection fund.*

To complicate matters further, we have a two-tier system of councils in most parts of the country. This means that district councils operate collection funds and recover the council tax, whilst the counties precept on the districts for their council tax income. Even in London and in the metropolitan areas, there are various authorities and bodies that precept on the unitary authorities actually collecting the council tax.

One of the advantages claimed for the new system of grant distribution is that it will enable the bill to a household to be clearly split between district and county needs. This is because RSG and redistributed NNDR income will be paid directly to counties. Under the old system, it was difficult to break down the funding of county and district expenditure each into its central and local element.

The relevant tax base

Because the tax rate is different for different values of property, and many households are eligible for discounts, both billing authorities and preceptors need

to know the exact tax base in an area. Put simply, if the council tax is set at
£500, how much money will this bring into the collection fund?

As well as councils' tax-setting decisions, a calculation of the tax base is
needed to share out government grant to councils, and to run the transitional
relief scheme. The way the calculation is made is to reduce all properties to
their mathematical sounding *band D equivalent*. The way this works is now
shown.

Preparing the tax base

The district council examines the valuation list for its area, which can rapidly
be analysed into the number of properties in each band. However, this raw data
needs to be adjusted by the council before it can be used for tax calculations.
Changes are made (which should be marginal movements in the numbers of
property per band) for:

- *newly constructed properties which the council has become aware of;*
- *an estimate of the number of properties which will be exempt, for the
  reasons outlined above (e.g. all the adult occupants are students, or the
  property is unoccupied). The numbers deducted are the full-year
  equivalent, since exemptions are granted on a daily basis and may not
  last the whole year (e.g. unoccupied properties are exempt only for the
  first six months, so 100 band D properties falling vacant would reduce
  the band D equivalent total by 50);*
- *the numbers in individual bands must be adjusted to take account of
  valuation appeals which are likely to be successful, and disability relief
  (which moves a property into a lower band).*

These adjustments enable the council to calculate the number of dwellings
in each band on which it will be collecting the council tax. In our example this
is as per the box.

Band			
	A	12,000	properties
	B	15,000	(full-year
	C	20,000	equivalent)
	D	18,000	
	E	9,000	
	F	6,000	
	G	3,000	
	H	1,000	

To complicate matters further, these numbers must be reduced for the
granting of 25 per cent or 50 per cent discounts. This calculation is shown in
the next box.

(1)	(2) 25% cases	(3) 50% cases	(4) Net (Column 1 less 25% of column 2 less 50% of column 3)
Band A 12,000	600	600	11,550
B 15,000	700	500	14,575
C 20,000	800	450	19,575
D 18,000	700	400	17,625
E 9,000	300	400	8,725
F 6,000	240	200	5,840
G 3,000	100	120	2,915
H 1,000	60	100	935
84,000	3,500	2,770	81,740

We can check this arithmetic as follows on the total number of properties:

Total number of properties	84,000
less 25 per cent discounts (3500 × 25%)	(875)
less 50 per cent discounts (2770 × 50%)	(1,385)
Adjusted number of properties	81,740

However, as we recall from our earlier review of the tax, each of the 935 equivalent properties in band H will raise twice the tax of a band D property. Thus, to calculate the tax base, we convert all our numbers to band D equivalents. So, for example, the 935 H properties are worth 2 × 935 or 1,870 D equivalents. This calculation is shown in the next box.

Band	Adjusted number of properties (from box above)	Multiplier to convert to band D (see p. 140)	Band D equivalents
A	11,550	67%	7,700
B	14,575	78	11,336
C	19,575	89	17,400
D	17,625	100	17,625
E	8,725	122	10,664
F	5,840	144	8,436
G	2,915	167	4,858
H	935	200	1,870
Totals	81,740		79,889

Thus the 84,000 chargeable properties produce a tax base equivalent to 79,889 band D units. Once this is known, it is easy to predict the product of a particular council tax level, because we simply need to multiply the number of D equivalents by the band D council tax.

One further adjustment is necessary, which is to estimate the likely level of collection. This is done on an accruals basis (see Chapter 2), reflecting income due for the year, rather than expected cash receipts.

Suppose, in our case, the assumed collection rate were 95 per cent, then the base would be reduced by 5 per cent, as it would be expected to produce 5 per cent less tax than the 100 per cent theoretical maximum. Our base would thus be:

Adjusted properties × Collection rate

or 79,889 × 95% = 75,895.

Calculating budget requirements

Both the county and district must then calculate their *budget requirements*. This includes the following items:

- —expenditure;
- —net expenditure of the council's general fund;
- —any increase in reserves (Councils may incur *special items* of expenditure which relate to only part of their area, and are only taxed in that area. This affects the local calculations but is not covered in this text.);
- —income;
- —fees and charges;
- —reductions in reserves.

Government RSG, NNDR redistribution, and council tax are not included in income at this stage.

Assuming in our (artificial) example, that our county area comprises a single billing district, the results of these calculations might be as follows:

	District £m	County £m	Total £m
Expenditure	80	380	460
Increase in reserves	—	10	10
	80	390	470
Income	(30)	(30)	(60)
Drawn from reserves	(10)	—	(10)
Budget requirement	40	360	400

Calculating the basic tax amount

Now that county and district each know how much their budget requirement is, they are able, by deducting the known figures of NNDR redistribution and RSG that they will receive directly from the government, to calculate the council tax they need to levy. The calculation works as shown in Table 4.3.

Table 4.3: RSG/NNDR DATA

	District £m	County £m	Total £m
Budget requirement	40	360	400
RSG	(20)	(280)	(300)
NNDR	(4)	(56)	(60)
Demand on collection fund	16	24	40
Band D council tax	£210.82	£316.22	£527.04

The band D amounts are derived by dividing the collection fund demands by the tax base calculated earlier. For the district this is:

$$\frac{£16,000,000}{75,895} = £210.82$$

A final adjustment to the calculations which might be necessary in an actual case is that any surplus or deficit on the collection fund should be shared between district and county when it comes to the stage of calculating the council tax demand. The allocation must be in proportion to their demands on the fund, though there is a special arrangement for financial year 1993/94 which allows districts or billing authorities to assume the entire surplus or deficit in their own calculation.

Having been through the calculation of the council in some detail, we might be entitled to feel that the process was even worse than paying the tax itself. However, the calculation process should have provided an insight into how the various financing factors affect the headline band D council tax. We conclude our look at council financing with a brief look at the benefits system they administer.

Council benefits administration

Councils are responsible for the distribution of two main categories of benefit: housing benefit which assists with rent costs (whether as a private tenant or in council property), and council tax benefit to reduce household tax bills.

The role of councils in paying such benefits to those in need has increased greatly over the last 15 years. Before 1982, any person receiving supplementary benefit claimed help with his or her housing costs from the Department of Social Security. But in 1982 these responsibilities were transferred across to councils, greatly increasing the benefits workload. With the introduction of the poll tax in 1990, many more individuals became liable for local taxation. This drove caseloads even higher.

Many councils have come to regard the government's 1982 gift of a large chunk of the DSS's benefits administration as a shrewd move, on the government's part, because housing benefit is a service for which councils are unlikely to win praise. Even if a claimant is paid with the utmost promptness and efficiency, they are likely to feel simply that they have received what was, in any case, their legal right. Conversely, any delay from receiving an instant service will reflect adversely on residents' opinion of the council's efficiency, but whatever the thinking behind the transfer, there was much sense in bringing housing benefits under a single unified control.

Although councils must expect a degree of dissatisfaction even when operating benefits efficiently, indications are that in some authorities the service is well below acceptable standards. A recent Audit Commission report 'Remote Control' highlighted the serious backlogs of benefit applications that had built up in some councils, leading to press reports of sacks of claimants' mail lying unopened in Town Hall corridors for months on end. The Commission called for independent quality assessments of the service provided by councils, and for greater financial incentives to councils to reward those operating the service to a high standard.

Councils, for their part, would point to the complexity of the benefit regulations set by government, and the difficulties of actually operating the service. Claimants often need considerable help in making applications. They might, for example, need a translator to explain the ramifications of the various benefit rules. Occasionally, claimants are difficult to deal with on a personal level, and counter staff are abused and even assaulted. In many councils the benefits section is not renowned for its high morale. Councillors, quite rightly, often take up benefits matters on behalf of ward residents. This can exert further pressures on staff as they try to operate the service.

Service delivery and probity

In operating the benefits service, there is usually a conflict for councils between satisfying claimants' service delivery requirements and ensuring only legitimate claims are paid. Whilst, in an ideal world, it would be possible to achieve both objectives, common sense dictates that the more effort put into paying claims promptly, the less can be spent on investigation and property visits.

Prior to financial year 1993/94, there was a positive disincentive to councils to carry out investigations. Any overpayments were subsidised at 25 per cent by the government, rather than the normal 95 per cent rate of subsidy. (Except in cases where the council could show the fault lay with the DSS in not promptly informing the council of claimant's changed circumstances). Thus, unless the council could recover more than 70 per cent of the overpayment from the claimant (unlikely given the limited financial resources of most claimants), the council would lose out by discovering the overpayment. (In the case outlined above, the 25 per cent subsidy plus the 70 per cent recovery would match the normal subsidy rate of 95 per cent). These rules have been changed for 1993/94 to allow councils much higher subsidy on overpayments. They could actually gain funds by achieving fraud detection targets.

A wider issue in pursuing errors and overpayments may be the political stance of authorities. Some vigorously pursued overpayments even when this was at a financial cost to the council. Others are unlikely to concentrate resources on investigations even under the new rules, as they see this as signifying undue pressure on claimants generally. Councils need to be aware, though, of the determination and skill of some individuals in exploiting any weakness in controls. In some areas of the country, there have been organised efforts to defraud councils on a significant scale. Once a claim is validated into the benefits system, a high value of payments can pass automatically before the case is scheduled for review.

A certain ennui at the ease of manipulating a government benefits system was evidenced by one culprit some years ago. Tiring of concocting aliases, he was forced to resort to the name Orig on one application. Staff processing the claim were obviously not crossword enthusiasts, as they failed to notice that Orig was simply 'giro' backwards (giro cheques being the medium of paying many claims).

Before we turn to the structure of the benefit schemes, it is worth commenting that there is a wide range of management structures used by councils in operating the benefits function. In some councils, the service is run by finance department. In others, it is split with housing department dealing with rent allowances and rent rebates, and finance handling council tax benefit. The structure in housing operations is often tied in to a decentralised or neighbourhood structure. It's also fair to say that given the 'no-win' nature of the service, the function has its fair share of reorganisations.

Rent rebates

These are given to tenants of council property. The rent due from the tenant is reduced by the level of benefit available, so no cash actually passes from council to tenant. It is advantageous to the council to bring as many tenants as are eligible into housing benefit, because all the rent income reductions are reimbursed by the government in housing subsidy.

Rent allowances

These are paid to private sector or housing association tenants. There is a greater risk of malpractice for these, as a payment is entailed. Tenants may opt to have their benefit paid directly to their landlord.

Council tax benefit

This is effected by reducing the demands on householders

Government subsidy rules

Rent allowances and council tax benefit attract 95 per cent subsidy from the government. This subsidy also covers bed and breakfast arrangements made by councils for homeless persons. (The council pays hoteliers, and levies charges on the tenants which are usually fully covered by rent rebate.)

Rent rebates are dealt with through the council's housing revenue account, or HRA, and are fully subsidised. If however a council's notional HRA is in surplus, then the subsidy on benefits is reduced £ for £. (As is explained in Chapter 2, government housing subsidy is based not on the actual accounts, but on a notional account using government formula figures. It is the balance on this account which determines the subsidy. If it is in deficit, then subsidy puts it into balance. If it is in surplus, that surplus is set off against benefits paid.)

Benefit levels

Rent allowances and rebates — Tenants' income (after various adjustments) is compared with financial needs (including number of dependants, any disability). If there is no excess of income over needs, then the full rent is covered by benefit.

There are limits to the level of rents for which government will subsidise benefits. Say, for example, that limit is £60 a week for a particular property, and the council pays benefit against a £100 a week rent. Only the £60 a week will attract subsidy (of about £50), and the council will need to find the additional £40 a week from its own resources. There is thus a strong incentive on councils to encourage tenants to achieve reasonable rents, particularly by use of the rent officer service.

Benefit tapers off at a 65 per cent rate for any excess of income above needs. Say a claimants rent is £50 a week. With an excess of income over needs of £30, then the benefit entitlement will be £50 (less 65 per cent of £30, or 30.50).

The scheme is complicated by the fact that not all payments to landlords fall within the benefits definition of rent.

Council tax benefit — This works in a similar way, but the benefit falls by only 20 per cent of the excess income. So a person with a liability of £10 a week, and excess income of £6 a week would get council tax benefit of £10 (less 20 per cent of £6, or £8.80). Unlike the former poll tax benefit scheme, benefit extends to 100 per cent of the tax in appropriate cases.

Councils' benefit expenditure

Expenditure in 1991/92 exceeded £6 billion. A majority of households in rented accommodation receive some support, representing one in six households for the country as a whole.

Summary

The review of the benefits system concludes our look at how councils finance their expenditure. Certainly any government wishing to introduce a simpler system would enjoy ample scope for rationalisation.

150

Further reading

The *PFA* magazine published by CIPFA usually provides a full analysis of the autumn statement as it affects local authorities, and the RSG settlement.

Various DoE publications give an exhaustive account of RSG and SSA calculations.

For an overview of housing benefit, the 1993 Audit Commission report 'Remote Control' is excellent. Also see CIPFA's 'Housing Finance' prepared by the housing finance expert, Bert Bucknall.

5 Capital finance and borrowing

The subjects covered by this chapter are at the centre of councils' financial operations. Despite government policy to curtail capital programmes, councils still carry out £billions of capital works every year: refurbishment of housing estates, new schools, roads, or leisure facilities. Any council manager therefore needs to be conversant with the capital finance system, how to bid for capital resources, and how to control the financial aspects of a capital contract. Whilst the law governing the capital finance area is undoubtedly complex, you will be in a much better position to negotiate with your finance department if you have a sound basic understanding of the system.

Over the years, much of this capital expenditure has been financed by long-term borrowing. A significant part of a treasurer's responsibility is to manage any new borrowing, and to replace old debt as it expires. This function, *treasury management*, has been a great deal in the news in recent years. In 1989, the local authority swaps crisis broke, when the London Borough of Hammersmith and Fulham were revealed to have some £3500 million of swaps. All such local authority agreements were later held to be unlawful, with considerable repercussions for the London money markets. Then, in July 1991, the Bank of Credit and Commerce International (BCCI) was closed down by the Bank of England. Over the next days, councils were discovered to be its main UK depositors culminating in the news that Western Isles Regional Council had a deposit of some £23 million, virtually all its spare funds, with BCCI.

These two incidents served to demonstrate that council treasury management was perhaps not all it ought to be. In fact, it has always been an area of council finance left to treasurers' better judgement. This, despite the fact that the cost of interest on borrowing forms a major element of many councils' budgets: over 25 per cent of expenditure in some cases. Accordingly, in the second part of the chapter we look at the basics of managing debt and investing cash surpluses. This should enable you to comment, in an informed way, on treasury issues, and perhaps even form a view as to how well the function is operated in your authority.

Capital controls under the local government and housing act 1989

To understand the system of capital controls we need to look briefly at the provisions of this act. The main controls are set out below. The terminology may be daunting at first, but the concept is simple. The aggregate credit limit (ACL) allows for all the borrowings a council has built up over the years. If it receives some new borrowing permissions, its ACL goes up and it can borrow the money to pay for new capital schemes. Conversely, if it sells assets its ACL goes down and it must eventually repay some debt. The ACL thus goes up and down as different types of transaction take place during the year.

- There is an absolute maximum on the amount of debt a council may have outstanding at any time. This is known as the *Aggregate Credit Limit* or ACL.
- Every year a council receives new borrowing permissions, known as *credit approvals*. These may be used to borrow for new projects, and raise the ACL.
- If the council sells any land or property, it must set aside at least half of the proceeds to repay debt, thereby lowering the ACL. The balance can be used to pay for new capital schemes. These sale proceeds are termed *capital receipts*. (The debt repayment was temporarily suspended for 1993).
- Each year, the council must make a *minimum revenue provision* (MRP) based on a percentage of its debt. This lowers the ACL.
- Borrowing permissions may only be used for works which meet a legal definition of *expenditure for capital purposes*.
- If councils want to pay for capital items straight out of revenue budgets, there is no limit on such expenditure.

We will now consider in more detail precisely how the ACL is built up. It has four elements: revenue limit, capital limit, credit ceiling, and approved investments. Two of these elements: revenue limit and capital limit, are straightforward.

The revenue limit allows the council to borrow in order to continue its day-to-day expenditure. Often (and not surprisingly!) payments such as salaries and running expenses run ahead of income collection. Provided the council has a balanced budget, and has identified income sufficient to finance all its activities, the revenue limit is designed to cater for all its temporary borrowing requirements. Often it proves the case that budgeted income is eventually not collected at all. The revenue limit allows arrears to be carried for 18 months after the financial year. After then, the lost income must be charged to the revenue budget.

Similarly, the capital limit allows councils to pay for schemes which are eventually to be funded by a government grant. Often such grants are only paid over after work on the scheme has taken place. The capital limit allows council the temporary borrowing facilities necessary to fund schemes in anticipation of the eventual grant.

Structure of the Act

A temporary revenue limit

This is defined as the lesser of:
      —expenditure already incurred;
      —income yet to be collected.
Arrears can be carried for up to 18 months.

A *temporary capital limit*

This allows the council to borrow for up to 18 months in anticipation of government capital grants.

A *credit ceiling*

This is the level of capital borrowing allowed to the council. In most authorities it is by far the largest element of the ACL.

Approved investments

This allows councils to hold money earmarked for repaying debt until the financial and economic circumstances are favourable.

The revenue and capital limits need concern us no further, and we turn our attention to the most important element of the ACL: the credit ceiling. It is through the credit ceiling that all the effects of capital transactions are reflected. The fourth element of the ACL: approved investments, is something of a technicality which we return to later.

The credit ceiling

What is the opening balance?

When the present system of controls began in April 1990, councils were able to take their existing long-term debt into their opening ceiling. (Certain 'creative accounting' items were disallowed, however.) It is important to remember that, once a loan is in the credit ceiling, it can be replaced when it expires. Suppose a council's credit ceiling is £100m, and its £100m of actual debt includes a £10m loan which is due to be repaid next month. The council can take out a new loan of £10m to repay the expiring loan without in any way breaching its ACL.

What increases the credit ceiling?

The government gives each council an annual ration of borrowing permissions known as credit approvals. The credit ceiling is increased once a council decides to use its approvals for capital schemes.

Can credit approvals be used for any other purpose?

They can also be used to enter into borrowing-like agreements which fall within the definition of *credit arrangements*. These include leases and hire-purchase agreements. Credit arrangements are not added to the credit ceiling. This means that, when they run out, new borrowing permissions must be wasted on renewing them. Also, the legal position behind a credit arrangement is not as strong for a lender as with a normal loan. This makes the interest cost of a credit arrangement much higher.

What decreases the credit ceiling?

A minimum revenue provision of at least 4 per cent of the credit ceiling (or 2 per cent for housing) must be made each year.

When any capital asset is sold, part of the receipt (the *reserved element*) must be set aside for debt redemption. This has been set at 50 per cent (or 75 per cent for housing) but were set at zero per cent for 1993.

Now we understand how the credit ceiling works, let us look again at that fourth element of the ACL: approved investments. This is a technical adjustment which allows for the practicalities of managing debt.

Approved investments and the ACL

- As soon as land or buildings are sold, a reserved element of the receipt arises.
- The reserved element reduces the credit ceiling.
- It is not always possible to repay immediately money borrowed by the council. Some loans have no facility for early repayment. Even if it is possible to repay a loan early, it can be very costly to do so. This would be bad value for money.
- The approved investment element of the ACL allows councils to hold both reserved elements from capital receipts and minimum revenue provisions until the time is right to repay debt. In effect, the approved investment is matched £ for £ with the loans it will eventually be used to repay.

Now that we have covered the basics of the ACL and its constituent elements, try running through the examples in Table 5.1 to test your expertise.

Table 5.1: Examples of how capital transactions affect the credit ceiling

Transaction	Effect
Housing Land is sold for £2,600,000. The money is placed on deposit with another local authority.	A reserved element of the receipt arises (75 per cent of £2.6m = £1,950,000). The credit ceiling falls by this amount, but is replenished by the approved investment. The balance of the £2.6m (£650,000) is a usable receipt which may be spent at any time for capital purposes.
The council applies £2m of its BCA to acquire land for a new school, borrowing the money to pay for the site.	The credit ceiling increases by £2m as soon as the credit approval is applied. This enables the council to borrow the money for the acquisition without exceeding the ACL.

Borrowing limits

The ACL sets a limit for council borrowing, but there are other controls in the act on what sort of borrowing may be undertaken. Essentially, a council is required to set three separate borrowing limits before the start of the financial year.

- Limits must be set before any borrowing can take place.
- An overall limit must be set for all forms of borrowing.
  As councils may carry approved investments matched for with borrowings, this limit may be higher than the basic ACL.
- A limit must be set on the percentage of debt due to be repaid in the financial year.
  It is regarded as bad treasury management to have more than, say, 15 per cent of borrowing falling out in any one year. The large borrowing requirement might coincide with a lack of borrowing facilities, or abnormally high interest rates.
- A limit must be set on the percentage of debt with a variable interest rate.
  When debt is in fixed interest rates (sometimes described as *funded*), the council's interest costs are predictable. However high interest rates rise or however low they fall, the council will not be significantly affected. If the council has a high proportion of debt in variable interest loans, its budget could be seriously affected in a period of high interest rates.
- The requirement for councils to set these limits in full council allows all councillors the opportunity to comment on these major financial decisions.

Before leaving the technicalities of the 1989 Act, we now look briefly at two key areas: what does and does not count as capital expenditure, and the rules on credit arrangements.

Capital expenditure

Each council has a capital programme. These schemes rely on a separate set of resources from the normal revenue budget. It is important therefore for you to understand what can and cannot be funded out of the capital programme.

Definition of expenditure for capital purposes

- The acquisition, reclamation, enhancement or laying out of land exclusive of roads, buildings and other structures.
- The acquisition, construction, preparation, *enhancement* or replacement of roads, buildings, or other structures.
- The acquisition, installation or replacement of movable or immovable plant, machinery and apparatus and vehicles or vessels.
- *enhancement* means:
  — lengthening substantially the useful life of the asset;
  — increasing substantially the open market value of the asset;
  — increasing substantially the assets use for or in connection with the council's services.

This definition of capital was introduced in legislation to stop councils using their borrowing powers for day-to-day repairs. It was felt that, as such repairs have no long-term value, it is unsatisfactory for councils to borrow to finance them.

Credit arrangements

Prior to the 1989 Act coming into force, many councils had developed 'creative accounting' schemes to achieve the substance of borrowing without falling under its statutory definition. The act therefore introduces the concept of a credit arrangement to control such devices. Credit approvals must be used to enter into a credit arrangement.

The definition of a credit arrangement used in the act is not exactly user-friendly, so we will not quote it word for word. Basically, it tests an agreement by checking how long after goods are supplied the council is still paying for them. This works as follows:

Take the financial year in which the agreement was signed, or any later financial year.

For that financial year, work out:
A: what value of goods the council had yet to receive at its beginning

B: how much the council had yet to pay at the end of the year

If B is greater than A, you have a credit arrangement.

Try a few examples. You will see that any deferred payment arrangement gets caught by the test if it stretches over more than two financial years. This is because you then come to a year where there is nothing left to receive (A = zero), but something left to pay (B = the remaining instalments). B is definitely greater than A, hence we have a credit arrangement.

There are certain types of credit arrangement which are exempt from controls, such as ordinary property leases for an annual rental. The most valuable exception here is the £10,000 minimum. This is a clear incentive to divide down contracts into sub-£10,000 chunks, hence avoiding the controls.

A credit arrangement arises when a council becomes the lessee of land, goods, or property. The amount of credit cover needed to enter into such an arrangement is calculated by multiplying the payments due in each future year by a statutory discount factor. The result of this calculation almost invariably exceeds the initial cost of the item. Certain exceptions are allowed:

- *leases of under 3 years (if the land was not previously owned by the council);*
- *operating leases;*
- *any credit arrangement worth less than £10,000;*
- *certain types of building contract where the council is committed to dispose of the completed dwellings to a housing association, or by shared ownership leases.*

How to maximise your position within the capital controls

As we have seen, the capital controls are complex. In most councils their interpretation is the responsibility of a specialist capital group in the finance department. Unless you are prepared to rely totally on their advice, it will be of some value to know the tricks of the trade set out below.

Capitalisation to free revenue budgets

Each council has two separate budgets: one for its revenue expenditure and a capital programme. In practice, these two budgets are not completely independent. You will find that tradition often determines what is charged where, and that not everything that could legitimately be financed from capital resources is. Table 5.2 lists a few such items. Are you happy that all your potential capital items have been included as capital programme bids? After all, if you can't get an allocation of capital resources, you can still continue to meet the costs as before out of your revenue budget.

Many treasurers are loathe to explain the full potential for capitalisation because they regard it as an easy way out which merely defers sorting out services which can't run within their revenue budget. It is worth taking a proactive approach in discussing this issue.

Table 5.2: Capitalisation Items

Item	Details
Salaries associated with capital schemes	The act doesn't specifically mention salaries as being capital, but it is a long-established tradition in council accounts to charge fees for architects, etc to capital. This could be extended to other disciplines such as planners, valuers and legal associated with a scheme.
Major repairs	In past legislation, any housing repairs could be financed by borrowing. Housing departments had to learn quickly under the 1989 Act what could and could not be capitalised, as this represented a major loss of spending power. Conversely, other departments which never borrowed for repairs are often not aware of the scope to do this. Check your revenue budget for major repair items, and compare with the definitions on page 156.
Leased items	In years of scarce capital resources, items such as vehicles and computers are usually leased. This is because certain categories of lease (termed *operating leases*) are exempt from capital controls. It is important to remember that this process can be reversed. When capital resources are available, it may be cheaper to borrow and acquire outright. Just because items have been leased in the past doesn't mean their replacements shouldn't be capital programme bids.
Receipt deductions	Just as the salaries associated with developing a scheme may be included in its capital cost, so the salaries associated with achieving a receipt may be deducted. This might include an allowance for valuers' work or any legal requirements.

Planning agreements

These are agreements between developers and councils. They usually entail the developer agreeing to undertake various works in return for planning permission which is more extensive than would normally be the case. For example, planning permission for 100 houses on a particular site might exceed the development guidelines for that locality in the council's approved plan. However, the council might grant such a permission if the developer undertakes to provide a community hall on an adjoining site, thereby redressing a lack of such facilities in the area.

The advantage of such an arrangement from the capital controls point of view is that any works so received do not count as capital receipts, and therefore come as a free good to the council. If you are aware of major developments planned close to your own service outlets or facilities, it is worth exploring the scope for planning agreements with your council's planning and legal departments. Most developers are not too concerned into which council service the benefits are directed, hence your service's claims need to be represented in any internal council discussions on such issues.

Operating leases

There is an established market in operating leases for equipment such as computers and vehicles. Under 1989 Act regulations, operating leases are exempt from control and do not require the use of credit approvals (credit cover). This means, providing you have the revenue budget to meet the leasing rentals, that operating leases are an excellent method of 'acquiring' capital items without using capital resources. You should always involve the finance department (and probably the legal department as well) in negotiating any lease. If you enter into an agreement that doesn't fulfil the criteria for an operating lease, you could find yourself having to pay the whole cost of the leased items from a single year's revenue account. Some of the main facts in relation to operating leases are listed below.

- The operating lease contract must not result in final ownership of the items passing to the council, even as the exercising of an option.
- Leased items must still be worth at least 10 per cent of their original cost at the end of the lease. This rule is not based on actual end values, but on the council's estimate at the beginning of the lease. Be careful of leases with options to extend, as the act uses the end of any possible extension as the calculation date. The leasing company may require the council to indemnify it as to the 10 per cent value. If the goods are sold and realise less than 10 per cent, the council will be required to make up the difference. Check out any such term in the contract with finance and legal departments.
- Some leasing companies are selective as to which manufacturers' products they will deal in. Items with a poor secondhand market are often difficult to lease.
- Although operating leases avoid capital controls, it pays to check the rate

159

of interest underlying the rentals. If this is inordinately expensive, it is better to use mainstream capital resources. On these, the council can achieve low-cost borrowing.

- Most leasing companies expect the council to buy the goods from the supplier as their agent. Check the company's requirements and timetables very carefully. It may not prove possible to include late items which are notified to the company past leasing drawdown dates. If you have already purchased the items, this can be more than a little embarrassing.

Extending old credit arrangements

Credit arrangements are not a very efficient use of credit approvals. Because they are not included in the credit ceiling, a new set of credit approvals is needed to renew them. However, you may find it is possible to renew very old credit arrangements without any credit cover.

The act was designed to prevent councils achieving control-free credit arrangements by multiple contracts. The multiple contract device entails bringing together series of contracts, each in itself exempt which, taken as a whole, have the effect of a credit arrangement. Accordingly, there are sections in the act which provide that a credit arrangement comes into operation on the date of the first of any such series of contracts.

Normally, a credit arrangement requires credit approvals to extend it. But credit arrangements entered into before 7 July 1988 have no meaning in law. Hence, if a credit arrangement came into force before 7.7.88, whatever contracts are added to it subsequently, the anti-series provisions leave the starting date of the credit arrangement unchanged. As these early agreements were free from control, the extension can be achieved without credit approvals. Consult your finance department or legal section on this possibility.

Maximising spendability of receipts

There are a number of cases in which you will not have to set aside a reserved element from any capital receipt. Where possible, it is worth structuring transactions to take advantage of these. You stand a much better chance of getting your capital programme bid accepted if you can promise to return any receipt 100 per cent for somebody else's turn. These 'in and out' rules are summarised in Table 5.3. (As a special budget measure to revive the economy, councils have been granted 100 per cent usage on most receipts in 1993.)

These rules are not as helpful as one might first assume. They don't allow additional expenditure on the 'in' element; councils must use their credit approvals to finance this. However, when the capital receipt comes in it is 100 per cent usable to the extent of credit approvals used in the first place. This effectively restores the credit approvals used. The problem with this approach is that the credit approvals are tied up for up to two years, so other capital programme schemes often have to be delayed to complete the 'in and out'.

Table 5.3: In and out rules

Type	Dispensation
Recently acquired interest	The cost of acquisition is deducted before applying the reserved percentage provided: — the sale is completed two years after acquisition; — a contract for sale is made after two years, and completed by three. An example of such a scheme might be a site bought on 1 April 1991 for £2m. If it is sold on 30 September 1992 for £3.5m, then £2m of that £3.5m would be 100 per cent usable. The excess of £1.5m would suffer the normal 50 per cent reserved element. In total, £2.75m of the receipt would be usable, as against the normal £1.75m (50 per cent of £3.5m). Don't forget that, in this example, the council would have had to use £2m of its 1991/92 credit approvals to acquire the land, not getting them back for other use until 1992/93.
Recently improved land	Enhancement costs incurred in the two years before disposal are deducted before calculating the reserved element. Don't forget you can use both this, and the recently acquired dispensation, on the same piece of land.
Replacement assets	For certain council services, it is possible to use 100 per cent of the receipts from selling an old asset to provide a like-for-like replacement. The replacement must be within three years of the disposal. Check with your finance or legal department as to what assets are covered.

Capital grants

A range of capital grants are available to fund capital schemes, both from the government and the European Community. Examples of various grant sources are outlined in Table 5.4. One problem with EC grants is that a £ for £ deduction is made from the councils' credit approvals. Still, such a grant will save your service the annual debt charges of council borrowing. It is worth making an analysis of grant options when considering any capital project.

Other capital devices

Prior to the 1989 Act, there was a whole financial industry based on creative accounting schemes. Much of this relied on fairly generous interpretations of council powers under S111 of the Local Government Act 1972. This permits councils to undertake anything which is conducive to, or ancillary to, one of their statutory functions. Recent case law has taken a fairly restrictive view of

Table 5.4: Types of capital grant (examples)

Grant	Purpose
Transport Supplementary Grant (TSG)	Funding for major transport and infrastructure projects, controlled by submission to Department of Transport.
European Social Fund	EC grants for training and development projects in particular areas of the UK.
Inner Area Programme	Job creation and training initiatives in designated areas.

S111, as in the Hammersmith swaps case, for example. These decisions, plus the tight controls of the 1989 Act, make it difficult to beat the system.

If a council disposes of land not for money, but for works, it is required to set aside a reserved element equal to the money foregone. Accordingly there is little point in undertaking these barter type schemes.

One useful exemption in the housing service relates to nomination rights. This enables a council to reduce its sale price for land to a housing association in return for being able to choose who occupies the properties which are to be built. No money need be set aside to make up for the lost reserved element.

As a general point, though, any proposed capital device needs to be checked out thoroughly with your finance and legal departments. If a scheme fails to avoid the controls as hoped, you might have to meet the whole of the cost out of your revenue budget.

So far in this chapter we have learned how the capital controls operate, and some ways to avoid them. Before we move on to the planning of individual schemes, the following 10-point checklist may be of use

- Capital means buying land or property, or major repairs that enhance the use of an asset.
- The council may only borrow up to its aggregate credit limit (ACL).
- The key element of the ACL is the credit ceiling. This moves up as credit approvals are used, and down as provisions are made from receipts or the revenue account.
- Provisions for repaying debt can be held in approved investments until used for repaying actual loans.
- Check your revenue budgets for items that could be capitalised.
- Use operating leases for vehicles and equipment provided the rentals aren't too high.
- Take advantage of the 'in and out' rules if possible.
- Be aware of the scope to claim capital grants.
- Check out any proposed scheme to avoid the controls very carefully.
- If in doubt, take expert advice. The act is very complicated, and even the Audit Commission admit to uncertainties about its precise interpretation.

Preparing a capital programme

So far in this chapter we have looked at the complex rules and regulations about how much councils can spend on capital schemes. The current system of controls concentrates on borrowing limits, and we saw how there are various methods of achieving capital schemes without needing to borrow. All the limits and controls such as the ACL and the credit ceiling, are expressed in overall terms. What we deal with now is the much more important business of translating these accounting figures into real schemes, such as building a new school or refurbishing a housing estate.

Capital programmes

The key factor in controlling capital schemes is the council's capital programme. This usually covers a period of three years or more. Not only are capital schemes notoriously unpredictable, but they often have a long duration from design through to the completion of construction. Hence it is impractical to control schemes on the one-year basis used for revenue budgets.

Having said this, the capital controls seem to fly in the face of these problems. Unlike the main revenue accounts, capital accounts are usually prepared on a cash basis. This means that work completed at the 31 March year-end is only charged in that year's accounts if the payment has actually been made on or before 31 March to the contractor. No year-end creditors are allowed for capital items. This requirement often leads to some curious practices. These have been known to include paying contractors for windows still in the course of manufacture (or, in reality, a pile of hardwood in a builder's yard marked 'property of the borough of XYZ').

A further problem is that the borrowing permissions granted by the government are restricted to a single financial year. Councils can't, for example, save them up to use for a major project in some future year. The only capital funding which is transferable from one year to another is the usable element of capital receipts. This means, other things being equal, that if capital resources are underspent it makes sense for a council to use borrowing in preference to receipts. Unused receipts can be used in a future year; unused credit approvals cannot.

How then are capital programmes drawn up? The main stages are set out below. The resources calculations are usually the treasurer's province, though it is worth other departments checking the assumptions used in such reports. Some treasurers like nothing better than to freeze the capital programme at the slightest hint of an overspend. Experience shows that the problem with capital is often more likely to be managing to spend as much as has been allocated to a scheme.

Drawing up the capital programme

- Calculate the overall resources available in each financial year. This includes the likely level of borrowing permissions (credit approvals) and the level of capital receipts.
- Calculate the remaining payments due on existing schemes in the programme. Generally, once a scheme is accepted into the programme, it is completed, however much its original cost escalates. Many councils find

163

that existing schemes take the lion's share of next year's programme (or more alarmingly, exceed available resources).
- Allocate the remaining resources to new schemes.

It is naturally the last of these three stages where there is the greatest dispute and discussion between different departments and between councillors. Essentially, this is a political process. New capital schemes provide the public with tangible evidence of council action. Accordingly, most councillors have one or more pet schemes they are anxious to see included in the capital programme.

Methods used to share out capital resources vary from council to council, but here are some of the more common methods.

Concentrate on:
- schemes supporting key policy objectives (e.g. if the council's main objective is to regenerate a particular part of its area, schemes in that locality will be prioritised);
- essential health and safety or statutory items. Some of these will be self evident, such as repairing a dangerous structure. Watch out for other departments' generous definitions of what constitutes 'statutory'. Most council functions have *some* basis in law!;
- a fixed allocation per committee. This seems to be less and less prevalent as the cake to be squabbled over gets smaller and smaller;
- schemes bringing in outside resources. If a scheme can secure half its funding from the government, for example, it will lead to much better value from each pound the council put in. Another aspect of this approach is to concentrate on schemes where a small council expenditure can trigger much larger investment from the private or voluntary sector. This was the philosophy underlying the 1992 City Challenge competition run by the government. This allocated funds to councils on the basis of their success in working in partnership with the private sector;
- points systems, with scores for factors such as the following:
    —Does the scheme save council running costs in the long term?
    —Is the scheme designed and ready to build?
    —Can the sponsoring committee afford the financing charges that will arise from the scheme?

One of the main factors in gaining acceptance for a scheme is credibility. Councillors and senior managers have an unerring knack of spotting the submissions based on a few 'back of a cigarette packet' calculations. If your scheme is properly drawn up and planned, it will therefore probably have a better chance of success. We now look at some of the essential elements of preparing a financial appraisal.

Most councils have a standard form or set of information for capital programme submissions. It is important to become familiarised with these precise requirements, as it would be unfortunate to lose a submission just for the sake of a technicality. Here are some of the main points to bear in mind.

- Consult and involve other departments who have either a service or technical interest in the scheme. Clearly, architects won't do much in terms of a design unless you have a budget to pay for this. However, even a small involvement from them is useful in setting realistic bounds for the cost of a scheme. Similarly, if the scheme entails land acquisition, discuss the practicalities with your estates department. There is no point in bidding for a scheme in the next financial year when the practicalities of land acquisition are bound to delay it.

- Be realistic in assessing costs. There is a great temptation to understate the expense of a scheme in order to improve its chances of acceptance. This may be a well-tried game plan for getting into the capital programme, but it can backfire with quite serious consequences. Significant overspends on a scheme will prevent new items coming into the programme, perhaps even yours. You may well be called on to provide a full explanation of the overspend, which will be difficult if your original calculations don't stand up to an appraisal.

- Clearly identify the revenue effects of a scheme. This will include not only the financing costs, but also the staffing and running costs associated with the scheme. There is nothing more galling to councillors than to see a scheme completed and then to be told that there are no resources to operate it. Again, it pays to be realistic about the true cost of operating facilities, or the level of income likely to be achieved where this is relevant.

- Explain how the scheme will enable the council to achieve its objectives, or improve its service performance. Try to be specific, and quote measurable improvements. This might be, for example, in the case of an estate refurbishment, that 100 void properties could be let and thus reduce the waiting list or number of homeless families.

- Pay particular attention to the phasing of payments likely to arise under the scheme. As we have stressed, capital controls are (excessively) based on actual payments made. This, just as much as the total cost of the scheme, can create financial problems. Various techniques and software are available to plan out the stages of projects, and these should be used where possible. The information gained will, in any case, prove extremely useful if the scheme does gain acceptance.

Letting contract work

Once a scheme is approved, the process of choosing a contractor to undertake the works begins. The relevant procedures will be set out in your council's standing orders and financial regulations. Needless to say, the letting of contracts is one that receives undying attention from auditors. It is sensible, therefore, to take particular care over the process and maintain a detailed record of your decisions, along with relevant documentation.

If the scheme is high in value, a formal tender document will need to be prepared by a quantity surveyor. This enables contractors to quote on a like-for-like basis. If the contract is worth only a few thousand pounds, it will probably be let by securing quotations from a range of contractors. Most councils have an approved list of contractors for different types of work.

If the contract is on a quotation basis, take particular care to specify the work before the quotations as much as possible. Once a contract has been let on a lump sum basis, the contractor will often seek to increase the price, claiming that the work includes items not foreseen in the contract. You will have a much better negotiating stance if you have already set out in writing precisely what the original quotation covered. As a general principle, it is much better to be telling the contractor what you want, rather than letting the contractor tell you what you need.

Remember that what is acceptable business practice in the private sector is not necessarily so in local government. Arguably it is an offence under the Local Government Act 1972 to accept any contractor hospitality. It may seem unremarkable at the time to meet contractors for lunch, or attend events as their guests. If the contract ever comes under scrutiny, these occasions, however innocent, will take on a very different appearance. Keep contractors at arm's length and deal with them in a businesslike manner.

Monitoring the financial progress of a scheme

Capital schemes are notoriously difficult to control in financial terms. Conversely, they often appear to be less closely monitored than revenue budgets. Here are a few pointers on how to do this capital financial monitoring more effectively.

- Monitoring relies on having a realistic plan of the scheme's progress against which to monitor. If this was not done at the appraisal stage, it is essential to do it now.
- Capital monitoring is notorious for the sudden introduction at the year-end of hitherto unexpected under/overspends. This is often taken to be indicative of a lack of control during the year, and should be avoided by careful monitoring from the start of the financial year. It may be in your own interest to identify an underspend as quickly as possible, as these resources might be redirected to another scheme for your service.
- Many councils have some form of interdepartmental capital monitoring group, which assesses likely spend for a monthly or bimonthly monitoring report to the relevant council committee. The size of capital programmes often prevents anything other than a superficial analysis on individual schemes in these groups. Better to set up an ad hoc project monitoring group in which all the departments concerned with the scheme are represented.
- Beware of the time-lag inherent in many councils' financial reporting systems. It's important to find out the basis of the figures in financial information you receive. Suppose for example the month 6 financial ledger is based only on invoices paid up to month 4. If you assumed erroneously that the ledger reflected six months' expenditure, you could be misled into significantly underestimating the likely out-turn for the year. Thus in preparing any forecast, it's well worth running over the figures with your financial department.
- Large contracts are usually paid for by a series of certificates, whereby contractors are paid on account for work to date. At the year-end it is worth devoting time to planning exactly when certificates are to be paid, as a few days' movement can change expenditure from one financial year to another.

- Meet with relevant departments to monitor internal fees during the year. These fees are often added at the closing of the council's accounts, when it is too late to do much about them. Get forecasts of fees from internal fee chargers in mid-year, and keep a record of any agreements reached on fee levels.

Before leaving capital programmes, we end with a checklist of eight key points.

- Be conversant with the procedures used to prioritise bids for scarce capital resources, and tailor your schemes accordingly.
- Consult widely in drawing up a submission. Reflect the practical problems of organising the scheme, such as delays inherent in acquiring land.
- Make a realistic plan of the financial elements of the scheme, including the phasing of payments.
- Make sure that your revenue budget will cover the running costs of the scheme once it is completed.
- Adhere carefully to your council's regulations on the letting of contracts. Keep the necessary notes and documentation to justify your action if this proves necessary at some future date.
- Monitor the progress of your scheme by establishing a project group.
- Meet regularly with finance staff to prepare forecasts and out-turns.

Borrowing and investments

In this chapter so far we have examined the complexities of the 1989 Act capital controls, and the financial aspects of a capital scheme. We end the chapter by looking at how councils manage their borrowing and invest any surplus funds. This *treasury management* function is normally dealt with by a specialist section in the finance department. In some councils, though, the cash management element is done by an external firm of investment managers. Treasury management is a major cost area in any council, as the amount of debt ranges from £10m upwards in district councils to £100s of millions or even £1000m+ in the larger metropolitan authorities. With a basic knowledge of the subject, you should be able to form a view as to how well the treasury function operates in your council.

What is the objective of a borrowing policy?

Some councils are now debt free, having sold their housing assets to a housing association, or having secured other large capital income. But most councils still retain a significant value of debt, and the interest costs of this debt is a large factor in their revenue budgets. In the case of housing debt though (which is by far the largest value of debt in most councils), there is a provision in the subsidy regulations which effectively protects councils from their own borrowing decisions. With certain provisos, interest costs are subsidised for housing at the actual interest rates paid. The higher the average rate paid on housing debt, the higher the £ for £ subsidy. Yet, as this policy may change at some future date, councils still seek to minimise their interest cost both on housing and on unsubsidised non-housing debt.

Table 5.5 is a synopsis of some simple rules of debt management.

Table 5.5: Debt management objectives

High cost, short life (fair)	High cost, long life (bad)
Low cost, short life (better)	Low cost, long life (good)

High cost, variable (fair)	High cost, fixed (bad)
low cost, variable (better)	Low cost, fixed (good)

The first block shows the trade-off between the *maturity* (life) of borrowing, and the interest rate paid. Clearly, the worst possible outcome (top right) is to be locked into paying a high fixed interest rate over a long period. This is because, whatever cheaper facilities become available during the life of the loan, you are locked into your high cost facility. If you must pay a high cost, better in a short-life loan which can soon be replaced.

The next stage in improvement would be to convert a high-cost, short-life, loan to a cheaper loan of the same duration. The saving in doing this is self-evident. Best of all, we could reach our goal (bottom right) of both a low cost *and* a long duration. Then, whatever happens in the way of interest rate rises, we are safely locked into our low cost loan for years to come.

Similar reasoning applies to the lower Table. Loans are generally available either with a rate fixed at the start of the loan for its duration, or with a rate that varies from time to time depending on market interest rates. When rates are high, it pays to borrow variable as this leaves the option to replace when fixed rates become more attractive.

Neither of these Tables tells us what constitute low rates. What seems like a trough in interest rates can be shown to have been only the prelude to a further decline, given the benefit of hindsight. Treasurers do, however, have two further guiding factors in trying to choose when to borrow long term. First, it is important to councils to have a predictable interest cost for budgetary reasons. This sets a limit to the proportion of council debt that ought to be held in variable rate loans, 15 to 20 per cent often being quoted as the safe maximum. Secondly, as councils already have accumulated large portfolios of loans, the average rate paid on this debt serves as a guide for future decisions. Any fixed rate borrowing at higher than average cost will need careful justification.

To set some figures to this theory, Table 5.6 illustrates the importance of timing borrowings correctly. Most council borrowing is from the government-backed public works loan board, or PWLB. This table, taken from financial year

1989/90, shows the wide range of interest rates that can apply in any one financial year. The PWLB changes its rates in line with money market rates at least once a week, so it is a real test for treasurers to pick the right week in the financial year for bulk borrowing. The Table also shows, at least for this year, that they just about got it right, as most money was borrowed at the lower rates offered during the year. Applying this test to your own council's borrowing results in any financial year can be quite informative.

Table 5.6: Incidence of PWLB drawings all councils 1989—90 15 to 25 year loans

Rate offered per cent	Amount borrowed by councils £million
$9^3/_8$	204.8
$9^1/_2$	163.1
$9^5/_8$	133.6
$9^3/_4$	54.2
$9^7/_8$	185.3
10	159.9
$10^1/_8$ to 11	195.7
$11^1/_8$ to 12	63.4
12 to $12^5/_8$	8.3

Source: PWLB Annual Report 1989—90.

Notice the wide range of interest rates shown in the Table. There is a $3^1/_4$ per cent differential between the cheapest rate offered ($9^3/_8$ per cent) and the most expensive ($12^5/_8$ per cent). Spread over the 15 year period of these loans, the difference in interest costs is truly remarkable and illustrates the significance of borrowing decisions.

One might also venture to suggest that the tail-off in borrowing above 10 per cent demonstrates the widespread use of this level as a safe funding level. Treasurers are usually reasonably happy to borrow long at rates below 10 per cent. Much above 10 per cent they will often choose to borrow short term or in variable rates.

Yield curves

As a further guide to borrowing policy, consider the examples of yield curves in Figs. 5.1, 5.2 and 5.3.

Figure 5.3 is the set of PWLB interest rates in force on 15 October 1992. As you will see, the shorter maturities are at much lower rates (e.g. $8^1/_4$ per cent for 3-year money) than the long maturities ($10^3/_8$ per cent for 25-year money). These interest rates are roughly similar to what councils would have to pay on the open market for loans (though the market in the longer maturities offered by the PWLB is very limited). This rising yield curve is often taken as signalling rising interest rates in the not too distant future, based on the following logic:

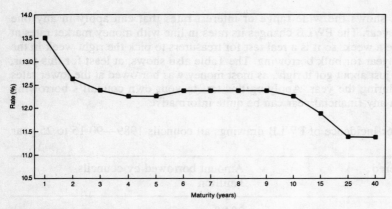

Figure 5.1: PWLB rates 5 September 1990

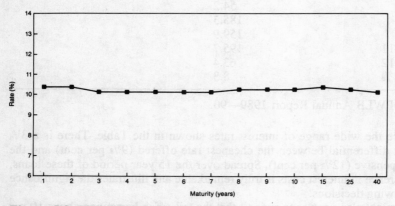

Figure 5.2: PWLB rates 12 August 1992

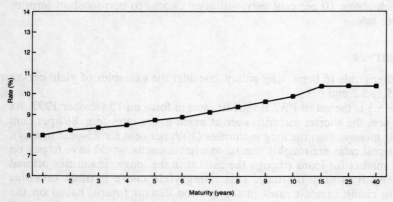

Figure 5.3: PWLB rates 15 October 1992

Short-term borrowing is cheap because short-term lenders are prepared to receive less interest. Short-term lenders are prepared to forego the higher interest they could earn on a longer investment because the market view is that rates will soon rise. Any short-term investment can thus soon be reinvested at the higher rates then prevailing.

Note that this view has an element of self-fulfilment in it. As short rates get cheaper and cheaper, the demand for short loans will increase, driving up their cost.

Figure 5.2, the rates in force in 12 August 1992, shows a flat yield curve. This is not giving a very clear signal either way of the market view. Contrast this with Figure 5.3, the rates in force on 5 September 1990. This yield curve is steeply declining, indicating a possible fall in rates. Lenders are demanding a high premium to lend short, as the view seems to be that the same high rates will not be available when the short loan matures.

The analysis of yield curves is a subject in its own right, but they certainly form a key element in borrowing policy.

Maturity profile

A further aspect of treasury management which deserves brief attention is the question of the maturity profile of the council's debt. There are a number of reasons why it makes sense to spread the maturity of debt smoothly across a number of years.

- *The council may find it difficult to raise a very large value of loans in one year, either because PWLB quotas are low, or because money market conditions are difficult.*
- *It might prove just the council's luck that, in the year the high maturities arise, replacement loans are particularly expensive.*

Until 1992, there was a voluntary code of practice requiring councils to have an average maturity of at least 7 years in each year's new borrowing. This was introduced at a time when councils had (from the Bank of England's point of view), a dangerously high proportion of short-term debt. As the average maturity of most councils' debt is now well above 10 years, the code was withdrawn having served its purpose.

The structure of council debt

As Table 5.7 shows, the main borrowing source for councils is the public works loan board, or PWLB. It rose to this prominence because during the 1980's, it was government policy to make extensive PWLB borrowing facilities available to councils. Previously, a significant proportion of council borrowing had been from banks. This bank lending boosted the M3 measure of the money supply, the restriction of which was then a key economic indicator. Hence councils were encouraged to switch to the PWLB by the offer of low interest rates.

Moreover, PWLB rates were then linked closely to the yield on gilt-edged securities of similar duration. Because, at that time, the government was buying back long gilts, long PWLB rates were artificially low. Treasurers, who rarely look a gift horse in the mouth, lined their councils' pockets with this cheap PWLB money.

Table 5.7: Council borrowing sources: Debt of UK local authorities as at 31 March 1991

	per cent
Internal borrowing	13.26
Temporary borrowing	4.66
Long-term debt	
PWLB	78.07
Other	4.01

Source: CIPFA debt statistics.

The internal borrowing shown in this Table represents the use of either council reserves, or the unapplied provision for credit liabilities, in place of external borrowing. Temporary borrowing refers to loans originally taken out with less than a year to maturity. In the past, there have been limits on the permissible level of temporary debt; none applies now other than the council's own borrowing limits.

The increase in the proportion of debt with the PWLB is shown in Table 5.8.

Table 5.8: PWLB debt as a proportion of total debt

Year	per cent PWLB
57/58	57.0
67/68	36.4
77/78	37.8
81/82	33.2
82/83	37.5
83/84	42.1
84/85	46.9
85/86	57.5
86/87	65.3
87/88	69.5
88/89	75.2
89/90	77.7
90/91	78.7

Source: PWLB Annual Report 90/91 Appendix A.

Although current government policy is to move council borrowing back towards the money markets, the PWLB is likely to remain the main borrowing source for some years to come. In the sections that follow, we look at what its facilities are, and how these are used to carry out borrowing policy.

PWLB borrowing facilities

The details of borrowing facilities provided by the board are usually set out in an annual circular. (The latest, Number 102, was issued in March 1993). Quota arrangements are planned annually, thus circulars arriving in mid-year usually signify a major change to the arrangements. This is not always good news.

The board has clearly stated for some years that the purpose of its loans is to enable authorities to meet their new, longer-term borrowing requirements. Money lent by the board, it warns, should not be used for on-lending or for the acquisition of investments. We saw earlier in this chapter how the ACL mechanism allows increased borrowing provided the money borrowed is held in approved investments. PWLB money on-lent short-term fulfils this equation quite neatly, and it is a temptation to which some councils have succumbed in the past. (In the late 1980's, PWLB 25-year money at 9 per cent was often 3 or 4 per cent cheaper than the rate which could be earned on money market deposits, allowing a substantial 'turn' to be made.)

The board has also said it may choose to make enquiries with councils as to whether they have adopted a balanced budget. It will not lend to an authority which, in its view, has chosen to act illegally.

Quota calculation

There is no uniformity as to councils' long-term borrowing needs. These range from zero in debt-free councils to very high peaks of demand in heavily indebted councils. Although PWLB quotas reflect (to an extent) the size of a council's capital programme, they are based on a fixed percentage of outstanding debt. This makes no account for particularly high levels of maturities in any one year. The situation is thus that some councils don't need their quota at all, whilst others don't have nearly as much as they would like. It is quite galling for councils in the latter category to note that only about 60 per cent of available quotas are drawn, taking councils as a whole.

The quota available to councils for financial year 1992/93 was set as shown in Table 5.9

Table 5.9: PWLB quotas 1992/93

	The aggregate of:
	75 per cent of a council's net reckonable capital payments in 1992/93:
	plus
	4 per cent of its total debt incurred for capital purposes as at 31 March 1992;
less	
	15 per cent of the authority's provision to meet credit liabilities unapplied at 31 March 1992.

Prior to financial year 1992/93, there was no reduction of quotas to reflect provision for credit liabilities. The board indicated that it intended to increase the deduction in future years to more than 15 per cent. The dedution was set at five per cent for 1993/4, less allowances for council SSAs and capital payments.

The reckonable capital payments referred to in the circular are defined similarly to 'expenditure for capital purposes under the 1989 Act'. To derive the *net* reckonable payments, the value of capital receipts is deducted. Note that the *gross* value of receipts is deducted, even though they may be only 25 per cent usable because of the requirement to set aside a reserved element.

Given the limited availability of long maturity market loans to councils, and the reasonably attractive rates charged by the board, councils with continuing borrowing needs seek to try and maximise their quota. Hence they often err on the side of overestimating quota during the year, in such matters as the level of the capital programme which will be achieved. Any overdrawing of quota which is revealed by the final accounts is merely deducted from the next year's quota. Hence little is lost by having taken the borrowing early.

Conversely, any carry-over into the next financial year is limited to 10 per cent of the actual quota. The quota must be finalised by 30 September in the next financial year, *and drawn by 31 October*. A further point to be borne in mind is that payments count as reckonable for quota calculation purposes whether or not they were financed from capital. Thus the fact that, say, architects' fees, which could have been capitalised, were met from revenue, doesn't stop that expenditure being added into the quota calculation.

The board also offers advances at non-quota rates, though these facilities were last used in the mid-1970s (see Table 5.10).

Table 5.10: Non-quota PWLB facilities

Non-quota A is as a lender of last resort where the authority can demonstrate no other source of finance is available (+ 1 per cent on quota rates).

Non-quota B. The council must prove the money is needed for capital finance, but need not demonstrate that no other funds are available (+ 2 per cent on quota rates).

Whilst these facilities are not important to councils, they should be understood by lenders to councils. They mean that, whatever difficulty a particular council had replacing a loan in the money markets, it could always rely on the PWLB. The availability of a government-backed lender of last resort should give councils a much higher credit status than some seem to enjoy.

Types of loan offered by the PWLB

We now discuss the types of loan offered by the PWLB (see Table 5.11). These are the means to put into operation the borrowing policy objectives we outlined earlier. The range of facilities is so diverse that it offers ample opportunity to practise good treasury management.

Figure 5.4 shows an example of a PWLB interest notice. Run through the various facilities offered to check your understanding of this chapter, and of the further facilities explained below.

PUBLIC WORKS LOAN BOARD

National Investment and Loans Office
1 King Charles Street London SW1A 2AP

Telephone: 071-270
GTN. 270
Fax: 071-270 3860

3873

INTEREST RATE NOTICE NO. 41/92   11 August 1992

RATES OF INTEREST ON PWLB LOANS TO LOCAL AUTHORITIES

FIXED RATE LOANS – The Treasury have determined that the rates of interest listed below shall apply to all fixed rate loans agreed with local authorities (as defined in paragraph 1 of the 4th Schedule to the National Loans Act 1968) by the Public Works Loan Commissioners on and after 12 August 1992. Changes from the rates previously in force are shown in brackets.

Period of loan Years	QUOTA LOANS		
	EIP	A	M
1			10 3/8
Over 1 up to 2	10 1/4 (-1/8)	10 1/4 (-1/8)	10 3/8
Over 2 up to 3	10 1/4 (-1/8)	10 1/4 (-1/8)	10 1/8 (-1/8)
Over 3 up to 4	10 1/4	10 1/4	10 1/8
Over 4 up to 5	10 1/8 (-1/8)	10 1/8 (-1/8)	10 1/8
Over 5 up to 6	10 1/8	10 1/8	10 1/8
Over 6 up to 7	10 1/8	10 1/8	10 1/8
Over 7 up to 8	10 1/8	10 1/8	10 1/4 (+1/8)
Over 8 up to 9	10 (-1/8)	10 1/8	10 1/4
Over 9 up to 10	10 1/8	10 1/4 (+1/8)	10 1/4
Over 10 up to 15	10 1/4	10 3/8	10 3/8 (+1/8)
Over 15 up to 25	10 3/8	10 3/8	10 1/4 (+1/8)
Over 25	10 1/4	10 1/8	10 1/8 (+1/8)

Loans made under the non-quota A arrangements set out in section 5 of PWLB Circular No. 99 will bear interest at 1% above the corresponding quota rate.

Loans made under the non-quota B arrangements set out in section 6 of PWLB Circular No. 99 will bear interest at 2% above the corresponding quota rate.

VARIABLE RATE LOANS – The rate of interest on all fresh variable rate loans made to local authorities by the Public Works Loan Commissioners until the coming into operation of a further determination shall continue to be the cost of government borrowing (GBR) plus a margin of 1/8%.

The GBR in force each day during the week commencing 3 August was as follows:-

	3 August	4 August	5 August	6 August	7 August
1 month	9 13/16	9 3/4	9 3/4	9 3/4	9 3/4
3 months	10	9 15/16	10	10	10
6 months	10 1/16	10 1/16	10 1/16	10 1/8	10 1/8

The LIBOR in force each day during the week commencing 3 August was as follows:-

	3 August	4 August	5 August	6 August	7 August
1 month	10 3/16	10 3/16	10 3/16	10 3/16	10
3 months	10 7/16	10 3/8	10 3/8	10 3/8	10 5/16
6 months	10 1/2	10 3/8	10 7/16	10 1/2	10 3/8

Figure 5.4: PWLB interest notice (example)

The rates charged on fixed rate loans are notified to councils weekly, and come into effect on Tuesday mornings. Emergency changes are effected for sudden changes in general interest rates (e.g. base rate cut). It therefore makes sense for treasurers to finalise borrowing decisions on Mondays. They then have the option of the old rates that afternoon, or the new rates the next day. On Mondays they will have most of the facts which will determine the (as yet unannounced) new rates, and with experience and some broker information it is possible to assess any likely change in the rates. This makes it possible to follow interest rates down to some extent before actually committing to borrowing.

Table 5.11: Types of loan offered by the PWLB

Two types of loan are offered:

> *Fixed rate* The interest rate is fixed for the duration of the loan when the advance is made.

> *Variable* The rate is variable at one, three, or six monthly intervals. The period of variability is fixed.

Variable rate loans may be replaced by fixed rate loans, and (new facility 1992/93) fixed by a variable.

Fixed rate loans may use one of three methods of repayment:

Annuity	fixed half-yearly payments of principal and interest
EIP	equal half-yearly instalments of principal, with interest on the balance outstanding.
Maturity	half-yearly interest with a single repayment of principal at the end of the term.

> Maturity is the favoured method for most councils, as it maximises quota in the short term, and often offers a marginally lower interest rate compared to other methods.

The durations available in fixed rate loans are as follows;

Annuity and EIP	Minimum is 2 years, maximum 60.
Maturity	Minimum is 1 year, maximum 60.

Variable rate loans

As we saw earlier, the use of variable rate funding is a very useful tool in treasury management. PWLB variable rate loans (see Table 5.12) are particularly attractive as at any time in their life they can be converted to fixed without needing to use precious quota.

The facility of being able to convert variable to fixed means that, in periods of high interest rates, councils often borrow in variable. They then wait for fixed rates to decline to the desired level before locking in. Also available is the facility to change a fixed loan to variable. This facility is likely to have a much more restricted application.

Table 5.12: PWLB variable rate loans

Variable rate loans are available for repayment by EIP or on maturity. (Durations 2 to 10 years, and 1 to 10 years, respectively.)

Interest is calculated at one-, three-, or six-monthly intervals.

The interest rate is calculated as follows:

> *A margin* currently 0.125 per cent
>
> plus
>
> *The cost of government borrowing GBR*

The cost of government borrowing:

> For one-month and three-month variables
>
>> the market rate for eligible bank bills (short-term money market instruments) of the same maturity, rounded up to the nearest 0.0625 per cent
>
> For six-month variable
>
>> the lower of the rounded six-month eligible bill rate, and the six-month LIBOR.

Conversion of a variable loan

On any roll-over date, a variable loan may be converted to a fixed loan of any maturity which exceeds the period the variable loan had left to run. *No quota is needed to make such a change.* Variable funds can thus be taken in times of high interest rates, and locked into fixed at an appropriate stage. If the ultimate aim is to take short (cheap) fixed, then the duration of the variable needs to be planned accordingly.

Conversion of a fixed loan

Any loan with at least a year unexpired can be converted to a variable rate loan. The actual principal is calculated on an actuarial basis (this is explained in the redemptions section below). The duration of the replacement cannot exceed the unexpired term, up to a maximum of ten years.

Once replaced, a loan cannot be replaced a further time.

Premature redemptions

As well as the range of facilities outlined above, the board will accept premature repayment of loans it has made. This can be used by councils to restructure their debt by swapping loans of one maturity to another, often with a high interest saving.

- The Board will accept the premature repayment of loans which:
  —have been advanced for over a year;
  —have at least a year left to run.

- The principal repaid is calculated by discounting the future payments due under the loan at the interest rate currently charged on advances of a similar nature.

Say a 9-year, fixed-rate, maturity loan were advanced at 11 per cent on 1.4.1989. It is repaid prematurely on 1.1.91, having 7 years still to run. The principal repaid is calculated by discounting the 11 per cent interest payments and the 1998 redemption at 9 per cent, the rate offered on 1.1.91 for 7 year loans.

As Table 5.13 demonstrates, the method of calculation means that a very substantial discount (i.e. less than the original amount to repay) or premium (more than the original principal to repay) can arise.

Table 5.13: Examples of premiums and discounts on redemptions

(All loans £1,000,000 principal, 10 per cent fixed rate)

Yrs to run	Discount rate %	premium/(disc)
5	9	£38,000
10	9	£62,000
25	9	£91,000
5	8	£77,000
10	8	£125,000
25	8	£183,000
5	11	(£38,000)
10	11	(£62,000)
25	11	(£91,000)
5	12	(£77,000)
10	12	(£125,000)
25	12	(£183,000)

As Table 5.13 shows, the effect of the discount calculation is as follows:

—If the current PWLB rate is higher than the original loan rate, a discount is achieved on redemption. This discount is higher the greater the rate differential, and the longer the loan period.
—If the current PWLB rate is lower, a premium is payable on redemption. This premium is higher the greater the interest rate differential, and the longer the loan period.
—If the current PWLB rate is the same, the loan is repaid £ for £ of principal outstanding.

The use of premature redemptions for restructuring relies on exploiting the PWLB yield curve. If you consider diagram C from Table 5.7 again, the interest rate offered on a 6 year loan is 12$\frac{1}{2}$ per cent. The interest on a 25-year loan is 11$\frac{1}{2}$ per cent. Suppose you have a loan already on the council's books with 6 years left to run and an interest rate of 12$\frac{1}{2}$ per cent. Because 12$\frac{1}{2}$ per cent is precisely the discount rate to be used in the premature redemption calculation, this loan can be repaid £ for £. Given available quota, the money to make this repayment could be borrowed back from the board for 25 years at 11½ per cent. This saves a clear 1 per cent on the annual interest cost (though at the expense of some increase in maturity).

Market borrowing

As the PWLB has had such a domination of council borrowing in the last few years, bank lending to councils (other than for short-term purposes) has become very limited. As PWLB quotas reduce, bank lending will be relied on to cover the balance of councils' needs. There is great wariness in the money markets as to councils' credit status following developments such as capping of council budgets and the swaps crisis. However, councils represent an extremely good risk for the following reasons.

- A loan to a council is legally enforceable even if the council has borrowed in excess of its statutory powers known legally as a 'safe harbour' provision).
- If any significant amount of interest or principal is more than 2 months overdue from a council, the lender can apply to a court for the appointment of a receiver to effect the repayment out of any of the council's income. Again, given the large property holdings of most councils and the large income streams they have (such as housing rents and government grants) this is a good security.
- The availability of the government-backed PWLB as a lender of last resort.

Running the treasury

So far in this review of treasury management, we have concentrated on the long-term borrowing function. This is only one part (if the most significant) of treasury management. We will now consider the other aspects of the function.

Monitoring the council's cash flow

Councils have very large variations in their cashflow from day to day. Some days, such as when an instalment of RSG is received from the government or a large land sale is completed, they are cash rich. Other days, such as when the monthly payroll is taken from the bank account, they are short of liquidity. These ups and downs are smoothed out by temporary borrowing or investments. Councils with small sums to invest will usually place these with the council's main banker. Bigger surpluses or borrowing needs are met through use of the London money market. This usually offers more attractive interest rates than the council's own bank. The treasury section will either deal directly with institutions (banks, building societies, other councils) or ask a money broker to place its funds. Brokers charge commission to borrowers, but not to depositors.

Making investments

As well as the short-term investments necessary to smooth out the cash flow, councils are often able to identify surpluses available for longer investment.

179

These might be, for example, usable capital receipts being saved towards a major project, or an unapplied provision for credit liabilities. Investments must be *approved investments* within the meaning of the 1989 Act. These are essentially deposits with authorised institutions under the Banking Act 1987, with building societies, or investments with other councils. If the council has a positive credit ceiling (i.e. still has long-term debt), the maximum duration of an approved investment is 364 days. If the council is debt free, the maximum permissible duration rises to five years.

Swaps, BCCI and the CIPFA treasury management code

Council treasury management has come under a great deal of public scrutiny in recent years. Many councils entered into interest swap agreements in the mid-1980s. Doubts about these transactions soon began to emerge and, in February 1989, the London Borough of Hammersmith suspended payment on its swaps. This led to extensive litigation between the council and the banks with which it had agreements. Later, in 1991, the House of Lords held that such agreements were outside the powers of councils. Restitution of sums paid over to councils is still proceeding through the courts. This episode naturally raised doubts in the money markets about the wisdom of lending to councils.

As the swap controversy began to die down, a further treasury management problem for councils hit the national headlines. They proved to be large depositors in the Bank of Credit and Commerce International (BCCI), which was closed by the Bank of England on 5 July 1991. BCCI was categorised as an 'approved investment' under the 1989 Act, being an authorised institution under the 1987 Banking Act. Many councils took this to be a comment on BCCI's creditworthiness.

The Department of the Environment and the Bank of England denied that the approved list had ever been intended to suggest that institutions on it were suitable for council deposits. Whatever the merits and demerits of these arguments (and the Bank of England accepted, it ought to improve its regulatory procedures following publication in October 1992 of the independent Bingham inquiry into the Bank's supervision of BCCI), both BCCI and the swaps episode showed all too clearly certain basic needs for good treasury management. These were covered in a Code published by CIPFA in 1992 'Treasury Management in Local Authorities'.

Clear reporting lines and delegation of authority

In both the swaps crisis and BCCI, it came as a surprise to councillors of some of the authorities involved that such transactions had been undertaken. Similarly, treasurers were not always aware of the very wide discretion staff in their loans sections were using.

All councils should therefore have a treasury policy, agreed by the full Council, covering the following areas:

- *guidelines on who the council will make deposits with, and who it will borrow from. (This might be, for example, that the council will only lend to banks with a sound credit rating, and that no more than £3m should be outstanding with any one bank at any time.);*

- *what types of loans or other agreements the council will enter into (as swaps and similar agreements are now clearly ultra vires, the range of possible agreements is now limited);*
- *how often treasury matters should be reported to a council committee, and what are the limits on the treasurer's delegated authority. (Many councils do this as an annual report on treasury activity, with quarterly updates on any significant matters. Treasurers usually are given wide discretion on day-to-day operations, such as when to borrow from the PWLB.)*

Good systems and documentation

Given the large value of treasury transactions, many councils have hitherto had fairly basic systems for controlling the treasury. A treasury should at least have the following:

- *a manual which explains all the treasury activities, including the limits on the authority of individual members of staff (e.g. the loans dealer may only place deposits with a value of £5m; any higher single deposit must be authorised by an assistant director of finance);*
- *a secure system (preferably computer-based) which is an authoritative record of all commitments. If for example you don't have a correct record of roll over dates for PWLB variable loans, you could miss the opportunity to lock one of these into an attractive fixed rate of interest.*
- *as much division of duties as possible. Treasury is an auditor's nightmare given the large amounts of money going backwards and forwards. The more the processes are broken down into separate elements by different officers, the better. Examples are:*
  —deciding how much the council has available for investment, and the period for which it will be deposited, should be done separately from negotiation of the actual deposits;
  —the placing and repayment of investments should be checked into the council's bank statement independently of the treasury section.

Although division of duties is an excellent principle, it can be difficult to achieve in practice in smaller councils. If the treasury section has only two staff, it proves quite difficult to ensure adequate division.

The use of credit ratings

The authorisation of a bank under the 1987 Banking Act merely signifies a lawful capacity to trade as a bank. The statutory depositor protection scheme is tailored towards private investors, and covers 75 per cent of any deposit up to a maximum compensation of £15,000. In the case of council deposits which usually run from £250,000 upwards, this figure of compensation is so low as to be virtually worthless protection. Councils should therefore have rigorous procedures to verify the financial status of institutions they lend money to. This may well include the purchase of a credit rating service. However, it should not be imagined that the use of credit ratings is entirely straightforward. The ratings are usually composed of a number of factors: the degree to which the bank is supported by its government, its capital reserves, its profitability. If you pitch your minimum acceptable rating too high (AAA), you would exclude even the main British clearing banks. The limited range of institutions would lead to a loss of interest earnings. Many councils rely on interest from balances as a significant source of income in their revenue budget, hence loss of interest could cause service cuts in other areas. If, on the other hand, you go too low, there becomes a risk (however slight) of default. The higher rates achieved in lending to the less favoured banks could never compensate for the loss of a single deposit, even were such a loss to affect the council only once a century. As if the use of credit ratings were not complicated enough, some institutions which have been traditional borrowers from councils were not credit rated at all as at October 1992, such as the smaller building societies. Even one of the clearing banks, which is the main banker for several large councils, was not credit rated at this time.

This review of treasury management should have provided you with a good basic knowledge of this technical area. We end with a checklist of points to use in assessing your own council's treasury operations. Your finance colleagues will perhaps treat you with new-found respect once you demonstrate your understanding of yield curves and premature redemptions!

- Compare any PWLB borrowings during the year with the range of rates offered for that particular maturity. Was good judgement shown in getting near to the lowest rates?
- Look at the spread of maturities over the ensuing financial years (any problems in producing this information may be indicative of a weak treasury system). Are there any unnecessarily high peaks of maturity in the next few years?
- Has the council lost any PWLB borrowing quota by failing to draw sufficient loans in the year, or by not exercising its carry-over options?
- Is the council carrying high-cost loans which could be replaced with cheaper ones in a debt restructuring exercise? If the council has not had to use its full quota for normal purposes (i.e. maturities and capital payments), the remainder could be directed to this purpose.
- Has the council taken advantage of the variable rate facility, which allows loans to be converted to fixed rates in periods of low rates? (If the council has recently taken expensive fixed rate loans which are much more expensive than the current offered rates, this could indicate a failure to use the variable loan facilities.)
- What is the council's policy on investments? Does it use credit ratings? How do returns achieved compare with money market averages?
- Does the council have a written treasury management policy, and does it clearly define the powers and responsibilities of councillors, the treasurer, and finance staff?

Further reading

Capital finance
Circular 11/90 published by the Department of the Environment explains the legislation section by section.

An extremely comprehensive guide to the capital and borrowing aspects of the act by Bob Davy, the treasurer of Chichester, is published by Longman.

Borrowing
'Treasury management in local authorities' is a code and guide published by CIPFA. As it is by way of being a regulatory document, it is somewhat lacking in practical examples and explanation.

The PWLB publishes a very readable annual report which provides a good overview of council borrowing activity during the year, explains any changes in PWLB facilities, and reviews interest rate trends, etc. It is available from HMSO.

Local Authority Borrowing by Sir Harry Page (published by George Allen and Unwin) is a fascinating history of council borrowing up to 1985, and well worth reading for a deeper understanding of the development of council finance.

Finally, borrowing is a frequent topic in local government journals such as *Local Government Chronicle* or *Public Finance and Accountancy*.

6 Pensions and investments

Most council staff have a keen interest in the local government pension scheme, if only to the extent of their own retirement benefits. What we hope to do in this chapter is to develop this interest to cover the whole area of pensions and investment management. This will enable you to answer such questions as:

- *how safe are my pension rights?*
- *how much influence do councillors have over the way the pension scheme is run?*
- *who benefits if the scheme's investments are successful?*
- *what influence is there over the employer contribution costs that must be paid by my service or department?*
- *how can a council measure whether or not its scheme is being run efficiently?*

We also look at the technicalities of managing investments, and the role of actuaries. With the benefit of this knowledge you ought quickly to become your own pensions expert.

The local government superannuation scheme

Local government pensions are termed *superannuation*. For the purposes of this chapter, we exclude staff such as teachers, fire and police who have their own separate schemes. However, we should note a very important difference between the main local government scheme and these other government-run pensions. That is that the local government scheme is a *funded scheme*.

A funded scheme is one where the cost of an employee's pension is provided for by collecting contributions during the employee's own working life. The contributions are used to buy investments, and it is the income from these investments, many years hence, that will pay a pension and other benefits when the employee retires.

An alternative to a funded scheme is one where all contributions and benefits are dealt with on a pay-as-you-go basis. The pensions of current pensioners are met directly out of the current contributions of employees and the employer. This is effectively the system used for the state retirement pension. The annual cost of these pensions is met out of the same year's tax revenues.

There is no reason in theory why the local government scheme could not be run on a pay-as-you-go basis. The same benefits could be paid, though the annual contributions from councils might rise. Public money tied up in £ billions of superannuation fund investments would be released, and could be put to a different purpose.

Whether or not such a policy would make better sense for the UK economy is a wider issue. A funded scheme, however, does have the advantage of stabilising the rate at which councils have to pay into the scheme.

Key factors of the scheme

The scheme is funded

Employers' pension contributions are part of the cost of employing a member of staff. A funded scheme ensures that this cost is met as the liability arises, during the employee's working life. If the scheme were not funded, the cost to councils might fluctuate widely from year to year. Any large inflation increase in pensions would fall directly on to councils as an additional cost. If the council reduced the size of its workforce, or chose to run one of its services by outside contractors rather than by its own employees, it would still need to pay on a current basis for the pensions of its former larger numbers of staff. This would produce a large overhead unrelated to its reduced capacity.

It is a final salary scheme

The pension earned under the scheme is a proportion of the employee's salary at, or near, retirement. It is not affected by the fund's investment performance. However much inflation increases an employee's salary over the years, it is still the final salary that will form the basis of the pension calculation. The employee's contributions in early years are thus effectively buying an inflation-proofed investment.

Thus in calculating council contributions, the effects of career progression by employees needs to be allowed for. Say an employee progresses from a trainee on joining the council to a chief officer at retirement. The employee will pay the same percentage of salary in pension contributions as both a trainee and a chief officer, but on retirement, a year's trainee contributions will have bought an annual pension of 1/80th of that final chief officer's salary. This is quite a good deal for employees, but the resulting cost burden needs to be covered by the fund.

The scheme is tax exempt

As with other pension schemes, profits and dividends on investments are exempt from taxation. Similarly, employees are not taxed on the proportion of their income that is paid into the fund.

The scheme is contracted out

On retirement, all scheme members will receive the basic state pension in addition to their local government benefits. They are not eligible for the state earnings related pension scheme (SERPS), because the local government scheme is guaranteed to provide a minimum pension at least equal to what could have been achieved had they been paying into SERPS instead. As members do not derive benefits from SERPS, their national insurance contributions are reduced.

The scheme is voluntary

Council employees are not obliged to enter the scheme, and are free to make their own pension arrangements. However, the council will not contribute towards the cost of a personal pension in the same way that it pays into the local government scheme.

Who runs the scheme?

The scheme's benefits, and employee's contribution rates, are fixed nationally, but the scheme investments, and the assessment of employer (i.e. council) contributions are organised locally. Just to make life more complicated, not every council has its own superannuation fund. In a shire county area, the county council runs a fund which caters both for its own employees and those of the district councils in its area.

The London boroughs each run their own fund. In the metropolitan areas (where the funds used to be run by the now-abolished metropolitan counties), there is a lead authority or separate pensions body covering all the former county's districts.

Even if your council does not directly operate a superannuation fund, it is important to be conversant with the principles involved. If nothing else, your council still has to pay in its top-up contributions. These can prove a very large budget item.

Structure of the scheme

Table 6.1: Summary of the local government superannuation scheme

Number of contributors	1,059,000
Number of pensioners	862,000
Value of investments	£40 billion
Number of superannuation authorities	89

Source: UKSC

Let's look a bit more closely now at the practical operation of an individual superannuation fund. This is shown diagrammatically in Table 6.2. Starting on the left-hand side, we have the three main sources of income into the fund: investment income, employees' contributions, and employer contributions. The investment income will hopefully be 50 per cent or more of total income. We say hopefully because the local government scheme is a long-established, funded scheme. It should therefore be in a position where the income from its investments alone can cover most of its expenditure. Pension schemes which have reached this stage of their development are often referred to as *mature*. Note that the contributions box exceeds the payments box. Provided the number of members in the scheme is not falling, we would expect a surplus to be achieved in most years. These surpluses are directed into the acquisition of new investments.

Second in importance on the income side are the employee (or staff) contributions. As Table 6.3 shows, these are currently set at 6 per cent of salary for officers and 5 per cent for manual workers. Finally, on the income side we have the employer's (or council) contribution. This is not fixed, rather it is set every three years following an *actuarial valuation* of the fund. Actuarial valuation is a technical process which seeks to match the investments of the fund with future pension obligations. As we see later, this is by no means an easy task!

From Table 6.2, we can now answer our earlier question as to who benefits if the fund investments are successful. The beneficiary is the council, because the council contribution (if any) is only as much as the actuary certifies is needed to keep the fund solvent.

Look at it this way. The payment obligations of a fund are determined by the nationally set criteria. We also know that the employees' (staff) contributions of scheme members are similarly a fixed percentage of salary, so, to balance the actuarial calculation, we have only the investment income and the council contributions. Hence the better the investment performance, the less the council will need to pay in over the years. Conversely, the worse the investment performance, the greater the top-up contributions required over the long term.

Table 6.2: Superannuation fund receipts and payments

Contributions	Fund	Payments
Employers		Pensions
Employees		Pension increases
Investment income	Investments	Other benefits
		Administration
	Transfer values	

Table 6.3: Summary of scheme benefits

Contribution rates
Officers   6 per cent of salary
Manual workers   5 per cent of salary

Pensions
$1/80$th for each year of service (maximum $40/80$ths age 60, $45/80$ths age 65) applied to final salary (best year in last three). Years of service accepted for pension purposes are termed *reckonable*.

Widow's pensions
On the death of a pensioner, a widow's pension continues in payment at half the original pension rate.

Inflation increases
Awarded annually, these take effect in April.

Lump sum on retirement
Three 80ths for each year of service, as per the pensions calculation.

Ill-health retirement
Up to ten years (usually $6^2/3$ is added to service already earned. Pension and lump sum immediately payable.

The expenditure side consists of pensions and other benefits paid (see Table 6.3), plus the costs of administering the scheme. Administration costs include running the pension payroll and managing the investments.

Transfer values

We have discussed the main items of expenditure and income met from the funds. This leaves the question of transfer values, shown in the lower box in Table 6.2. Transfer values arise when an employee leaves or joins the council. Consider first the example of an employee leaving the fund to join a different local authority. During their service, their contributions and the matching employer contributions have been accumulated in investments. In order to maintain the funding level of the new employer's superannuation fund, the value of these investments must be transferred across to it. It is the last employer of a retiring officer who must pay all the retirement benefits. Hence the need for the transfer value system. Similarly, if a new employee joins the council from another local authority, and becomes a member of the scheme, a transfer value is recovered from the former employer.

Transfer values are calculated according to a standard formula, based on the contributions paid into a fund and the number of years of service. The use of transfer values is complicated by the fact that staff are often moving from outside the local government scheme. Generally, if an employee joins from another part of the public sector, the transfer value will purchase equal benefits in the local government scheme. In other words, if the employee has 20 years' service with a previous employer, the transfer value will have bought 20 years' reckonable service in the council's scheme.

In the case of other employers, the value of the transfer may not be regarded as sufficient to buy equivalent benefits. Thus 20 years' service with a previous employer might only buy 10 years' service in the local government scheme, restricting the employee's eventual pension entitlement. Conversely, the transfer paid by the local government scheme may not be acceptable to a different employer.

There are, however, further options open to most employees leaving local government. One is to leave their benefits frozen or 'preserved' in the local government scheme. Thus if an employee had 20 years' service with the council before moving to the private sector, the $^{20}/_{80}$ths pension could be stored in the council scheme until retirement. (The $^{20}/_{80}$ths pension would be based on the salary received on leaving local government, increased for annual inflation.)

Another is to take out a personal pension using the value of benefits accrued in the fund. This latter option is one requiring expert advice, as the benefits payable under a personal pension are determined by its investment performance—low performance, low pension!

The net effect of the transfer value system is thus that fund investments are lost or gained as employees leave and join the council. Moreover, the fund investments also need to cover the preserved benefits of staff no longer with the council, who have chosen to store their pension entitlement in the fund.

Example of fund accounts

Before examining the investment aspect of the funds in more detail, we look at an actual example of fund accounts being those of Humberside County Council for 1990/91.

Table 6.4: Superannuation fund accounts

Humberside 1990—91	£000	£000
Income		
1. Contributions — employees	11,328	
2. — employees	6,642	
3.		17,970
4. Investment income		24,082
5. Transfer values (in)		3,748
6.		45,800
Expenditure		
7. Pensions	22,411	
8. Retirement grants (lump sum)	4,726	
9. Death grants	329	
10.		27,446
11. Other expenses		1,190
12. Transfer values (out)		5,061
13.		33,697
14. Net income available for investment		12,103
		45,800

Notice that income and payments are not in balance, with a surplus of £12.103m (line 14). As the employer's contribution rate is calculated on actuarial principles, rather than accounting, we would expect this to be the case. Note also that the investment income (nearly £24m) is almost sufficient in itself to cover the fund benefits (£27.446m — line 10). This is clearly a mature fund.

The accounts also show some of the advantages inherent in a funded scheme. Suppose, for the sake of argument, that the £27.446m of benefits had had to be met on a pay as you go basis. Instead of the £6.642m paid in by employers on actuarial assessment (line 2), they would have needed to pay £16.118m (the total benefits less employee contributions). Once a funded scheme has developed to the maturity of our example, the saving against pay-as-you go rates is large.

It is also informative to look at the considerable value of investments that underlie such a scheme (Table 6.5)

Table 6.5: Net assets statement Xyzshire 1990/91

	£000	£000
Net assets 1.4.90		450,539
New money for investment in year (line 14 of table 6.5)		12,103
Increase in market value of investments		
realised	8,555	
unrealised	9,844	
		18,399
Net assets 31.3.91		481,041

Thus to generate the £23.995m of investment income used to fund benefits, the value of investments held was over £480m by the end of the year in question. The average yield on these investments was quite low at 5.2 per cent, reflecting the fact that 77 per cent of these were equities or ordinary shares.

Investment objectives

Thus far, we have examined the overall structure of the local government superannuation scheme, and the expenditure and income arising for individual funds. We now turn to the investment aspect of the funds. As we have seen, the scheme benefits are provided for on a funded basis, or matched by investments. What sort of investments should a fund make? What sort of investment performance are funds expected to achieve?

Table 6.6 and Fig. 6.1 show in different forms the investment distribution of the average superannuation fund over recent years. As shown, in 1991 some 78 per cent of the funds was held in equities, or ordinary shares. (56 per cent UK, and 22 per cent overseas). For the more equity-oriented individual funds, the equity proportion was in some cases as high as 95 per cent. Before we examine in more detail the reason for this equity predominance, it is interesting to note the changes in the proportions of investment types since 1981. Technically, this distribution into the different categories of investment is termed *asset allocation*.

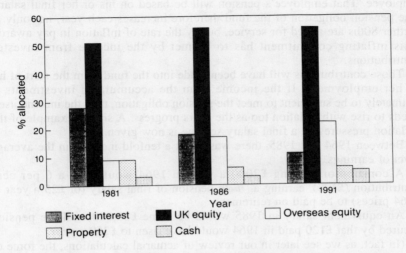

Figure 6.1: Superannuation investments: 1981, 1986 and 1991

Before 1983, investments were classified under local government law as narrow range (basically government bonds) and wider range (equities and property). The value of the wider range was not permitted to exceed three times the value of the narrow range. This meant that at least 25 per cent of the fund had to be held in government stocks or *gilts*. A further restriction was that the total of property and overseas stocks (part of the wider range) must not exceed 25 per cent of all investments.

Once these restrictions were removed in 1983, many councils followed a policy of replacing their large bond holdings with overseas equities. As at 1992, over 40 council funds had 25 per cent or more of their value in overseas equities. Conversely at least five funds had either reduced their bond holdings (UK and foreign) to less than 0.1 per cent of holdings or eliminated them entirely.

Table 6.6: Superannuation fund investment asset allocations

Type of investment	1981 %	1986 %	1991 %
Fixed interest (1)	28	18	11
UK equities	51	56	56
Overseas equities	9	17	22
Property	9	6	6
Cash	3	3	5
(1) includes overseas bonds and index linked bonds			

Source: CIPFA statistics.

191

The popularity of equities as a pension fund investment is that they appear to offer inflation protection. Consider this from the simplified example of a single employee. That employee's pension will be based on his or her final salary. The pension obligation of the fund therefore increases each year, not only as further 80ths are added for service, but by the rate of inflation in pay awards. This inflating commitment has to be met by the income from invested contributions.

Those contributions will have been made into the fund from the start of his or her employment. If the income from the accumulated investments is ultimately to be sufficient to meet the pension obligation, then the income itself needs to rise with inflation too as the years progress. A simple example of the inflation pressures on a final salary scheme is now given.

Between 1964 and 1985, there was about a tenfold increase in the average level of earnings.

A contributor earning £2000 a year in 1964 would pay a 6 per cent contribution (£120), earning a $^1/_{80}$th pension of final salary (or £25 a year at 1964 prices) to be paid on retirement.

An equivalent salary in 1985 would be some £20,000, and the pension secured by that £120 paid in 1964 would have risen to £250 *a year*.

(In fact, as we see later in our review of actuarial calculations, the force of wage growth usually runs ahead of ordinary inflation.)

Clearly, the type of investment required by a pension fund is one on which the investment income keeps pace with inflation, or better still achieves a return in excess of inflation. The credentials of equity investments to meet this criteria are shown in Table 6.7. In the nine 5-year periods since the war, equities failed only twice to make returns in excess of inflation. In those periods when they failed (1947/51 and 1972/76), so did gilts and cash (bank deposits).

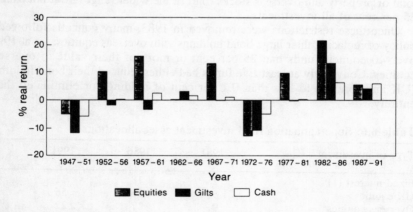

Figure 6.2: Annualised real returns: five year periods

Over the period as a whole, equities averaged a remarkable 6.2 per cent a year *above inflation* though a great deal of this relied on the exceptional 21.6 per cent a year average return achieved during 1982/86.

Table 6.7: Historical investment real returns (5 year annualised)

Period	Equities	Gilts	Cash
1947–51	–5.0	–11.7	–5.7
1952–56	10.2	–1.8	0.2
1957–61	15.9	–3.3	2.4
1962–66	0.3	3.0	1.5
1967–71	13.2	–0.2	1.0
1972–76	–12.7	–10.7	–4.8
1977–81	9.7	–0.3	0.2
1982–86	21.6	13.3	6.2
1987–91	5.5	4.0	5.8
1946–91 (entire period)	6.2	–0.9	0.6

The term *real return* is used for the percentage achieved after deducting inflation. For example, the return on equities in 1979 was 11.4 per cent, but inflation was higher at 16.3 per cent. The real return achieved on equities was thus minus 4.9 per cent (11.4–16.3).

Returns reflect both capital growth and dividends paid. If, for example, a £100 investment paid a £5 dividend (5 per cent) and grew in capital value to £110 (10 per cent) the return achieved would be 15 per cent.

Annualised returns are an averaging of the return achieved over a several year period. If an investment returned 10 per cent in each of two successive years, and then 0 per cent in the next three years, the result would be the same as a steady rate of 3.89 per cent in all five years, and this is therefore calculated as the annualised rate.

We have seen that investments need to show income growth that keeps pace with inflation. Let us look now, in more detail, at the main categories of investment that are available, and what their particular properties are. We deal first with bonds (Table 6.8)

Table 6.8: Types of investment—bonds

Type of investment	Benefits	Drawbacks

Gilts

A gilt is a fixed interest security, issued by HM Government. Gilts are dated, an example being 'Treasury 9 per cent 2008'. This stock when first issued cost £100 to buy. Each year the holder receives interest at 9 per cent on the £100 par value. In 2008, the Government will repay the £100 originally borrowed. Gilts can be bought and sold on the stock market during their life. It may cost more or less

Gilts are the most secure form of investment, literally as safe as the Bank of England.

There is always a ready market for gilts, which can be bought or sold immediately as required.

Investment in a gilt is not inflation-proof. Whatever the intervening rate of inflation, the investment will only be repaid £ for £ of original value at maturity. Similarly, the interest earnings do not rise with inflation.

Table 6.8: continued

Type of investment	Benefits	Drawbacks

to buy the gilt, depending on current interest rates.

As an example, 'Treasury 9 per cent 2008' was trading at about £104 in November 1992. As the interest paid on the gilt never changes (9 per cent of £100), a buyer at £104 is accepting a lower rate of interest on the investment. The £9 earned each year on the £104 will be an interest only yield of 8.65 per cent.

The price of gilts rises and falls with general interest rate trends, and stock market expectations of long-term economic performance and inflation.

Gilts are classified as shorts (up to 5 years to run), mediums (5 to 15 years), and longs (15 years plus). A small value of undated stocks is still in issue, which could be redeemed at any time, or left to run indefinitely.

The value of a gilt is composed of two elements: its interest earnings and the final redemption. The shorter a gilt, the higher the effect of the redemption element. This means that short gilts are usually less price sensitive to interest rate trends than long gilts. Long gilts, on the other hand, are very interest rate sensitive, as their value lies almost entirely in the annual interest element. Their price adjusts to bring the interest paid (or coupon) in line with current rates. Thus if a long gilt has a 15 per cent coupon, and current rates are 7.5 per cent, its price may increase from £100 to nearer £200. Conversely, a 7.5 per cent coupon is likely to fall in price to nearer £50 in a period of 15 per cent interest rates.

This explains why gilts are sometimes referred to as a fair weather friend. Gilts bought at the start of a period of falling interest rates and optimism re-inflation can show very significant capital gains.

If gilts are to be held to redemption, it is possible to predict with complete accuracy the return that will be achieved.

If investment in gilts is correctly timed, substantial capital gains can be achieved.

The price of gilts is at the mercy of government policy. If the government has a large borrowing requirement, it will need to issue a high value of gilts, driving down the price of the stocks already in issue.

Table 6.8: (continued)

Type of investment	Benefits	Drawbacks

Conversely, gilts bought immediately before a period of rising interest rates can show heavy capital losses, whilst not even earning the rate of interest that could be achieved on a straightforward bank deposit.

Index-linked gilts

There is a special set of gilt stocks known as index-linked. With these gilts the redemption value is increased annually in line with the RPI. Moreover, the annual interest coupon is calculated not on the original sum at which the stock was issued, but on the RPI-increased value. Given this inflation protection the coupon is much lower than a traditional gilt, usually between 2 and 2.5 per cent.

Index-linked gilts combine the high security of a government stock with an inflation proof return.

Index-linked stocks have been surprisingly unpopular with funds, especially as they guarantee a real return. Perhaps this is because recent years have shown very low inflation, and high returns in other types of investment.

Overseas bonds

The equivalent of gilts is available in overseas stock markets. The price and yield in another country is affected by that country's economic situation. Factors such as whether local pension funds or banks are obliged to invest to a significant degree in the bond market can affect prices.

Because an overseas bond is an investment denominated in a foreign currency, the value of the investment is dependent on exchange rates.

Overseas bonds in many countries (e.g. Germany, Japan) carry virtually the same security as UK bonds.

Overseas bonds are a good hedge against bad UK economic performance, and do particularly well in periods when the £'s value is falling.

Because they have the double drawbacks of not being inflation proofed, and an inherent currency risk, foreign bonds are not obviously suited to form a major element of the fund investments. If investment and disposal are well-timed, very good returns can be achieved.

As a further summary on bonds, try Table 6.9 and Fig. 6.3. Column 1 is the yield (the current return on gilts) at the end of the year in question. So, for example, at the end of 1985, the average £100 holding of gilts was generating £10.43 of interest income. The second column is the total yield achieved in that year, interest and capital appreciation (or loss) combined.

The Table enables you to test your understanding of the gilt price/yield relationship. Between 1985 and 1986, yields fell only slightly and thus the level of capital appreciation was minimal. The return was thus only slightly better

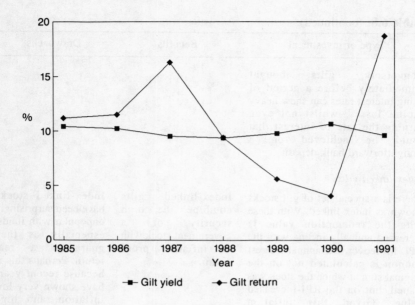

Figure 6.3: Gilt yields and returns: 1985–91

than the interest yield. But look now at 1987. Yields fell from 10.24 per cent to 9.55 per cent, leading to a significant rise in gilt values. This rise, when added to the yield, produced a total return of 16.3 per cent.

The opposite situation applied in 1990. The yield rose from 9.78 per cent to 10.66 per cent, producing a major fall in gilt values. When deducted from the 10.66 per cent yield, this capital loss caused the actual return achieved to reduce to only 4.0 per cent.

Table 6.9: Gilt yields and returns 1985 to 1991

Year	Yield %	Return %
1985	10.43	11.2
1986	10.24	11.5
1987	9.55	16.3
1988	9.39	9.4
1989	9.78	5.6
1990	10.66	4.0
1991	9.60	18.7

Source: FTA share indices.

Table 6.10 shows a similar summary of overseas bond performance. Column 1 is the annual return achieved, and column 2 a measure of the £'s strength: its trade weighted index. A high index signifies the £ buys more foreign currency, a low index that it buys less.

Column 1 demonstrates the volatility of overseas bonds as an investment. But more interestingly, relate these returns to the sterling index. 1987 was a poor year for overseas bonds because the £ rose by 10 per cent, making any investment denominated in foreign currency worth proportionately less. Conversely when the £ fell in 1988, overseas bonds received a considerable boost, turning in a 20.4 per cent return.

Table 6.10: Overseas bond yields and returns 1986—1991

Year	Return %	£ trade-weighted index
1986	18.4	100
1987	−11.5	110
1988	9.5	113
1989	20.4	100
1990	−7.6	109
1991	19.6	106

Before we move on to equities, let's summarise our understanding of bonds investments.

- Gilt-edged bonds offer the highest security of any investment, the guarantee of HM Government.
- Gilts can be purchased on the stock market, and their price reflects current interest rates, and expectations of inflation.
- Bonds perform well when interest rates are falling, and poorly when interest rates are rising.
- Gilts may beat inflation in the short term, but there is no long-term guarantee of such a performance.
- A special category of gilt, index-linked, does offer an inflation proof return. These stocks have not been as popular with funds as might have been expected, perhaps because of the unusually good performance of alternative investments during the 1980s.
- Overseas bonds are a good hedge against UK underperformance, but are a fairly volatile investment. They have the double risk of interest rate variations *and* exchange rate variations.

Some key factors in equity investment

As we saw earlier equities, whether UK or overseas, are the favoured investment of pension funds. When we read the financial pages of our newspaper, equity investment can come across as a matter of spotting the winner; which of the hundreds of well-known companies on offer will beat the market, and which are better avoided.

In fact, the fund investments are much more concerned with general properties of the equity markets than whether, say, Sainsburys will out-perform Tesco or vice versa. Superannuation funds are looking to long-term dividend growth. They benefit greatly from the large scale of their investments. A typical

197

fund might hold 200 or more different individual equity stocks. Hence, although these will include winners and losers, the diversification virtually eliminates the risk of disaster.

Similarly, the frequent sudden variations in the value of the stock market indices is not such a pressing consideration as might be imagined. A classical case of this was the rapid fall of the UK equity market in October 1987, beginning with 'Black Monday'. The stock market index fell by 25 per cent or more over a few days, but for council funds this was something of a non-event. The sudden collapse in prices was a disaster for investors obliged to meet their losses immediately at the end of the monthly account. For a pension fund with 20 or 30 years as its investment horizon, it was an irrelevance. A year later, the indices had recovered and the net effect on council funds was negligible.

In fact, in discussing this with an actuary at the time, he felt that Black Monday was an excellent opportunity for councils. In purchasing equities, funds are buying a future stream of dividend income. Provided nothing has happened to undermine the basic profitability of the companies concerned, the lower their share price the better, as the cheaper it is to buy that dividend stream.

It is interesting to note that, when actuaries value a fund, they sometimes reduce the market value of investments if they feel the market is too high, and the yields on shares stretched too low. Conversely, they will increase the market value of the fund if they feel yields are too high and the market has fallen too low. So much for index watching.

The concept of yield brings us to a traditional tool of investment analysis, the bond/equity yield ratio (see Table 6.11).

Table 6.11: Gilt equity yield ratio

Year/ quarter	UK equity yield %	Gilt yield %	Yield ratio
1986 Q1	3.78	9.00	2.38
1987 Q1	3.45	9.16	2.66
Q2	3.04	9.18	3.02
Q3	3.01	9.95	3.31
Q4	4.32	9.55	2.21
1988 Q1	4.38	9.03	2.06
1989 Q1	4.22	9.34	2.21
1990 Q1	4.82	11.57	2.40
1991 Q1	4.80	10.12	2.11
1992 Q1	5.09	9.77	1.92

The third column of this Table is not as esoteric as it might first appear. The value of this gilt/equity yield ratio has a sort of mystical significance to investment pundits, a bit like the way car salesmen kick the tyres of a used car. The rule of thumb is that the ratio is within reasonable bounds between say $1^3/_4$ and $2^3/_4$. If the ratio falls much below $1^3/_4$, then this seems to show that the additional risk of an equity investment as against a bond is more than compensated for by the price of equities (which is low, giving a high yield). To correct this anomaly, one is likely to witness a surge in equity prices, or a rise in bond yields.

Conversely, if the ratio nears three, this would indicate that yield on equities is getting too high, and is insufficient to compensate for the extra risk as against gilts. To demonstrate (with hindsight of course) the value of this adage, look at the yield figures in the table for 1987. The figure of 3.31 in the third quarter obviously forebodes some mishap. Hey presto, came the Black Monday fall in share prices (driving up equity yields) and a general cut in interest rates (reducing gilt yields). Thus by the end of the year (quarter 4) the ratio had returned to a more usual 2.21 per cent.

Investment analysts use many ratios, but it is worth remembering the importance of the yield on the market. Managers talk about 'the market looking cheap' or, alternatively, 'overpriced'. These are judgements on whether the dividend stream an equity purchase will produce represents good value. The equity yield and its ratio to gilt yields will quickly give you a synopsis of the market situation and can be a better guide than the fluctuating FTSE numbers of the financial pages. To allow you to exploit the better known equity indicators, we cover some of the main factors.

The FTA-actuaries all share index

The index 'FTA all-share' is a measure of the general trend in share prices. It is calculated in a way which:

- *uses price data from 653 stocks;*
- *gives due allowance to the size of the constituent companies. This means that the same percentage price movement in one of the largest companies (such as British Telecom) will produce a larger variation in the index than the same movement in a smaller company's price;*
- *was set at 100 on 10 April 1962. Since then its highest level was 1326.36 (11 May 1992), and its lowest 61.92 (13 December 1974). As at November 1992, it stood at 1250.*

The FT-SE 100

The 'Footsie' is a quick reference index covering only the 100 largest companies. This index is available continuously during the trading day. The smaller number of shares make it easier to update than the all-share. It is not as reliable a measure of the overall market, because sometimes (perhaps in a recession) large company shares outperform the average.

Sector indices

For analysis purposes, companies are grouped into *sectors* (e.g. oil and gas, telephone networks, banks, building materials). This enables the all-share to be subdivided into 35 sector indices. Sector indices are informative, because individual sector prices often move at a different rate to the main index (or even in the opposite direction). As an example, high interest rates may depress share values generally. At the same time, bank stocks could perform better than the average on the prospect of higher income likely to be earned on their loan books. Conversely, property stocks might perform worse than average, as they would suffer higher costs on their borrowings.

Yield

Yield is a measure of the rate of dividend paid on shares. As the all-share, 100 and sector indices are calculated for share prices, so the yield on these indices is reported.

A comparatively low yield is often taken as an indicator of long term growth potential, whereas a high yield may show limited potential for capital advancement. It is interesting to note the variation in yields between particular markets. Japan is a particularly low yielding market: yield is between 1.5 per cent and 2.5 per cent. Highly regarded companies can yield as low as 0.5 per cent. This reflects a very optimistic perspective as to such companies' long-term growth potential.

Between 1985 and 1992, UK equity yield has moved between 3 per cent and 6 per cent.

Price/earnings ratio (P/E)

Price earnings is, in some senses, the reverse, or reciprocal, of yield. The calculation includes not only dividends paid but profits earned and retained within the company.

A high P/E may indicate long-term growth potential, a low P/E a pessimistic market view of the share. P/E and yield vary considerably from sector to sector. The quality of individual stocks needs to be judged against their own sector rather than against the market as a whole.

Capitalisation

The capitalisation of a quoted company is essentially the total market value of all the shares in issue. Capitalisation is a valuable indicator for the following reasons.

- It gives a measure of the comparative size of the company, and may qualify it for inclusion in the FTSE 100.
- By comparison with the value of the company shown in its accounts, the market capitalisation may show whether the stock is under- or overpriced.
- Capitalisation also shows the relative scale of the different types of security. As at the end of 1988 for example, the London Stock Exchange was capitalised as shown in Table 6.12.

Table 6.12

Category	Market value £ billion
Gilts	140
Eurobonds (Bonds issued by UK companies in several markets denominated in a foreign currency)	23
Company stocks	
Loan capital	12
Preference capital	15
Ordinary shares	393
Total capitalisation (UK companies)	583

Additionally, there was a much higher capitalisation (over £900 billion) for the shares of overseas companies who are quoted on the London Stock Exchange as well as their own domestic exchange. The domestically quoted equity for 189 US stocks and 11 Japanese stocks included in this total amounted to some £2,811 billion! Against the scale of these figures, the investment influence of the local authority pension funds is set in perspective.

As at November 1992, a sample of 'household name' companies were capitalised as in Table 6.13.

Table 6.13

	£m
National Westminster Bank	6,313
ICI	7,318
Shell	17,658
British Telecom	22,994
Next	404
Ratners	32

Sources: *Financial Times*; Stock Exchange Quality of Markets reports.

Sector weightings

Thus far, we have looked at some of the general properties of equities, and how these are measured. All these can be applied in assessing the stocks of the fund in which you are directly interested. We look now at two factors which give a deeper understanding of an individual set of investments (or *portfolio*).

Recall that, in the FTA all-share, each sector of the market has an appropriate weighting. An individual fund's investments will have sector weightings too. This is essentially a strategy decision, as per the following example.

- *The bank sector forms 5 per cent of the all-share in value.*
- *A fund holds 10 per cent of its equities in bank stocks.*
- *If banks out-perform the index, so will the fund. A 20 per cent rise in bank shares will increase our particular fund value by 2 per cent, but the index by only 1 per cent.*
- *If banks underperform the index, the fund will be below average in its performance.*

Stock turnover

Equity management is less dramatic and exciting than might be supposed. The image of frenetic, shouting traders may hold good for foreign exchange spot traders or swap dealers. Fund management is a much more measured process. The core holdings of a fund may run on unchanged for many years. Not only is there the cost of dealing (the 'spread' between bid and offer prices) but the depth of market is not always there to buy and sell large values of equities at fair prices.

A high rate of buying and selling may indicate unclear investment strategy. Wholesale reorganisations of the portfolio should be undertaken as rarely as possible.

Overseas equities

Overseas equities allow funds to diversify, and avoid undue reliance on UK equities. As with overseas bonds, there is not only the normal equity risk, but a currency risk as well. Rather than buy shares of overseas companies directly, it is possible to gain overseas exposure by buying into UK companies which derive a high proportion of their earnings overseas.

The main opportunities for investment are:

North America;
Europe;
Japan;
Pacific Basin.

We cannot allow the topic of Japan to pass without a digression. An investment manager, asked to explain farcical results in comparison to the Tokyo index, was soon able to hoodwink the council's investment committee. Off the record, she later explained to the council treasurer the true reason.

Without any real understanding of the respective merits of different Japanese companies, her team of investment 'experts' relied on their recognition of well-known brand names and car marques for technical analysis. This had led them disastrously away from better performing companies such as banks, the names of which were unknown to the team.

The sheer volatility of returns in Japan is captured in Table 6.14. Between 1985 and 1991, returns ranged from a handsome 96.3 per cent (1986), to a debilitating minus 46.8 per cent (1990). Clearly, a market to be approached with the utmost care!

Table 6.14: Returns on the Japanese equity market 1985—1991

Year	Return %
1985	15.3
1986	96.3
1987	12.2
1988	41.4
1989	16.2
1990	−46.8
1991	40.1

We have now covered (in equities — UK and overseas — and bonds) over 89 per cent of the value of fund investments shown in Table 6.6. The type of knowledge you may have acquired will enable you to take a much more informed approach to questioning why your fund is invested in a particular way.

Investment managers rank amongst the best of salesmen, and they have a particular ability to divert attention to the performance of specific shares rather than the portfolio as a whole. We all like to hear a bit of expert analysis on a well-known high street retailer, or famous company. In reality, a fund will probably have many winning investments and many losers. From our long-term viewpoint as pension fund members or employers, it makes a lot more sense to concentrate attention on broad factors such as the overall asset allocation of the fund and how the yield of the market as a whole is moving. Keep up to date with the sort of indicators we have described, and your questions to finance staff or investment managers will be much more respected than 'why did we buy share X?' or 'how much have we lost in last week's stock market fall?' Try the equity checklist set out below.

- Equities offer a good prospect of inflation-proofed returns.
- From a pension perspective they need to be viewed long-term. Temporary volatility is largely irrelevant to fund objectives.
- The ratio of equity yields to gilt yields is a fair indicator of whether the market is expensive or cheap.
- Yield and price/earnings are possible indicators of share potential. Care needs to be exercised in using this information; these indicators vary widely from sector to sector.
- Other key measures of individual portfolios are the relative weightings in particular sectors, and the rate of turnover in stocks.
- Overseas equities are a good method of diversifying risk. Expert knowledge is needed to operate successfully in these markets.

Property

Property has certainly fallen from investment favour with council funds as Table 6.6 showed. Yet it should fulfil most of the basic objectives of a pension fund investment. It is a real asset, and ought to provide a return which compensates to a large extent for inflation. The normal lease in the UK for commercial and industrial property operates as a ratchet, with upward only rent reviews. Thus buying into property at a time of depressed property prices (i.e. high investment yield) should present an excellent long-term growth opportunity. Some of the pitfalls of property investments are set out below.

Direct property

The fund buys and owns the property. It can therefore choose the precise type and location it favours, but unless the property is in demand in all stages of the economic cycle, the fund could find itself saddled with an asset that is hard to sell. This is a major failing with direct property. At least with an equity (which we would hope to hold for many years) you can sell out of problems and cut your losses.

Although prices have fallen lately, prime property is expensive. To buy sufficient direct property to have a suitably diversified portfolio will soon eat into the typical 5 per cent or 10 per cent property asset allocation. For a £200m fund, buying a single London office block would probably bust a 5 per cent property allocation.

Unit trusts/property funds

Rather than buy property directly, funds can subscribe to some form of pooled arrangement. This allows them to benefit from a spread of different types of property. Fees, however, can be expensive, and the type of fund established is often a long-term commitment. Again, it can be difficult to realise anything like your original investment if you want to do so quickly.

Location

Probably the corniest investment joke around runs as follows:
'What are the three most important factors about a property investment?'
'Location, location, and location.'
Given the current oversupply of property of all descriptions, tenants are notoriously fickle as to their location. What started out a few years before as a state-of-the-art office building, in a prime location can quickly become not quite 'comme il faut'. Any prolonged period of voids can undermine returns.

Unquoted investments

Council funds sometimes carry a small level of unquoted investments. In some councils these are directed towards investment in the council's own area. Certainly a difficult question to answer about a 1 per cent or 2 per cent exposure is why bother at all. The diversification afforded by such a low allocation is hardly worth having.

Whilst it's true that successful unquoted investments (or venture capital) produce high returns, this is usually at the cost of nearly as many failures. Moreover, unquoted investments are hard to sell. It's only the successes that are saleable.

Once locked into a pattern of decline, venture capital funds can take on a somewhat bizarre aspect. If returns are not forthcoming, councils start to look on the managers as enjoying some sort of fee trip. Venture capital investments do need higher than average scrutiny, so high fees are not always unjustified.

More amusing are the unlikely inventions or businesses espoused by managers in an ever more desperate search for a winner that will compensate for past losses. These can range from a briefcase-sized folding bicycle that somebody has been designing in a shed at the bottom of their garden for the last 20 years, to some new fast food outlet opened in direct conflict to the internationally established companies we hardly need name. The latter usually last a few days.

If a fund is serious about making an asset allocation to venture capital, then the utmost care needs to be devoted to developing strategies and choosing the investments. If a fund 'loses' a £1m in value on a quoted equity, the external auditor will never bat an eyelid. If that loss is the entire value of a hastily made unquoted investment, watch out.

Cash

Cash, or bank and money market deposits, are possibly a neglected area of asset allocation. On the face of it, cash has none of the requirements of a pension fund investment. It will never produce a capital gain, and the return (interest) received will not rise with inflation.

The author often daydreams of situations in which, had he converted the whole council portfolio to cash, the ensuing fall in the stock market would have enabled him to buy back in at some huge profit. In practice, such strategies are unlikely to be carried out, not least because the market could just as rapidly move the (wrong?) way. One still meets the odd treasurer though who claims to have been on the brink of 'going liquid' just before Black Monday.

If a large fund liquidated its equity holdings quickly, not only would it probably get a poor price for its assets, but it would prove a long and expensive process to reassemble the portfolio.

Cash though is an area where councils or managers are entitled to exercise a reasonable discretion in putting new funds into equities. Take, for example, a situation where the US market is falling rapidly. If a council is timed to invest new money in this area, surely it makes sense for it to invest later, rather than put money into an immediately devalued asset. Put more technically, we want to buy our dividend stream at the lowest possible cost.

As a note of warning the level of cash holding is likely to be of interest to auditors. They often take the view that the entire fund value must be in equities, gilts and property. If a council wishes to develop an asset allocation policy, perhaps short term, which includes a high allocation to cash, it is advisable to keep a full record of the decision. There should also be clear criteria as to when the money will be reapplied to the more normal categories of investment.

Options and futures

The technicalities of these products (or *derivatives*) are beyond the scope of this book. A very brief explanation is given here.

Options and futures are a method of investing in a stock without the need to buy the stock itself. They are also a way of insuring fund investments against underperformance. Interested? Then read on:

- A *future* is a contract between buyer and seller to deal in a stock at a fixed future date at a fixed price.
- An *option* is just that. There is a contract to buy or sell a stock at some future date, but it may or may not be exercised depending on whether it is in the option holder's interest to do so. A *call* option is the right to buy a stock at the option price. A *put* option is the right to sell at a particular price.
- Imagine a fund wishes to invest in a company, but is worried about the downside of the investment. If it buys the stock, it is taking the whole risk of any loss in its value. The stock's market value now is 600p. Suppose though it buys a put option to sell at 10 per cent below the current market price, 540p, three months hence. As this option is well below the current market level, it will probably cost a few pence, say 20p. Why would it do this? Because the fund's investment is now protected as follows:

—if the price of the share in three months time has risen significantly (say to 800p), the fund will have gained 200p per share. Against this it must set the cost of the option which is now worthless, 20p. Still a good gain though.

—if the price does fall to say 400p in three months' time, then on its actual shares, the fund has lost 200p. However, the option now has value. The council could exercise the option and require the counterparty to buy its shares (worth 400p each), at the option price of 540p. This would gain the council 140p per share, and would probably be settled in cash. The council's net position would then be that rather than having lost 200p per share, it would have lost only 80p (the 60p fall down to the option price, and the 20p cost of the option).

The properties of derivatives are invariably difficult to grasp unless you are dealing in them on a regular basis. Back in the mid-1980s, a swap broker visited a council to extol the virtues of these agreements. His sales pitch revolved around the clear distinction between the council paying fixed, and paying variable. In swap parlance, these are about as different as driving on the left-hand side of the road, and driving on the right-hand side.

The treasurer and his assistants listened with ever more sage nodding to the broker's explanations. The broker really couldn't have put it more clearly. However, as he prepared to leave after an hour or so's address, the treasurer indicated he had just one final question. What is a swap?

More seriously, if your fund is using derivatives, seek confirmation of the legal advice underlying this decision. Derivatives are not specifically cited as an investment in the superannuation regulations, and after the swaps fiasco (see Chapter 5), it pays to be cautious.

Thus far we have looked at the scheme in general terms, and investments at a 'macro' level. In the remainder of the chapter we consider the practicalities of managing the investments, and how we can objectively measure manager performance. We finish by looking at the techniques of actuarial valuation. In fact, armed with all this know-how, I should think the treasurer will start beating a diplomatic retreat the next time you ask him or her a question on the subject. Before we move on, check your knowledge against the summary below.

Pensions and investment synopsis

- The local government superannuation scheme is a funded, final salary one.
- Even if your council is not a superannuation authority, it will be required to pay a top-up employer's contribution for all its enrolled staff.
- The funds are mature, and most of their benefit outgo is financed by investment income.
- Employee contributions are fixed. Employer contributions are set by a three-yearly actuary's valuation.
- If investments perform well, it is the council employers who benefit in the form of reduced employer contributions.
- A very large value of investments is needed to support the funded basis.
- Equities are the favoured investment because of their expected capacity to

show real growth in investment income.

- Taken together UK and overseas equities dominate council investments.
- Other investments are fixed interest, property, unquoted and derivatives.
- Gilts (UK government fixed interest) are responsive to interest rate trends and market views on inflation and economic prospects. When their yields fall, they show capital growth and vice versa. Index-linked gilts — which guarantee a positive real return — have not enjoyed the popularity with funds that might be expected.
- The gilt/equity yield ratio is often taken as a key market indicator. It rarely exceeds three.
- Key equity indicators include stock market indices, yield, and capitalisation. Temporary market fluctuations are likely to have limited effect on long-term fund performance.
- Property and unquoted investments are useful for diversification, but require specialist advice.
- Derivatives can be used to insure against losses on stocks held, or to gain on stocks without actually having to invest.

Managing the fund investments

The councils running the funds, the superannuation authorities, operate an investment panel or committee. Its members are councillors, sometimes assisted by non-voting employee representatives. They are advised by finance staff in the same way as any other committee.

Quite often, the panel members refer to themselves as 'trustees'. This is not strictly correct. Superannuation is a council function just as highways and education are. The councillors do not have the independence of action of trustees, and all the superannuation fund's activities must be conducted in accordance with the relevant local government law and regulations.

However, certain law governing trustees serves as a good guide to what is or is not reasonable as regards the council's investments. It has been held in the courts, for example, that trustees must not have regard to extraneous matters in managing investments. This would prevent the trustees proscribing a particular company's shares for political reasons. Similar logic must apply to council panel decisions.

Investment panels usually meet quarterly. This is the minimum frequency of meeting required by the superannuation regulations. A quarterly cycle also fits in with the investment performance companies that analyse fund results. They produce their reports on results up to the end of a quarter: 30 June, 30 September, and so on. These reports are usually the main item on the panel's agenda.

The investment regulations

In 1991 there was an unexpected confrontation between councils and the Department of the Environment on the subject of investment panels. A Department official wrote to councils to the effect that they had no powers in law to delegate their investment decisions to external managers. As such delegation had been practised by the majority of superannuation authorities for many years, the new interpretation was greeted with some alarm.

Amendments were quickly effected to the regulations. These are now fairly clear as to the responsibilities of the council, and that it is lawful to delegate day-to-day management of investments to outside firms.

In fact, whether councils manage their investments using their own staff or employ an outside company, the role of the panels is fairly limited. Beyond setting tolerances for the different categories of investment (e.g. the gilt allocation to be over 5 per cent and less than 15 per cent), it is in any case impractical for panels to exercise much influence on individual stock selection. Choices made at a panel meeting on 1 April could be obsolete by 8 April, given the volatility of stock markets. The pace of a council's committee cycle is simply not fast enough for the cut and thrust of share dealing.

The main duties of the panels are:

- *setting the broad bands of asset allocation;*
- *appointing and dismissing external fund managers;*
- *monitoring investment performance, including receiving the reports of an external performance measurement service;*
- *appointing actuaries to the fund, for valuations and for other investment advice.*

Given the large sums at stake, panels are well advised to buy in as much expert advice as they feel they need to assist them in some or all of these duties.

Superannuation investment regulations

The regulations were last revised in February 1993. They cover the following requirements:

- Councils must have regard to the need for diversification of fund investments, and to avoid placing excessive funds with any one manager.
- Managers' appointments must be terminable at not more than one month's notice.
- Councils must receive a manager's investment report, and review performance, at least once every three months.
- Unquoted investments in total must not exceed 10 per cent of the fund.
- No single holding of any description may exceed 10 per cent of the fund, unless it is invested in unit trusts, in which case there is a 25 per cent limit for the total of trusts under one body's management.
- The investment limits are for making new or further investments. There is no need to sell investments which have grown to exceed the limits.
- The amount deposited with an institution authorised under the Banking Act 1987 should not exceed 10%.

All these requirements are sensible. More than 10 per cent of a pension fund in unquoted stocks would be on the risky side by most standards.

If funds use a single external manager, finance staff need to keep a check on the amount of cash held by that manager. Cash is usually invested via the banking arm of the investment manager's holding group. Temporary cash richness could cause the 10 per cent to be exceeded, and the need to check credit ratings (see Chapter 5) becomes a consideration. Banking registration is no guarantee of creditworthiness, and it would be quite risky to place such a huge sum as nearly 20 per cent of the fund with a single institution, however briefly.

Many managers effect specialist investments not by buying securities directly for the fund but by using their own company's unit trusts. If this were done for mainstream assets (say Japan and property), the total of unit trusts with that manager could soon threaten the 20 per cent limit.

Choosing a fund manager

Before a manager can be appointed, the council needs to determine the basic structure of its fund. If the fund is to go all equity, there is no need for any property investment expertise and so on. There are basically two routes to go down in setting up the investment structure. The first, which is declining in favour, is to appoint a single, *discretionary* manager who will have the power to switch funds around as he or she determines. The second, which is enjoying something of a vogue, is to commission actuaries to set the allocation. This is known as an *asset liability study*. It is intended to tailor the allocation to the particular age profile of fund members, any service issues such as high expected redundancy levels, and other local factors.

All that we have seen so far in this chapter stresses the importance of a correctly conceived asset allocation, which can then be left to run for some years. Actuarial advice is expensive, but it is worth spending a few tens of £thousand to improve the investment of hundreds of £million.

Having decided on one of the two types of approach, there are a whole range of options as to how managers are organised to make the structure work. The investment community is constantly seeking to expand this choice. A major divide within these is that into *passive* and *active* approaches.

Achieving even the same return as the index in any market is quite a fair investment performance. (Recall the indices we discussed on page 199). Very few managers beat the index by more than 1 per cent or 2 per cent in a year, and certainly not on a consistent basis. The objective of achieving exactly the index return with complete reliability year on year led to the development of passive (or indexed) funds. These are simply made up of the same shares as are used to calculate the relevant index, held in exactly the same proportions as in the index. Not surprisingly their investment return is also that of the index.

For funds which are not large enough to justify acquiring, say, all 653 stocks in the FTA-all share, computer applications are available which will choose smaller selections to track the index almost as faithfully.

Nothing is more underwhelming than receiving the quarterly performance report of a passive manager. There is no discussion about the pros and cons of individual stocks as these are totally irrelevant. The single measure of manager performance is the *tracking error*, this being the percentage deviation from the index. In fact, a passive manager is the only manager you can get annoyed with for doing significantly *better* than the index (think about it!).

Active managers occasionally get the last laugh out of their passive colleagues. Some passive funds are designed to track the FTSE 100 index and, as promotion or relegation of stocks into the 100 is only done at monthly intervals, it is pretty clear in advance who the new entrants will be. This is the signal for the active managers to buy the stocks in question, as they know they will have a ready buyer a few days later in the shape of their passive competitors.

Setting asset allocation

The average allocation

Some funds, even if not explicitly, are structured to replicate the average allocation of other similar funds. This average distribution is readily available from performance measuring agencies. The strategy has the advantage of ensuring your performance never varies too sharply from the rest of the pack.

Asset liability studies

The results of such a study rely on a statistical concept termed *the efficient frontier*. This is a technique to find the particular allocation that produces a desired return with the minimum risk. A very oversimplified and artificial example will explain.

- Based on the data of council employees and pensioners, the actuary and finance staff determine that the investment objective of a fund is real income growth of 2 per cent per annum over the next 10 years.
- Two main options are available with the following properties:
  —20 per cent bonds and 80 per cent equities. This is likely to produce an average return of 10 per cent per annum, but the range of possible average returns runs from -5 per cent per annum to +25 per cent per annum.
  —40 per cent index-linked gilts, and 60 per cent equities. This is likely to produce an average return of 3.5 per cent per annum, but the range of possible average returns is from 2 per cent per annum to 5 per cent per annum.

It thus becomes a choice for the council of going for the better average return (option 1) with a significant risk of failing to meet the 2 per cent, or ensuring the objective with dull but worthy option 2. Option two shows the price of relative certainty, because it is expected right from the start that average performance will be well below that of a typical, equity-dominated fund.

Fund management structures (examples)

In-house management

Many of the most successful investment teams consist of council staff. This is an option both for passive and active management.

Fully discretionary manager

This is simple to operate, and there is certainly no lack of accountability for performance.

Specialist managers

The big investment houses claim to provide high-quality cover for all world markets. It may be preferable though to designate separate managers for assets demanding specialist knowledge, such as property, overseas, unquoted.

Core : satellite

The majority of the fund is placed in a 'safe' core, which is run passively or with a conservative performance target. A smaller satellite is run with a more ambitious brief.

Using a specialist or tactical asset allocator

A central manager is retained with the brief of choosing how much should be placed each quarter in the various asset categories. The sums so allocated are then managed on a day-to-day basis by specialists in those categories.

Competing managers

Some funds retain several managers, each with the same brief and an equal share of the fund. Advocates of the method believe the element of competition, and the likelihood of being sacked if you get the worst results stimulates better performance. Critics point out that the system often eliminates manager strategy all together. If manager A's strategy is to be long (overweighted) in property, but manager B's is to be short in property, they will ensure quite nicely between them that the fund overall is basically right on the property average.

Value added passive

This is a technique to exploit a view that a particular category of company, or companies with a particular set of indicators will outperform the index. Similar computer programs to indexation methods are used, but the stock selection is skewed by a pre-determined degree towards the particular stocks favoured. This combination of active and passive seems fairly paradoxical, but has produced good results for some funds. It certainly puts the emphasis on analysis of wider market indicators, rather than picking individual stocks.

Once the investment allocation has been set, the manager selection process begins. This is an area in which it is best to rely on expert advice.

The investment management market is dominated by a few large firms, and these are likely to figure in any short list, along with some hopeful newcomers. Here are some key factors to bear in mind.

- How much experience does the firm have of local authority funds? These are significantly different from most company schemes.

- Make sure you establish which people will be dealing with you on a day-to-day basis. There is nothing worse than being 'persuaded' by the firm's leading light, only to find that you never see that person again once the contract is won.
- Realism and common sense are far more desirable than ambitious promises about performance results, which are worthless. If the fund loses value through bad management, it is the council that will pick up the bill, not the manager.
- Don't make fee levels the overriding issue. At between 0.1 per cent and 0.3 per cent a year of fund value, they are tiny in comparison to the return differential between good and bad management. Some firms are prepared to operate on performance-related fees. Again, this can prove of limited advantage to the council. There is not a great deal of evidence that such fees achieve better performance, and the fees saved when performance is bad will never compensate for the actual investment losses suffered.
- Ask about the firm's approach to soft commission. It may secure commission from brokers on bargains undertaken on behalf of your fund. They may agree to redirect this by paying the fees of your performance measuring company, or some similar expense.

Once a manager is appointed, it's essential to put in place a proper contract which covers such matters as who within the authority is empowered to instruct the managers, the basis of any performance fees, or the tracking error permissible on an indexed fund. By the nature of investments, things can go seriously wrong from time to time, and it is essential that the respective responsibilities of council and manager are clearly set out. Otherwise it becomes very difficult to achieve redress for any manager mistakes or incompetence.

Performance measurement

Our analysis of investment management has thus far proceeded on Beatonesque lines: first catch your manager. We now look at how their results are monitored. At first, the process may seem unduly mathematical, but we hope to simplify it by appropriate diagrams and charts. If you are involved in assessing manager performance, then the sort of outside independent measurement that is available is priceless. It therefore pays to become conversant with the principles, otherwise you will be reliant on the manager's own sales pitch.

The comparison universe

The basis of performance data is to compare the individual council fund with the average of all the other funds covered by that particular survey. This could be the 'universe' of all council funds, or perhaps a wider combination of both council, other public sector, and company funds. This explains why performance reports appear at fixed quarter ends, as all the funds in the survey need to return comparable data.

The type of data you receive might be as set out on page 215. This is based on a simplified example of funds with only two types of assets: overseas and UK equities. See how the variation in performance between our funds and the universe is split between the effects of *asset allocation* and *stock selection*.

Let's work through the example of Tables 6.15 and 6.16 to see how these are worked out.

Table 6.15 deals with the asset allocation effect, and assumes there is no difference in stock selection performance. Note that the measures of fund allocation are always expressed in percentages, rather than the actual values of investments. This *normalisation* makes it straightforward to compare one fund with another.

Table 6.15: Calculation of effect of asset allocation

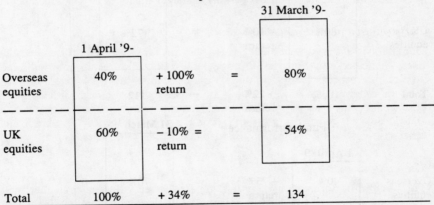

Universe performance

	1 April '9-			31 March '9-
Overseas equities	20%	+ 100% return	=	40%
UK equities	80%	− 10% return	=	72%
Total	100%	+ 12% return	=	112

Fund performance

	1 April '9-			31 March '9-
Overseas equities	40%	+ 100% return	=	80%
UK equities	60%	− 10% return	=	54%
Total	100%	+ 34%	=	134

Difference in performance in this example is 134—112 = 22 per cent. The effect of asset allocation for a particular class of asset is therefore defined as:

Difference from the universe allocation x Universe return for that asset

To find the effect of asset allocation for the fund as a whole, we simply total the effect for each category.

That is, in our example:

Overseas equity asset allocation effect = 20 x 100 = 20 per cent
UK equity asset allocation effect = 20 x 10 = 2 per cent.
Total asset allocation effect = 22 per cent.

In our example, the average of the universe is a 20/80 split. The overseas equities returned 100 per cent for the year (must be Japan again), and UK equities returned minus 10 per cent. These two factors, combined as in the Table, produced a total overall return of 12 per cent.

Our fund, however, was longer in overseas, being split 40/60. This was good management because the manager had directed more value into the better performing of the two assets available. At the same time, there was also less value in worse performing asset. Calculating these two effects as per the formula, we have an analysis of the effect of being under or overweight in each asset. Don't forget in a real example there would be more asset classes.

If you move to Table 6.16, we combine the effects of asset allocation and stock selection. The manager has still gone for a 40/60 split at the start of the year, but neither of the assets has made the universe return for the class. Overseas equities have returned only 75 per cent, for example, not the universe return of 100 per cent. So, even though the manager got the asset allocation decision right, the manager partly spoiled the result by bad stock selection within that category. On the worse performing UK equities though, the manager chose good stocks, because the return was above average.

Table 6.16: Calculation of effect of stock selection

Universe performance

	1 April '9-			31 March '9-
Overseas equities	20%	+ 100% return	=	40%
UK equities	80%	– 10% return	=	72%
Total	100%	+ 12% return	=	112

Fund performance

	1 April '9-			31 March '9-
Overseas equities	40%	+ 75% return	=	70%
UK equities	60%	+ 0% return	=	60%
Total	100%	+ 30%	=	130

The performance difference is thus now 18% (30% – 12%)

Of this, the effect of asset allocation we know would have been 22 per cent, had there not been stock selection differences. This is the calculation we made in the previous Table. The stock selection effect for the fund as a whole is thus the difference between the total variation (30 per cent) and the asset allocation effect (22 per cent), or –4 per cent.

Let us test this out against our definition of the stock selection effect for a particular category of asset:

Stock selection effect = Difference in return x fund allocation on asset

To calculate the effect for the fund as a whole, we simply add the effect for each of the asset categories.

Total stock selection effect in this example is –4 per cent.

That is:
Overseas equity stock selection effect = –25% x 40% = –10%
UK equity stock selection effect = 60% x 10% = 6%
Total effect therefore is –10% + 6% = –4%.

We are now able to summarise the total variation as follows:

Universe %	Fund %	Asset	Allocation %	Selection %
20	40	Overseas equity	+20%	–10%
80	60	UK equity	+2%	+6%
100	100			
12	30	Total return	+22%	–4%

Total variation +18%

This type of analysis is a very powerful tool. It might reveal one or more of the following.

- A manager who scores well on stock selection, but poorly on asset allocation. This may be a case for running this part of the fund on a fixed asset allocation.
- Weak performance in a particular asset category. This might suggest redirecting those particular assets to a new, specialist manager.
- Sometimes you can get analysis for different managers from the same investment house. You may be able to use this to get a change.

Performance statistics are like the camera that never lies. I heard of one manager who had a bad run over several quarters. He never tired of assuming a baffled expression at the investment panel and insisting that the performance was there: 'it just doesn't seem to be in the figures . . .'

You can measure performance against a different benchmark than the universe average. If you have set a manager the benchmark of outperforming the index by 1 per cent, this should be used as the basis of the performance figures.

Turnover and risk

Further statistics that can be measured are the rate of turnover in stocks, and risk. If you look at Table 6.17, we can see a fairly rudimentary graph of the risk to reward relationship experienced in investments. Basically, this is that the higher the potential reward, the greater the potential variation of that investment. Line A (dotted) on the graph is a neutral line. Line B (heavy) is a more risky combination of investments, with a higher gain in a rising market and a greater loss in a falling market.

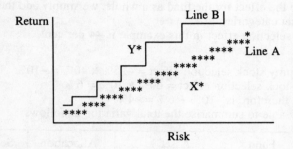

Table 6.17: Risk/reward

It is possible to analyse a fund's investments mathematically to calculate the underlying risk of a particular strategy combination (e.g. all equity would be high risk compared to 80 per cent equity/20 per cent gilt). It is then very informative to compare the actual return achieved with the risk inherent in the portfolio.

Look at point X on the graph. The return is below the heavy line. This means that the portfolio was structured with an unnecessarily high risk for the return achieved. Conversely, Y is above the line. That indicates good management because the return which would normally entail a higher risk has been achieved with a less risky portfolio.

Time-weighting and deciles

Two other practical points on performance measurement are worth examination. The first is the concept of time-weighted return. In our earlier examples, we measured return as simply the differences between opening value and closing value. The reality of fund operations is quite different. It might be, for example, that a manager achieves a 5 per cent return for a quarter. However, two-thirds of the way through the period the council asks for an equivalent sum back from the manager, as the investments must be realised to pay transfer values. This leaves the manager with the same value of investments at the end of the quarter as at the beginning. Clearly, it would be misleading to categorise this as a nil return achieved. Performance measurers therefore use a technique termed *the time-weighted rate of return (TWRR)*.

We need not go into the mathematics, but essentially the quarter is broken down into the little periods between each cashflow. A return is calculated for each, and these are combined to give a more reasonable measure of results.

A separate consideration in running the funds is the avoidance of sudden, large demands on managers for cash. If a large quantity of shares have to be sold in a thin market, the council may not get very good value. Councils should prepare a prediction of their cashflow needs for the year, and take any sums required as a regular monthly transfer.

Performance analysis often refers to a fund's results being in the 9th decile, and so on. This simply means that, if the results for all the surveyed universe were listed in order, yours would be in the next to last tenth. The decile statistic can be very misleading, because the degree of variation from the *median* (the middle of the order, not the mean or average) is often quite low. It sounds quite disappointing to be, say, in the seventh decile, but if results are tightly grouped, there is probably nothing to worry about.

The dangers of performance measurement

We have seen that performance measurement can give us a deeper perception of why a particular percentage return was achieved. Unfortunately, performance measurement has in some ways grown too successful for its own good.

The use of quarterly figures to assess manager ability is really a nonsense, as this is far too short a time period for proper judgement. Remember that long-term growth objective. So long as the fund gets into the right assets and stocks, a quarter's delay in getting on the train shouldn't really matter. A manager should be given at least a year to settle in. Unless something is seriously amiss, they need to be allowed a three-year tenure.

The performance statistics can drive investment panels into some ridiculous situations. What is not as well publicised as the results is the unavoidable degree of error arising in their preparation. Criticising a manager for being 0.2 per cent under a benchmark is ill-conceived, as the actual performance might be 0.1 per cent over if capable of exact measurement.

Performance statistics also cause an unhealthy concentration on relative as opposed to actual performance. Thus in the high-returning 1980s, managers were sacked for being 2 per cent under the index. This seems a bit nitpicking if the fund has still achieved 32 per cent in the year against the 34 per cent average. The moral seems to be that statistics should be used sensibly. If you are seeking to make decisions on the basis of them, think very carefully about what you are doing, and take expert guidance if possible.

In our final section of this chapter, we turn to actuarial valuation. Although this is perforce a rough guide, I think we will see that the actuarial process sets a very different perspective to investment. Small investment variations have a minimal effect on the 'bottom line' of the whole superannuation function: the council contribution.

Once you are in a position to start checking over your fund's actuarial valuation, you will justly be entitled to claim at least a passing knowledge of superannuation. More importantly, it will bring together the benefits and investment side of the fund and allow us to confirm the knowledge we have already gained.

Actuarial valuation

The objective of an actuarial valuation is to establish whether the fund's investments are in balance with its future obligations. Depending on the result, the council is required to pay in a greater or lesser contribution over the period to the next valuation. The regulations governing the valuations are set out in Table 6.18.

Table 6.18: Actuarial valuation requirements

All superannuation authorities to obtain an actuarial valuation of their fund's assets and liabilities as at 31 March 1992, and every third year thereafter. (Next valuations will be as at 31 March 1995, 31 March 1998, and so on.

The actuary's report must be obtained within 12 months of the valuation date.

The authority must then secure an actuary's certificate and apply the certified employer's contribution for a period of three years beginning 1 April following:

Valuation date	Financial years in which the valuation applies
31 March 1992	1993/94, 1994/95, 1995/96
31 March 1995	1996/97, 1997/98, 1998/99

The actuary must certify two different rates:

The common rate — This applies to all bodies which are members of the fund. In the case of the shire counties, for example, this would include the district councils.
The secondary rate — This increases or decreases a particular authority's contribution in the light of its special circumstances.

The common rate must be sufficient to ensure the fund is solvent.

Actuaries must have regard to the desirability of maintaining as nearly constant a common rate as possible.

As at November 1992, the principles of council actuarial valuations had just reverted to the 100 per cent solvency basis outlined above. For the 31 March 1989 valuation, where the rates certified first came into force on 1 April 1990, special rules were introduced by the Government. This was the date on which the first year's poll tax bills were issued. To reduce poll tax levels, it was decided by the government to value the funds on only a 75 per cent solvency basis. Accordingly, it was expected that councils would be able to reduce their contribution costs and keep the poll tax down.

A further change made in the 31 March 1989 valuation was to allow the annual inflation increases on pensions to be met from the fund investments. Before 1989, these costs had been met directly from revenue, meaning that the scheme was only partly a funded one.

The funds were thus required to meet increased costs, whilst reducing their solvency. The deficits that have accrued in many funds under this short-lived 75 per cent policy are now a significant problem.

In order to make sense of this period of change in the regulations, Table 6.19 lists the main changes for reference purposes.

Table 6.19: Fund valuation principles 1984 to 1992

DATE/BASIS	YEARS IN WHICH THE RATES APPLIED
31 March 1984 (quinquennial)	1985/86 to 1989/90
Funds to cover level of pensions as at retirement. Increase act payments charged straight to revenue.	
During the intervaluation period, some authorities undertook interim valuations. This allowed contribution rates to be reduced, given the excellent investment performance, outlined in Table 6.7.	
31 March 1989 (triennial)	1990/91, 1991/92, 1992/93
To cover all benefits, including inflation increases but on a 75 per cent solvency basis.	
31 March 1992 (triennial)	1993/94, 1994/95, 1995/96
To cover all benefits, including inflation increases, but now on a 100 per cent solvency basis.	

Actuarial valuation

To understand the principles behind valuation, let us consider the example set out in Table 6.20.

Table 6.20: Example of DCF cash flow calculation

(1) Year	(2) Discount Factor (%)	(3) Cash In £m	(4) Cash Out £m	(5) DCF Cash in £m	(6) DCF Cash out £m	(7) Net DCF value £m
0	100.00	1.000	1.000	1.000	1.000	1.000
1	90.00	1.600	2.000	1.440	1.800	−0.360
2	81.00	1.500	0.800	1.215	0.648	0.567
3	72.90	0.500	1.100	0.365	0.802	−0.437
4	65.61	0.300	0.500	0.197	0.328	−0.131
5	59.05	1.000	0.500	0.590	0.295	0.295
		5.900	5.900	4.807	4.873	−0.066

If we look at our example, we have in columns 3 and 4 a set of predicted cash flows over our 6-year period (£5.9m in, £5.9m out). However, we wish to express this as a single present value. To do this, we multiply each year's actual cash figure by the relevant discount percentage (column 2). This has the effect of giving greater value to items paid or received in the earlier years.

The logic underlying this approach is that income received in the earlier years of the period could be invested to earn interest and dividends. Thus by the end of the 6-year period, it would have produced a higher value than the same sum of income received in a later year.

Applied to the actuarial valuation, the DCF leaves open the question of in precisely which year a sum is received or paid. We simply know that if it is later, it will need to be a higher cash figure than if it is earlier.

To express this mathematically, we reduce the value of the later years rather than increase the value of the earlier ones. The effect is the same, but doing so enables us to operate the calculations more easily.

In our example, the discount rate is 11.1 per cent, which produces a 90 per cent value for cash flows in the second year. The next discount rate is 81 per cent (90 per cent of 90 per cent), and so on. Note that DCF can produce a different result to simply adding outflows and inflows. In our example the actual cash flows are expected to balance (£5.9m in, £5.9m out). Under DCF there is a 0£.066m deficiency (total of column 7).

Example of actuarial valuation

The valuation is calculated on a *discounted cash flow* basis. It would be impossibly complicated to make the valuation by trying to plan the cash flow for the next 60 years or more. Thus all the inflows and outflows are reduced to *present values* by discounting at the *valuation rate of interest*. How this works is shown in the following simplified example.

Actuarial assumptions

Before calculating the present value of assets and liabilities, the actuary needs to make assumptions about various factors shown in Table 6.21.

Using all the above assumptions, data as to the scheme's membership and pensioners (age, salary, and so on) and its investments is fed into a computer program. This produces the type of result shown in Table 6.22.

Let's work through Table 6.22 in detail. The calculation is really in three parts. Perversely, line 7 is the easiest place to start. 100 per cent is actuarial terminology for the fact that the council needs to contribute 100 per cent of whatever the employees pay in. Thus if the council payroll is £100m a year, and employees pay in £5m, the council too must contribute £5m.

The 100 per cent in line 7 is a rate for future service. This means that, whatever the current surplus or deficiency of a fund, the rate of 100 per cent should build up enough investments to cover all the new pension entitlements earned by employees as they pay into the scheme.

What though of the current pensioners, and the pensions that employees have already earned? These values are shown in lines 1, 2 and 3. Now we see the merit of the DCF method. Were the calculation not abbreviated in this way, we would be faced with a huge cash flow exercise running over decades. Given our assumptions, the current value of these benefits (which are already in pay, or certain to be paid at some future date) is set at £400m (line 4). By comparison, the value of the fund's investments is currently £375m, or a deficit of £25m. A deficit of this scale could quite easily have arisen by natural variation from the statistical assumptions used in the previous valuation. It might have been, for example, that the expected investment return was not achieved because of an underperforming equity market. We should also note that the following the change back to 100 per cent solvency (see Table 6.19), many funds are carrying deficits in the 31 March 1992 valuation.

Table 6.21

Factor	Range of assumptions
Inflation	On historical experience, the assumed rate is usually between 4 and 6 per cent.
Pension increases	These are virtually identical to RPI, and the same rate is usually used.
Earnings growth	This is an important factor because it will affect two aspects:
	— the retirement salaries achieved by current employees
	— the rate that employee contributions into the fund rise
	It is usual to assume that earnings will outpace inflation by between 1.5 per cent and 2.5 per cent a year. (Assumed growth is 5 per cent to 8.5 per cent a year.)
Dividend growth and investment returns	These will determine the income available to the fund in future years. A total return of between 8 per cent and 10 per cent a year is usually used, with dividend growth accounting for between 4 per cent and 5 per cent.
Retirements, life expectancy, etc.	The actuary should take into account any known abnormal incidence of retirements. National statistics can be used for the more cheerful factors of the calculation, such as how long current pensioners are expected to survive to draw their pensions.

Table 6.22: Valuation of XYZ superannuation fund as at 31.3.92

Past service liabilities	£m
1. Contributors	140
2. Pensioners	220
3. Preserved pensioners	40
4. Total liabilities	400
5. Total assets	375
6. Surplus/(Deficit)	(25)
7. Future service rate	100%
8. Past service adjustment (Clear over 12 years)	25%
9. Total contribution rate	125%

(Valuation assumptions)

Dividend growth 4 per cent a year
Inflation 4 per cent a year
Earnings growth 6 per cent a year

In order to recover this deficit over a reasonable period, an additional rate of 25 per cent is calculated to be sufficient to clear the deficit in 12 years. Remember that the actuary is required to keep as constant a contribution rate as possible. If the deficit were eliminated more quickly, then a much higher contribution rise would be forced on the council.

Let's now look at how slight changes in the actuarial assumptions will vary the council contribution rate, by looking at Table 6.23.

Table 6.23: Effect of varying actuarial assumptions

Item	Option 1 (Original)	Option 2 (Medium to high investment return)	Option 3 (Clear deficit more quickly)	Option 4 (High investment assumption)
Liabilities	400	400	400	400
Assets	375	400	375	425
Surplus/(deficit)	(25)	–	(25)	25
Future service rate	100%	100%	100%	100%
Adjust deficit/(surplus)	25%	–	75%	(75%)
Council contribution	125%	100%	175%	25%

The first option in this table is the original valuation whose assumptions we examined in Table 6.22. You will recall that our investment value (or assets) were based on a DCF of the expected future income. This assumed a 4 per cent dividend growth. If, instead, we assumed a 4.5 per cent growth, our existing assets would become more valuable. This is reflected in the higher value of £400m in option 2 of Table 6.23. It is important to remember that the asset value in an actuarial valuation is not necessarily the actual market value of the investments at the valuation date. Suppose, for example, the actuary considers the market value is unusually depressed, and the investments therefore high yielding. The asset value used in the calculation might be higher, because the actuary's DCF (based on a lower standard yield) will come to a higher value.

Were the adjustment between options 1 and 2 to be agreed and accepted between actuary and council, the council's top-up over the next three years would fall by 25 per cent of the employee's rate (from 125 per cent to 100 per cent). This would save it about 1.5 per cent of its payroll cost. The actuarial assumptions are thus no mere technicality.

Option 3 demonstrates a reverse effect. This writes off the deficit by the next triennial valuation, lifting the overall contribution rate to 175 per cent. There is a variety of practice between authorities as to how quickly deficits are eliminated. This is linked to the actuary's desire to maintain as constant a rate as possible. However, instances could arise of conflict between shire counties (who run the funds), and their district subscribers as to the best rate to eliminate a deficit. Whereas one tier might have the budget to eliminate the deficit as quickly as possible, this could cause unnecessary problems for the other tier who would appreciate a more leisurely adjustment.

Option 4 is a yet more extreme option (though still realistic), which changes the deficit round to a surplus. Here the rate of dividend growth is an optimistic 5 per cent. This lifts the asset value to £425m, a £25m surplus. If this is credited back to the fund over the next three years, only a minimal 25 per cent contribution arises.

These examples show the irrelevance of mere day-to-day investment fluctuations in the light of the longer term actuarial view. They also advise very careful attention to the basis and assumptions of any actuarial valuation.

Summary - pensions and investments

Given the scale and complexity of our subject, this has been only an introduction to the main issues. Whether you are simply a contributor, or have a more direct interest in the running of the funds, you now ought to be able to deal on more equal terms with finance and investment professionals.

7 Competition

In this chapter we look at the financial and accounting effects of competition on council services. There are many functions which councils may provide by direct labour only if they have won a contract competition with outside firms. These include building work to council property, or refuse collection. The process is termed *compulsory competitive tendering*, or CCT.

But many other activities and functions are now also being operated under a market discipline which is self-imposed. The contracts which control these markets are known as *service level agreements*, or SLAs.

This chapter will provide you with a fuller understanding of both forms of competition, including how to bid for work as an internal manager, and the control of contracts once they have been won.

Compulsory competitive tendering

Before 1980, there was no legal requirement for councils to test the cost of direct labour work against outside contractors. Councils did, however, make extensive use of contractors for a number of reasons:

- *to cover unusual peak workloads, so that councils would not have to carry an excessive workforce;*
- *for specialist work, where it would not be viable for a council to establish its own permanent unit;*
- *in some councils there was a political disinclination to place undue reliance on direct labour.*

In many of the metropolitan authorities though, a strong political commitment to direct labour meant that only a small proportion of work was let exernally.

The 1980 Local Government, Planning and Land Act

The act introduced CCT for four different categories of building and engineering work. The main measures introduced were as follows.

- Councils have to quote DLO prices, or at least the method by which they will be calculated, in advance of carrying out work. (Under traditional accounting procedures DLOs simply charged whatever it cost them to carry out work, with an on cost to cover overheads.)
- Work of types or values specified by the secretary of state has to be competed for. The only work currently exempted from competition is:

—highways jobs under £25,000 (provided these total less than 40% of all highways work);
—emergency work (such as making safe a collapsing building);
—winter gritting;
—extensions (basically of up to 10 per cent of the value) to existing jobs already won in competition.

- DLOs are required to earn a 5 per cent rate of return on capital employed for each of four categories of work. Failure to achieve the return in successive years enables the secretary of state to order the DLO to stop doing the failed type of work.

Categories of work under the 1980 Act

- *General highways, including new construction and maintenance;*
- *new construction over £50,000;*
- *new construction under £50,000;*
- *maintenance work.*

Since the act's coming into force, competition-free allowances granted to councils by the DoE have reduced or disappeared entirely for all categories of work. There was some gamesmanship in the mid-1980s as to exactly what constituted 'work', and thus fell under the statutory controls. An oft-cited case revolved around whether painting was maintenance work. (It was.)

CIPFA has played a major role in the interpretation of CCT law and the operation of DLO accounts, through its code of practice for compulsory competition. This is used by authorities to determine their detailed accounting procedures, and is claimed to have prevented prescriptive DoE regulations in this area.

The effect of CCT on councils' internal structure

In the pre-CCT period, council building departments were often organised as a subsidiary section of the housing department. Similarly, highways works units would come under the control of the chief officer also responsible for scheme design, and other highways functions.

In order to operate the charging rules of the 1980 Act, most councils decided to split the affected departments down into separate *client* and *contractor* units. After all, it requires a strong mental discipline to settle fairly a dispute with oneself. These new structures have proved very helpful in:

—clarifying precise objectives for the service (e.g. what new roads are needed, rather than how much work the highways works unit wants);
—enabling construction and maintenance sections to concentrate on precisely those functions, rather than a wider service role. So, for example, a DLO should have the management information system it needs to run its operations and charge clients. It ought not to have to bear additional costs to collect client-side information needs.

This method of structuring departments has had a continuing and increasing influence on many council functions.

The 1988 Local Government Act

In 1988, CCT was extended to a further eight categories of work (see Table 7.1).

Table 7.1: Categories of work under the 1988 Act

Work	Financial Target		National timetable		Contract period	
	5% rate of return	Break even	First batch of work	Last date for 100% to be CCT tested	Min (years)	Max
Refuse collection	X		Aug '89	Jan '92	5	7
Cleaning of buildings		X	Jan '89	Jan '92	3 LEAs 4 other	4 LEAs 6 other
Other cleaning (i.e. street)	X		Aug '89	Jan '92	4	6
School and welfare catering	X		Aug '89	Jan '92	4	5
Other catering	X		Aug '89	Jan '92	4	6
Grounds maintenance	X		Jan '90	Jan '94	3 LEA 4 other	4 LEA 6 other
Vehicle repair and maintenance	X		Aug '89	Jan '92	4	6
Sport and leisure management		X	Jan '92	Jan '93	4	6

- Whilst these are all separate work categories in legislation, this does not oblige councils to set up separate DSOs for each. (Though they must calculate the separate statutory financial target for each.)
- Emergency work is excluded from controls.

- There is exemption if the value of a council's annual workload in any one category is less than £100,000.
- In Inner London, dates were later for some of the work transferred from ILEA to the boroughs.

The Local Government Act 1992

This act provides the framework under which CCT may be extended to professional services. Government is still considering the precise extent and timetable for professional CCT, though activities most likely to be affected include computing and architectural services. In early 1993, the progress of CCT was called into question by disputes over whether European Community law protecting transferred workers' rights applied to CCT contracts. If it were held to apply, this might stop contract-winning companies taking on ex-council workers because they would be forced to continue expensive council conditions of service.

How charges are made for CCT work

There are two main methods in use to charge for CCT work. A method needs to be chosen at the planning stage of letting a CCT contract, as it forms the basis on which tenders are invited and evaluated. The methods are as follows.

Lump sum

The council specifies the total work required under a contract, and the tenderer offers a single price bid.
Examples of lump sum contracts are:

— a cleaning contract comprising a list of the properties to be cleaned, and how often the various types of cleaning should be done (e.g. carpets vacuumed daily, desks dusted weekly);
— for grounds maintenance, a list of playing fields and how often they should be mowed.

Lump sum tenders are easy to evaluate, and the client department should know very accurately how much the service will cost each year. Problems with lump sum contracts include how to deal with work not foreseen when the contract was planned (such as newly acquired premises which need to be added to the cleaning schedule). If the lump sum is supported by a priced *bill of quantities*, then it is easier to negotiate such variations.

Schedule of rates

A list of individual standard jobs is issued to tenderers. There is no commitment to how much work will be ordered against each standard item in the schedule (though a fair indication is usually given). Tenderers are asked to quote for the whole schedule in one of two ways.

- *A guide price is provided for each item, and the tenderer must quote a single percentage discount or premium which will be applied against the whole schedule.*
- *Tenderers are asked to quote a price for each individual item. Councils assess which is the best tender by multiplying the expected workload by the tendered price for each item, and then comparing total costs for the whole schedule.*

An example of a schedule of rates contract would be a building maintenance contract, where tenders might be given a list of hundreds or even thousands of standard building jobs (e.g. 'fit new door', or 'reglaze window').

Schedule of rates contracts are useful when the precise amount of work that will be needed under a contract is uncertain (perhaps housing repairs, or vehicle maintenance). Also, because work is charged in detail, the contracts are easier to analyse for management information purposes.

A disadvantage of the schedule of rates approach is the higher volumes of charging information that need to be processed.

Rate of return calculations

Under the legislation, there is an important distinction between the DLO or DSO accounts themselves and the rate of return calculation (see Table 7.2).

The figure of surplus or deficit shown in the council's main accounts will not necessarily be the same as the rate of return achieved. That is because, at the time the legislation was introduced, current cost accounting (CCA) was in vogue. This was a method of adjusting accounts to show the effects of inflation, which was introduced in company accounts to prevent the traditional historical cost accounts from exaggerating profitability. It was soon abandoned as unworkable, especially as the rate of UK inflation was no longer high enough to undermine accounting presentation, but at least, in DLO rate of return calculations, CCA lives on.

More interesting than the CCA adjustments are the grey areas of expenditure and income which can make all the difference as to whether a set of DLO accounts are in surplus or deficit. Let's look at a few examples.

Redundancy

It has long been a source of contention with DLO managers that, when staff are made redundant to improve profitability, this is self-defeating because the DLO accounts must bear the costs of redundancy payments. If DLOs could charge these costs to another account of the council, their profitability would be enhanced. The CIPFA code's ruling is that in two special circumstances redundancy costs need not be charged to the DLO.

—If the staff made redundant were doing a category of work for which the DLO has now lost all contracts.
—Suppose, for example, that a building DLO was doing both maintenance and new construction work. It loses the tender for new

Table 7.2: DLO accounts and the rate of return calculation

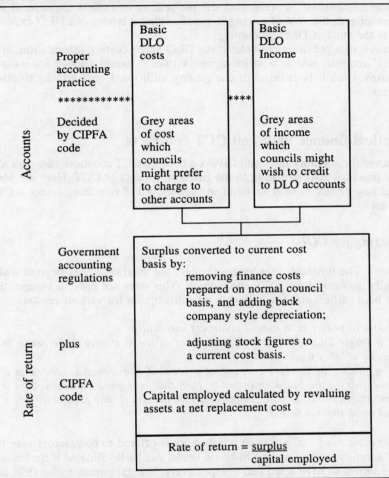

construction, and has to make staff redundant. Those costs will be charged not to the remaining maintenance operation (perhaps driving it into failing to meet the rate of return), but can be met by the accounts that were clients of the new construction DLO. (The council still has to meet the costs, but it may be politically expedient to save the DLO at the expense of a higher reported cost for other services.)

—Redundancy costs for staff shed before the DLO commenced that category of work.

Client costs

There is often no clear demarcation line between what is a client expense (and need not be borne by the DLO accounts), and what is a contractor expense. The code goes into some detail on this. If, for example, a schedule of rates used in a tender competition is pre-priced, the pre-pricing is a client expense. If it is not pre-priced, the cost of pricing it in submitting a tender is a DLO expense. This is the stuff of DLO accounting!

To revisit a previous example, if the DLO keeps costing information, at its clients' request, which is more complex than it would choose for its own purposes, then it is entitled to charge any additional cost arising to client accounts.

Practical finance issues on CCT contracts

Whatever the statutory rules and CIPFA advice on CCT accounts, there are also many practical issues relating to the financial aspects of CCT. Here are some of the key points to bear in mind in preparing and operating under a CCT contract.

Preparing for CCT

Timing   The timetables set by government are legal deadlines beyond which councils may not delay CCT competition. This does not prevent competition being held earlier, and councils may take this option for various reasons.

- *Political policy is to award contracts externally.*
- *If a single DLO does several categories of work, it may make sense to tender all this work in one go.*
- *The timing of tenders can affect prices. If, for example, there is a recession in the building industry, then that is a good time to secure a low external bid. Conversely this may be the worst time for the in-house bid to be market tested.*

Tender conditions   The way in which work is offered to contractors may fall under scrutiny, and a winning in-house tender can be invalidated if the council can be shown to have acted anti-competitively. In legal parlance (the 1992 act) this is known as 'conduct which has the effect of restricting, preventing or distorting competition, or is likely to have that effect'.

Whether or not particular tender conditions are anti-competitive may be assessed retrospectively. If there is very little serious external interest in tendering, this might indicate something wrong with the way the work has been offered. In June 1992, the DoE issued draft regulations proposing strict controls over the way tenders were prepared and evaluated.

Tender conditions which could stray into anti-competitiveness include the following.

The way the work is packaged   In the early stages of CCT, one council fulfilled its competition obligations by tendering its entire housing maintenance in one-day duration contracts. This extreme ploy illustrates how the packaging of work can be a deterrent to possible bidders. Factors to consider are:

—the council's work as a whole might well be subdivided into geographical areas, or smaller contracts
—generalised and wide-ranging categories of work such as building maintenance could be broken down over specialist trades.

Use of council assets Contracts may be offered on the basis that the winner will operate the contract using council assets and equipment. It might be unduly restricting to suggest the successful contractor must buy these outright. After all, what private company would want to take over a worn out fleet of refuse collectors.

A more subtle approach is to allow the winning contractor free use of the assets. These then become a clientside cost. Their depreciation will not be charged against the CCA return, and their value will not count in the capital employed (see box).

A building contract is run from a depot valued at £2m, which has a 20 year life. Other capital employed is £2m, making a total of £4m.

The DLO is expected to achieve a nil rate of return on the contract after charging CCA depreciation on the depot of £100,000 a year.

$$\text{Rate of return} = \frac{\text{CCA surplus}}{\text{capital employed}} = \frac{0}{£2m} = 0$$

But if the depot becomes a client cost:

New CCA surplus = Old surplus + depreciation on depot

The depreciation which was charged in the original calculation is added back as it is now a client cost.

So new CCA surplus = 0 + £100,000 = £100,000

New capital employed is:

Old total less depot = £4m – £2m = £2m

So new rate of return = $\dfrac{100,000}{£2m}$ = 5 per cent

Such a decision would have to be made before the contract was let. It does illustrate how a different accounting treatment of precisely identical circumstances can make all the difference.

Information systems

Preparation for CCT usually entails a comprehensive review of information systems. As this coincides with other workload peaks such as departmental restructuring, and preparing the in-house bid, mistakes can be made. This is a heavily marketed area, and the sales or demonstration copy of a system may not reveal the true operational quality.

- The system needs to interface effectively with the council's main accounting system, if only so that DLO charges can be made promptly and accurately.
- It should be capable of dealing with the relevant volume of transactions. If, for example, repairs orders are being placed through terminals, nothing is worse than a slow system with long waiting times for reaction to prompts. Conversely, an unnecessarily powerful solution will be an overhead burden on the financial target required.
- It's easy to become carried away with information demands, and different types of analysis that the system must offer. Experience shows that the more sophisticated elements of systems are often left unused, even though these are the very facilities that swing the decision at the procurement stage.

Preparing the in-house bid

Detailed knowledge of a service is a tremendous advantage in bidding for the work under CCT. Tenderers might be asked say to include a weekend emergency service in their price. If council managers know full well that this facility is never called upon, the in-house tender can be priced accordingly, but an outsider might assume there would be numerous Saturday night calls for work. They might thus overprice their bid, and lose the tender competition, even though their price for routine work would have been cheaper.

The government is clearly concerned that DLO staff should not be able to secure an unfair advantage in future CCT competitions. Under the 1992 draft regulations, any officer (except a chief officer) or councillor that works for the DLO or sits on its controlling committee will be prevented from taking part in certain activities. These include:

- *selecting the number of contractors to tender and who those contractors are;*
- *issuing the tender documents;*
- *receiving and evaluating the tenders.*

A different area where the role of council staff needs to be carefully monitored is if one of the CCT bids is some form of management buy-out. Once such an interest is either declared or becomes apparent, the potential contractors must be excluded from determining the shape and form of the new contract. If not, they could potentially be writing their own pay cheques.

Tender evaluation

However the in-house bid is prepared, and whatever the tender conditions, the most controversial stage of a CCT contract competition is often the evaluation of the tenders. External bidders and the council will often have different views as to how the result should be decided.

As far as outsiders are concerned, price alone ought to be the consideration. Moreover, if the council has imposed any tender conditions that are not strictly relevant to the work in question, the price of such extras ought to be disregarded in assessing who is the cheapest.

Suppose, for example, a council, anxious to promote job opportunities in its area, insisted that any successful tenderer would be required to include a certain number of apprentices in the contract workforce. Then any additional cost to the company in meeting that provision should not be allowed to disadvantage it in comparison to the in-house bid.

From the council's point of view, however, there are all manner of costs which it might wish to add to the basic outside tender to ensure a like-for-like comparison with the in-house bid. Suppose the loss of the in-house contract would lead to redundancies. Although some costs would fall to the superannuation fund, revenue accounts would have to bear payments in lieu of notice and the costs in future years of some enhanced pension rights.

If these increased costs were £50,000 a year, the council might argue that any outside tender needs to be at least £50,000 a year lower than the in-house bid before it is better value to the council. The more associated costs are brought into the calculation, the more difficult it is for an outside tenderer to win. Accordingly, government intentions are to limit the factors allowed in tender evaluation as follows.

The pay-back period

A method is prescribed which:

—will favour an external bid if its total cost is lower over a notional ten year period (in reality the contract period could be much shorter);
—converts the difference between in-house and external bids to a present value, and compares this to the present value of extraneous costs;
—sets the discount factors councils may use in the calculation.

Redundancy costs

Statutory redundancy payments may be included in extraneous costs. The council should only include staff who would have continued to be employed had the council won the contract. So, if the DLO has had to make staff redundant to achieve its tendered figure, it is not allowed to use those costs to improve the competitiveness of its own bid.

Payments in lieu of notice will only be allowed in the calculation if the new contractor actually began work before the end of the notice period.

Disabled staff

Many councils pride themselves on their progressive employment policies. It is intended to limit extraneous costs to the extra cost that has arisen in comparison to an able-bodied person, and to those persons relevant to the completion of the contract.

Apprentices

Councils will be able to treat the costs of organising an apprentice scheme as an extraneous cost.

Costs which councils may not use to discount their own bids

Some councils add in the 5 per cent rate of return that councils are expected to achieve. This may soon be forbidden.

Other councils bring in frozen entitlements to holiday pay. This too is likely to be prevented.

Contract monitoring

Once a CCT contract has come into operation, its financial position must be monitored as with any other large contract. These are some of the factors.

Inflation increases

Most contracts provide for prices to be updated in accordance with a standard index, such as the RPI or a specialist trade index. These increases may be substantial, and it pays to check thoroughly that contractors are not overclaiming or allowing themselves a generous interpretation of the contract provisions. Many contractors are extremely claims conscious, so take care.

Non-scheduled items

Given the scale of council activities, and the long duration of CCT contracts, new work usually arises that is not covered in the original contract. Ideally, a contract should incorporate clauses as to how such problems are resolved. Any disputes as to charges need to be promptly resolved, as the exception rate of charging (often based on staff time claimed by the contractor) is usually higher than the equivalent contract rate.

Performance penalties

Councils should be as zealous as contractors in maximising their financial position under an agreement. Monitoring arrangements can easily pay for themselves in the shape of recouped charges. Performance monitoring should not be confined to the staff ordering against the contract on a daily basis, as they may develop a tolerant attitude to the friendly contractor.

Contractor payments

Depending on the nature of the contract, various control difficulties may arise.

- *It can be difficult to establish the exact expenditure under a schedule of rates type contract. Some form of commitment recording is advisable, as by the time charges are actually invoiced it may be too late to correct a large variation from budget. One possibility is to use an outside expert, or quantity surveyor to keep payments under a rigorous control.*

- *Contractors should be allowed a maximum period in which to claim charges. They are notorious for timing their financial demands to suit their own financial agenda.*

Budgeting for CCT services

Theoretically, clients should find it much easier to budget for CCT contracts. But if the contract is demand led, such as a transport repair contract, clients still need to operate normal budget controls.

From the DLO point of view, budgets need to be flexible and are closer to the type of budgets used in commercial operations. These are points to bear in mind.

- Contract profits need to cover overheads, both within the DLO itself and in the form of charges from outside departments.
- Close links need to be maintained with finance as year-end accounting adjustments can wreak havoc on assumed financial results. You may, for example, be expected to provide for likely losses on incomplete contracts.
- Clients need to be kept in the picture as to likely charges, and the price of contract variations. These can degenerate into accounts closing disputes, where the limiting factor is time rather than the merits of the DLO's case.
- Remember the rate of return calculation is not the same as the accounting surplus, so there needs to be a budget for this objective too.

CCT for professional services

In 1991, the government published the Citizen's Charter, promising to promote increased efficiency in council services by further extension of the CCT approach, but this time sights were set squarely on the professional functions within councils, including of course finance.

Not surprisingly, this concept met with some opposition from the relevant professional bodies and associations. Earlier functions subject to CCT had traditionally been carried out with a mix of contractor/in-house provision. With the exception of architectural and engineering services, the central professional functions had been run entirely by council staff in most councils. How would an outside contractor be able to deliver the politically sensitive advice councillors had come to expect from loyal chief officers?

As Table 7.3 shows, government acknowledged there were certain of the professional areas into which it would not be prudent to extend CCT but, at the same time, whole fields of professional activity could be placed in the hands of outside contractors.

In 1993, a clearer CCT timetable was set, with legal (contracts let by October 1995) and competing (July 1996) amongst the first services for competition. There were indications that the planned 1991 percentages might be raised. Two proposals which would have greatly hampered councils' discretion over CCT

Table 7.3: Professional CCT proposals in the 1991 'competing for quality' white paper

Function	Proposed CCT	Traditional use of outside contractors
Architectural services and engineering	All aspects of the function suitable for CCT. This would include design work, and project management.	Most councils use consultant architects or quantity surveyors to a greater or lesser degree. There would appear to be no major impediment to extending CCT to these functions.
Property management	All aspects suitable, ranging from devising the council's property strategy down to providing security for premises.	Councils often restrict the use of external firms to the more complex, specialist areas. Small local firms can be a cost-effective method of marketing and selling properties.
Corporate and administrative services	Corporate strategy work, and member and committee services are too closely allied to the democratic process to be externalised. Printing of council papers and typing or word-processing services are suitable. About 15 per cent of all work might be a suitable level to pitch the first tranche of competition.	Not usually an area in which there is a high degree of work placed externally.
Legal services	Corporate advice, and ensuring the propriety of the council's affairs are not suitable for CCT. About 33 per cent of legal work should be exposed to competition, particularly in the areas of litigation and conveyancing.	Legal work is often a well-guarded fiefdom within councils, though use is made of external solicitors for specialist work, or dealing with peak workload on process-driven work such as dealing with right-to-buy conveyancing.
Financial services	Financial planning and corporate accounting are not suitable for CCT. Areas such as internal audit and cash collection are. About 25 per cent of	The use of external firms for income collection is growing rapidly, but their use in areas such as internal audit is still at a low level.

Table 7.3: (continued)

	finance work should be subject to competition in the first instance.	
Personnel	Corporate strategic work is not suitable, such as employee relations. Training and recruitment are. About 25 per cent of the work is suitable for CCT.	Many councils use an external recruitment agency for particular categories of post, and external trainers in a similar way. Few have outsourced such functions completely
Computing	All aspects of the function, including systems development, are suitable. Up to 80 per cent of the work could be subject to competition.	There is a growing market over the last few years in facilities management (FM) contracts.

contracts appear to have been abandoned: the double envelope tender system, and the introduction of statutory trading accounts.

Double envelope would have processed tenders rather like the awarding of TV franchises. Councils would have been asked to set a *quality threshold*, and any tenderer failing to meet this would have been eliminated from the competition, but for tenderers passing the quality threshold, price alone would have determined success. As most of the professional services intended for CCT are difficult to specify methodically, the government later conceded that councils could consider price and quality at all stages of tender evaluation.

The prescription of statutory trading accounts for professional CCT services was also shelved, though councils will be expected to publish various information about their professional functions. This could be of use to potential tenderers.

Finance and CCT

Some aspects of finance department work are likely to prove more appropriate for competition than others. One particular likelihood is computing, though this is not a finance department responsibility in every council. Not only is there a ready market of contractors able to bid for the work, but the function promises various advantages under external operation. An external company, if able to secure contracts from a number of councils, could ensure its computing facilities were used to peak efficiency. With an individual council's in-house operation, it is unlikely that computing power will be perfectly matched to the number of applications currently in use.

A further saving available to external contractors is the ability to run several councils' applications, say a payroll, for the cost of a single software licence. As individual operators, each council would have its own licence fee to pay.

Many treasurers acknowledge systems development to be not without its problems. Hence the chance of externalising the function, and making service quality and delivery somebody else's problem has its attractions. Similar arguments apply to other no-win responsibilities such as benefits and council tax administration. As large companies each gain dozens of contracts, it will be difficult for the small district council to match their in-depth knowledge of the function and economy of operation. Moreover, expert staff are likely to be attracted to the firms with greater security of employment, as employment with a council is at the mercy of a sudden death contract competition.

In the area of internal audit, the benefits of externalisation may be less clearly defined. Audit is a powerful source of information on council activities, and often provides the first warning of wider financial management problems. Many treasurers would be reluctant to allow this valuable resource to pass into external control but, for smaller councils, where the audit section numbers one or two staff, the expertise offered by accounting firms must seem attractive.

Whatever timetable for professional CCT emerges, it will be interesting to see to what changes it effects on the traditional power of central department chief officers.

A CCT checklist

We end this section of the chapter with a brief checklist of CCT issues to consolidate our knowledge.

- The range of functions covered by CCT is wide. The 1980 Act rules cover building and engineering work, and the 1988 Act extended CCT to other manual labour areas such as refuse collection and grounds maintenance.
- There are statutory rules as to the timing and duration of 1988 Act contracts. For building and engineering work, councils have greater local discretion.
- Statutory financial targets have been set for council DLOs and DSOs. The type of target depends on the category of work undertaken. The targets are either to break even or to earn a 5% rate of return on capital employed.
- The rate of return calculation uses special accounting rules. The return may be different from the surplus shown in the DLO's accounts.
- If a DLO fails to achieve the statutory financial target, particularly in successive years, the DoE may order the council to cease carrying out that category of work.
- The packaging of work for CCT is a key factor in the competitiveness of the in-house bid. Councils should be able to demonstrate they have not acted anti-competitively.
- Effective DLO management information systems are important for the control of CCT contracts. They need to be operated carefully to ensure that the DLO's up-to-date financial position is known.
- New government rules will prescribe what factors may be considered in evaluating rival tenders. Councils' ability to weigh extraneous costs, such as redundancy payments to contract-losing staff, will be strictly controlled.

- The client department for a CCT contract needs to exercise budget control, particularly where the charges are demanded, as under a schedule of rates type contract.
- Government plans to expose professional services to competition are not yet completely defined, though voluntary externalisation is becoming more prevalent in problem service areas such as income collection or bendfits administration.

Service level agreements

Competition, as we have seen, is an established force in shaping council services. A parallel trend has become equally deep rooted, and this is the use of *service level agreements or SLAs*.

The popularity of SLAs marks a long-term change in the accountability of councils' central professional departments. Prior to 1980, central department costs were widely treated as a cost in their own right. But new CIPFA accounting arrangements from 1981 onwards required central costs to be charged to main services in council's published accounts. This was perhaps the worst of both worlds, as service managers often had little say over the costs their accounts had to bear. So, by 1988, CIPFA was espousing the SLA concept as a means to complete the circle of accountability.

What is an SLA (service level agreement)?

An SLA is an internal contract between the provider and user (or customer) of any service.

The SLA will specify some or all of:

—what services will be provided;
—the quality of service that will be provided, and the expected volume of service;
—how the internal recharge for the service will be calculated;
—how any complaints or deficiencies in the service will be dealt with, and how any disputes will be resolved.

Examples of finance functions which lend themselves to the SLA approach include payroll, internal audit, and creditor payment.

The main benefit of an SLA is that central and service managers decide jointly the central support that is needed (and can be afforded!) for front-line services.

Some councils have developed SLAs to a high degree. Central departments are dependent on the demand from service departments to finance their operations. Service departments have the power to reject the internal supplier and choose an outside source.

The growth in SLAs since the mid-1980s must prompt concerns at the haste with which they have been embraced. As one chief executive asked, was it entirely appropriate that so many senior council managers devoted much of their time to 'playing shops'? But as they have become so widespread, it is important to be conversant with the mechanics of their operation. In the remainder of this chapter, we look at how to get the best out of SLAs.

Introducing SLAs into a council

The framework for SLAs

The implementation of an SLA system is far from being a formality. Much of the difficulty arises from the various strategies adopted by managers once it is realised that real money and service influence are at stake.

In one council, the process of SLA introduction led to a curious result. Under council rules, central charges in year 1 were to be non-negotiable. These charges would form the budgets held by service departments in year 2, when they would have real power over the value of central services purchased.

As the first year charges were buying year 2 spending power which could be used for pet spending projects instead, departments were eager to maximise their costs. Negotiating teams from the central departments were thus pleasantly surprised at the alacrity with which proposed charges were accepted.

This example demonstrates the need for clear and sensible rules to control the SLA process. At the same time, it is important to avoid excessive paperwork and bureaucracy; the whole reason for having SLAs in the first place. The dangers of overcomplexity can be seen by taking the case of a council with five central departments and five service departments. That would mean no less than 25 central/service SLAs (on the assumption that each service department uses each central department's services), and ten central/central SLAs (assuming again that each central department uses the services of every other). This basic set of 35 SLAs could be augmented by intra-departmental SLAs, say, between a department's own administration section and its operational units.

Clearly, unless the SLA process is operated with a good deal of common sense, management energies can be wasted on fragmenting the delivery of professional functions to no good effect. Here are some of the key issues which might be covered in setting up an SLA system.

Timetable

Ideally SLAs should be integrated into the budget process, and last for one or more financial years. If some central departments become more advanced with SLAs than others, this could cause unfairness in calculating central budgets. All departments ought to be under the same pressure of competition. A common timetable for all departments is a big advantage, though it should make a realistic allowance for the effort entailed in preparing and negotiating SLAs. This usually comes as an added bonus on top of managers' ordinary work. Given the considerable effect of SLAs in operation, some form of member or committee oversight of the process is likely.

What is, or is not negotiable?

Not all central costs are suitable for the SLA treatment. CIPFA accounting recommendations recognise that not all central costs should be allocated out to services. Take, for example, the role of the council's *monitoring officer*.

One of the council's officers (usually the head of its legal services) is, in accordance with legislation, designated to monitor the propriety of its affairs. This scrutiny might not be the top purchasing priority of service departments with SLA buying power. But the council has no choice as to whether such a function is carried out. So it is logical to exempt such a function from the SLA process all together.

Services could perhaps be split into the following categories:

Corporate These are activities in the council's overall interest, such as meetings of the full council, the cost of the chief executive, and the publication of the statutory statement of accounts. These costs are not recharged to services, and not covered by SLAs.

Chargeable, but not negotiable There are some activities which it may not be advisable to place at the mercy of service manager discretion. But as the central activity is clearly linked to a particular service, a charge would be made in the published accounts.

Many councils treat some of their internal audit service in this way. A little thought shows that the departments most in need of audit are likely to be the most reluctant purchasers of the service. If functions under a chief officer's personal control are in a mess, it takes an enlightened management attitude to invite in audit to publicise the fact.

Chargeable and negotiable The main run of central services should fall into this category. It may be that negotiability extends to the use of an outside agency to provide the services. If so, there ought to be some overall control on the externalisation process. This is because a single customer going outside could prejudice the costs of all the other internal customers. If, for example, ten departments share the cost of a software licence, then one department dropping out could increase the cost of servicing the other nine by 11 per cent. If SLAs have already been negotiated on a ten customer assumption, irrecoverable costs could put the central budget into deficit.

SLA contracts

SLAs may be set out in a formal contract document, and there will probably be a standard format for use within the council.

From a provider point of view, the longer the contract period the better. If the period exceeds one financial year, there will need to be a mechanism to calculate price increases.

Most of the service information will be incorporated in schedules to the contract. The greater the degree of specification, the easier it will be to operate the contract from the provider's point of view. In particular, there will be the opportunity to charge for work not provided for in the schedule.

Say the SLA with finance department entitles social services department to receive 12 budget monitoring reports a year. Then if a thirteenth is required, finance could reasonably ask social services to meet the extra cost.

If, however, the SLA was expressed in more general terms, say, that 'the finance department will provide a budget monitoring service', it would probably not affect the SLA recharge whether the number of reports produced was 12, 13 or more.

The contract obligations will work both ways. It is usually not lost on central departments that there is a high degree of co-ordination with service departments in carrying out the central role. Unless service departments do their bit, delays can arise. This again provides charging opportunities.

Finance may have contracted to provide social services with a payroll service at £100 per employee a year. Suppose the SLA schedule stipulates that social services managers must return signed weekly timesheets to the central finance payroll office by Monday of each payweek. If social services frequently fail to adhere to this condition, and usually send the sheets over on Tuesday instead, finance may need to pay staff overtime to achieve the Friday pay day. Those extra costs, and some form of penalty to discourage repeated non-performance, may well be imposable under the SLA.

The contract must state clearly how charges will be effected. The main methods are:

—an annual lump sum for the service;
—charges based on an hourly rate for staff engaged on the relevant work;
—unit costs for service received, such as the number of staff paid (payroll), or the number of invoices paid;
—work outside the scope of the SLA may be charged at a premium rate.

To facilitate budget monitoring, clients may ask for charges to be billed monthly. This creates a hitherto unknown pressure on providers to promptly identify and recharge work for particular clients. There may well be a presumption that charges made cannot subsequently be varied. SLAs thus require providers to operate accurate and efficient charging systems, including time recording systems.

SLA contracts should provide a clear basis on which disputes may be resolved. Often, this entails arbitration by an independent chief officer or the council's chief executive.

Tail chasing or central/central charges

The fact that central departments provide services to each other must be allowed for in calculating recharge levels.

Say, for example, the finance department provides personnel department with services such as financial accounting and audit. Personnel, in its turn, provides finance with various items such as maintaining employee files and organising training courses.

Before finance can calculate how much to charge personnel, it needs to know how much it will be charged by personnel. Otherwise, charges will be levied which are insufficient to cover total costs. These cross charges cannot be ignored otherwise the discipline of controlling work by the internal market would break down.

Various methods of calculating such recharges are in use. These usually take an algorithmic approach, as follows.

Step 1 Finance estimates the charge it will have to bear from personnel, and makes an estimated charge to personnel accordingly.

Step 2 On the basis of finance's first estimated charge (Step 1), Personnel makes a charge to finance. This will be closer to the final figure than finance's own original estimate that was used in Step 1.

Step 3 The revised charge from personnel is fed back into the Step 1 calculation, and the process continues until the change between successive steps is down to a minimal agreed level.

Negotiating the agreements

Having seen how SLAs work in overall terms, and some of the contractual problems, we now turn to the key task of negotiation. Selling or marketing a service is a skill all its own, as is effective purchasing of any supply or service. Here are some basic ideas which may be useful for those in the relatively new role of purchasing central department work.

• Discuss the proposed SLA as widely as possible within the department. It is particularly important to get the views of those dealing with the central department on a daily basis. What seem like fairly innocuous provisions in the contract may have much greater practical significance than you first appreciated.
• Don't allow the central department to rush the negotiations. Typically, the central department will have spent a lot more time and effort on preparing its case than the purchasing client. Unless clients are able to judge the value of what is being offered, the SLA process degenerates into a formality.
• Overdetailed specifications may indicate either a desire to up the charges for unspecified items, or an attempt to dress up a weak service for more than it really is. It should be permissible within the negotiating structure to ask for the specification to be changed to a mutually acceptable format.
• Read the small print for the conditions placed on you. Check these out with the staff directly responsible for meeting them, so that you can assess the likelihood of failing to meet them.
• To combat the specialist knowledge a central department has of its own service, it may be a good idea to combine with other service departments to negotiate as a team on common services such as payroll, or personnel advice.

- Go into the negotiations with as much comparative information on the service in question as possible. This may include:
    - prior year figures from your own council;
    - the cost of the function in other councils of similar size;
    - information on the cost of buying from an outside agency.

  The last of these three needs to be handled with caution. If you simply ask an outside contractor for a guide price, they will probably quote an unrealistically low figure to advance their case for getting on some future tender list. Does their quote reflect the costs they would have to bear to integrate into the council's other systems and procedures? Simply bandying about unlikely figures in the negotiation process will only serve to diminish your negotiating credibility. It may, though, be possible to get reliable data from other councils who have held proper tender competitions.

- Try and achieve the charging basis that suits you best. If you are unclear as to the rate at which you use a particular service, it might be best to opt for a fixed annual charge. Conversely, if you have tight control of the throughput and hope to reduce it, a unit-based charge is better. Providers will hope for some limitations on the extent to which the throughput can be varied before the whole contract becomes invalid. Worse still, you might be tied into high costs however little your usage. Go for the maximum flexibility on your side, or SLA charges could be preserved at the expense of other budget heads.

- Avoid any conditions on charges and performance that it is unrealistic to control. If, for example, your service will be charged monthly, you might be allowed only one working week to check the charge and contest it. Don't accept such a condition if it is impossible to check thoroughly in this time.

- In negotiating the SLA, have an eye to how you will monitor the performance standards. You will probably need to keep entirely new records and set up systems to do this.

  If, for example, your charge for a computer system is rebated once its down time exceeds a certain percentage, don't rely on the central provider to inform you when this is the case.

- Finally, be sensible in your negotiating position. Allow a reasonable timescale for central functions to improve themselves. The whole point of SLAs is realistic joint discussions. If you try to crowd your central colleagues too much, they may resort to padding out your charges with hidden extras and so forth.

Budgeting and accounting for SLAs

We end our review of SLAs with a brief look at some of the associated budgeting and accounting problems. Remember your friendly central department has now become a predatory contractor, trying to squeeze every last penny out of the contract in order to pay their salary bill.

Many of the budgetary issues are thus the same as we discussed earlier in this chapter with regard to CCT contracts. What though are the particular problems with SLAs?

- Be clear which elements of the central recharges you receive are negotiable, and which are not. As we saw earlier, there are some costs over which you will have no discretion.
- Beware of any post-negotiation adjustments to agreed SLA charges. The figure agreed should be the cash figure met from your budget, other things being equal.
- During the financial year, you will need to monitor SLA expenditure as if it were incurred with any outside supplier. If you are overspending because of over use of the function, you must either cut your use or transfer funds from another budget.
- Find out what happens to any surplus earned by central departments on SLAs. There are two schools of thought on this:

Cost basis

Any 'profits' mean that services have been overcharged, and the surplus should be returned to them in proportion to the charges made.

Trading basis

Trading 'profits' add reality to the market discipline. To return them to users would undermine the SLA negotiations. Profits should be held in reserve to meet future losses, and to develop the efficiency of central services.

- If central departments run up losses on their SLAs, find out whether your department could become responsible for meeting part of the deficit.

Before leaving the subject of SLAs, we end with a few pointers on how to get the most out of the system.

- Find out which are the negotiable services and concentrate your attention on them.
- Watch out for central department strategies to exploit your own service management and impose extra charges.
- Be sure you are capable of monitoring central department performance, and checking their charges thoroughly.

SLAs may not be straightforward, but at least they are a great deal better than having no say at all, a situation which appertained only a few years ago.

Conclusion

We end this chapter, and indeed this book, in the artificial market place of the service level agreement. Hopefully, your new-found knowledge of the local government finance function will allow you to drive a hard bargain next time that particular SLA comes up for negotiation.

Further reading

CIPFA has published numerous documents and publications on competition and SLAs, some under the auspices of its Competition Joint Committee, whose membership includes every conceivable local government interest.

Competition is the favourite topic in most local government journals. It is covered virtually every week in both *Local Government Chronicle*, and *Municipal Journal*.

Index

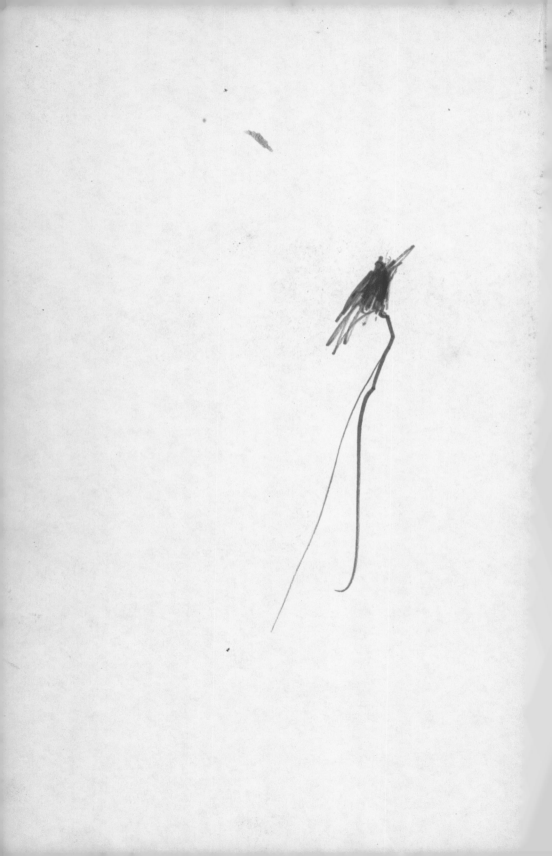